# WATERING HOLES

## YOUR GUIDE TO DETROIT'S BARS, PUBS, AND TAVERNS

MIKE KLINE

Author: Mike Kline
Editor: Mamie Sepulveda



First American Edition, 2017
10 9 8 7 6 5 4 3 2

ISBN 978-0-692-92738-0

www.wateringholesbook.com

www.facebook.com/WateringHolesDetroit

@wateringholesdetroit

Author's photography website: www.notkalvinphotography.com

Photography by
Mike Kline - Notkalvin Photography
Canton, Michigan, USA
Text, descriptions and opinions by
Mike Kline - Notkalvin Photography
Canton, Michigan, USA
Published by Notkalvin Photography
Canton, Michigan, USA
Printed and bound by PrintNinja in PRC

# Introduction

Welcome to your copy of Watering Holes. In order to create this guide, I visited every bar in person, gathering information, observing, and in many cases, sampling. The guide is meant to provide knowledge that will help you to figure out where to go in Detroit. Besides the basic info; name, address, phone, hours, website, there is a picture of the outside, a brief description of the inside, and a smattering of details about the bar and kitchen offerings. On many of the pages, there is also information about where to park, what is near, and if the QLine or the Detroit People Mover have nearby stations. Finally, there are some pages which have an italicized snippet which may contain info about a drink or food item I really enjoyed, additional information, or some advice. The bars in this guide are south of Warren, north of the Detroit River, east of 96, and west of Jos Campeau Street.

Each page has a check box at the top allowing you to keep track of the places you have visited, and at the bottom there are three colored rectangles. The intention is that these will be used to record what you liked (green), what was just OK (yellow), and what you wouldn't order again (red). How else are you going to know who had the good fries, which bar had the cute bartender, or who served the best Moscow Mule?

The guide is organized alphabetically by color coded neighborhood. At the start of each new neighborhood, there is a street map of the area showing the bars locations and where many of the event venues are located. Detroit People Mover Stops are marked with a DPM, and QLine stops are marked with a Q.

Word of warning: Many places in Detroit have seasonal hours and even seasonally variable days of operation. This not only pertains to the four seasons, but also to the sports seasons. There are also quite a few places which have flexible closing times. As a rule of thumb, confirming in advance is the safest bet. Any prices I have listed in the guide are subject to change. The bars have the final say.

As with any city, over time there will be new places opening, and there will be others that go out of business. As this happens, I plan on sharing the information through Facebook: www.facebook.com/WateringHolesDetroit. Stop in and let us know what you think of the guide, and any corrections you might find along the way.

I hope you enjoy the guide and have fun visiting some or all of Detroit's wonderful watering holes.

Mike Kline
Notkalvin Photography

# Gratuitous Quotes

"Fill with mingled cream and amber,
I will drain that glass again.
Such hilarious visions clamber
Through the chamber of my brain —
Quaintest thoughts — queerest fancies
Come to life and fade away;
What care I how time advances?
I am drinking ale today."

- *Edgar Allan Poe*

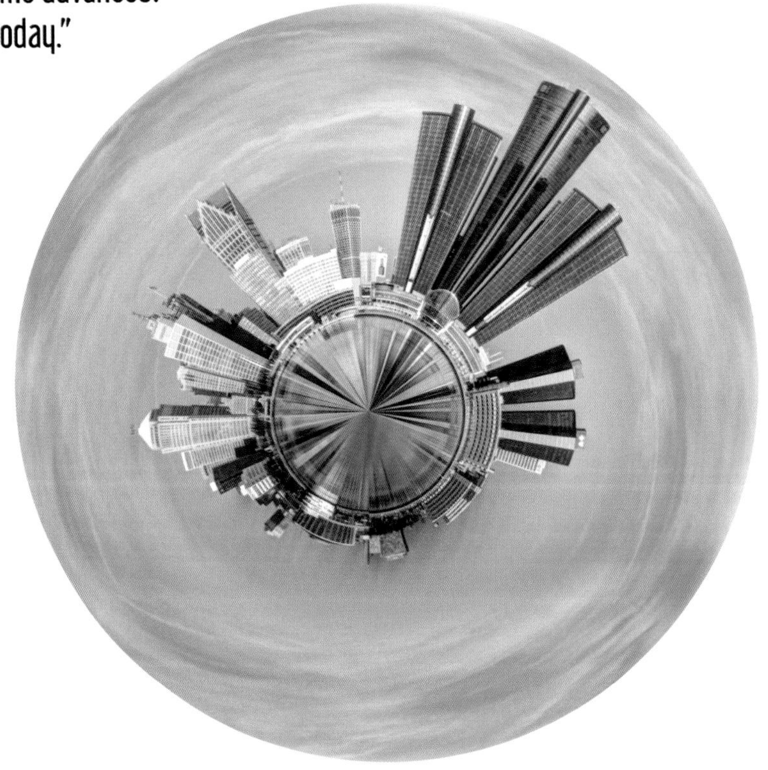

"I could have written a guide
to office supply stores, but where's the fun in that?"

- *Mike Kline*

# Contents


Bricktown . . . . 2

Corktown . . . . 14

Downtown . . . . 34

Eastern Market . . . . 68

Foxtown . . . . 75

Greektown . . . . 110

Midtown / Cass Corridor . . . . 132

Riverfront . . . . 158

Southwest . . . . 162

Honorable Mentions . . . . 166

Index . . . . 167

Acknowledgements . . . . 169

About the Author . . . . 170

# Bricktown

DPM = Detroit People Mover station

Q = QLine station

**519 E. Jefferson Avenue**
**(313) 656-4820**

# Briggs Detroit

**Full bar:** ✓ **Draft beer:** ✓ **Full kitchen:** ✓ **Shuttle service:** ✗ **briggsdetroit.com**

HOURS:
Sun - Thu: 11am - 2am
Fri - Sat: 11am - 2am

HAPPY HOUR:
Mon - Fri: 3pm - 6pm

This large sports bar is located across Jefferson Ave from the Renaissance Center. The interior is spacious, with a large rectangular bar dominating the middle space. The walls are decorated with Detroit sports related pictures and a large scoreboard. Of course, being a sports bar, there are numerous TVs in all directions.

The bar is well stocked from the alcohol standpoint and features 20+ beers on draft, with around 20 other varieties in bottles and cans. For the beer drinker, it may be of interest to note that **Briggs** offers the option of 24oz drafts. It is common for Briggs to offer drink specials; they vary, so check when you get there. They also have specials to coincide with Detroit sporting events, such as $10 Coors Light pitchers during Lions games.

Burgers, sandwiches and bar sides are the main fare out of the kitchen, and many of the items are named after something or someone in Detroit sports history. **Briggs** prides themselves in prepping all of the food fresh daily, and their most popular item is the 1939 sandwich, which is their version of a Rueben.

Parking is pretty easy to find in this area, with parking structures, surface lots, and metered spots on the streets. **Briggs** is close to Cobo Hall, St. Andrews Hall, and Greek-town, but a bit of a walk to Comerica, Ford Field, and everything else out that way. The Detroit People Mover has a stop in nearby Millender Center, and that can get you close to the parks.

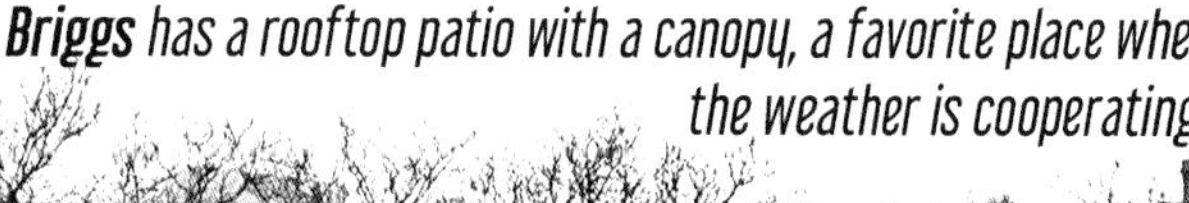

***Briggs** has a rooftop patio with a canopy, a favorite place when the weather is cooperating.*

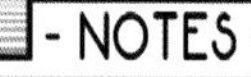

- NOTES -

Been there! ☐

Bricktown

# Checker Bar Detroit

124 Cadillac Square
(313) 961-9249
checkerbar.com

**Full bar:** ☑ **Draft beer:** ☑ **Full kitchen:** ☑ **Shuttle service:** ☒

HOURS:
Mon - Sun 11am - 2am

HAPPY HOUR:
Mon - Fri 4pm - 7pm

Just a block from the bustle of Campus Martius, **Checker Bar**, with its iconic red and white checker board mural, is a time-tested standard in Detroit. Come in for their "Sloppy Hour" on weekdays from 4-7pm and get $2 sloppy joes, hot dogs, Stroh's, and well drinks, and $3 cans of Atwater's Dirty Blonde. Thursday nights are for karaoke, starting at eight.

The menu at **Checker Bar** is chock-full of Michigan products - Wigley's corned beef, Kowalski hot dogs, Dearborn kielbasa, Aunt Nees tortilla chips, and others. All of these can be washed down with a solid mixed drink, or with a beer from their selection of drafts, bottles, and cans.

When you step inside, you'll find the glare and hustle of the city melts away behind you, leaving you in a cozy environment perfect for a group meet-up. When the weather is nice, the **Checker Bar** offers limited outdoor seating. This is a fun place to go for good food, cold drinks, and socializing.

There are numerous parking garages in the area, metered parking on the street, and surface lots. There are several stations for the Detroit People Mover nearby, and the QLine is just a short walk away.

*__Checker Bar__ has good, fresh burgers, and some of the best onion rings I have ever had.*

There's a bonus bar upstairs; **Pop+Offworld**. Besides being a bar, they are an 80s style arcade and a pizza joint with New York style pizza, either off the menu or designed by you from a long list of ingredients.

- NOTES -

655 Beaubien Street
(313) 963-3355

# Detroiter Bar

**Full bar:** ☑ **Draft beer:** ☑ **Full kitchen:** ☑ **Shuttle service:** ☒

HOURS:
Mon - Sun 11am - 2am

HAPPY HOUR:
Mon - Fri: 3pm - 5pm

Another stylish old Detroit building receiving some love. The **Detroiter Bar** is a neighborhood bar in the big city. Fitting of the neighborhood, the exterior is beautiful old brick. Cross the threshold and you are taken away from the bustle of the city streets and inserted into a welcoming, albeit on the loud side, environment with intimate tables arranged around a central bar. TVs bring you the current game, while a juke box belts out someone's favorite playlist. If you like the street activity, during the warm months there is limited outdoor seating available.

The bar features around twenty beers on tap, a cooler full of other beers in cans and bottles, and a fully stocked array of liquors. There are daily drink specials, and if you are there during happy hour, Monday thru Friday, 3pm-5pm, you get your domestic drafts for $3.

The **Detroiter Bar** is just outside of Greektown, but still an easy walk to Greektown Casino, Campus Martius, St. Andrew's Hall, and any number of other downtown Detroit destinations.

They keep the menu pretty simple, with mostly burgers, which is what they are known for, sandwiches, and a range of fairly standard bar-style appetizers.

*The daily drink specials change from time to time. When you get there, check the chalk boards in the back.*

- NOTES -

Been there! ☐ Bricktown

# Granite City Food & Brewery

100 Renaissance Center #1101
(313) 309-9120

**Full bar:** ✓ **Draft beer:** ✓ **Full kitchen:** ✓ **Shuttle service:** ✗ gcfb.com

HOURS:
Mon - Sat: 11am - 11pm
Sun: 10am - 9pm

HAPPY HOUR:
Mon - Fri: 3pm - 6pm
*and* 9pm - close

BRUNCH:
Sun: 10am - 2pm

While **Granite City Food & Brewery** is part of a larger chain, that does not take away from what they have to offer. This location, attached to the first level of Detroit's iconic Renaissance Center, is massive. The restaurant portion easily can seat a couple hundred people, and the bar area serves up a variety of their namesake craft beers as well as a large selection of signature cocktails and traditional drinks.

The layout is modern and well thought out, with walls breaking up the large space to keep down noise and avoid having a warehouse feel. The warm colors used in decorating make this a very comfortable location capable of serving anything from singles to massive groups.

The granite-topped bar is a great place to peruse the descriptive drink menus and enjoy happy hour, during which there are discounts on craft beers, premium house cocktails, hand-crafted cocktails, wine, and a variety of apps. Large flat-screen TVs also provide the opportunity to catch a game.

The food covers a wide range of tastes, from traditional items to more creatively crafted offerings. Prepared fresh in house, there is most likely something for everyone in your party. Servings are large, artfully assembled and delicious.

Due to their location in the RenCen, the weekday lunch crowd tends to be large. Plan accordingly.

***Granite City*** *has a rewards program which allows for specials and discounts, as well as occasional tapping parties when a new beer is introduced. Sign up in-house or through their website.*

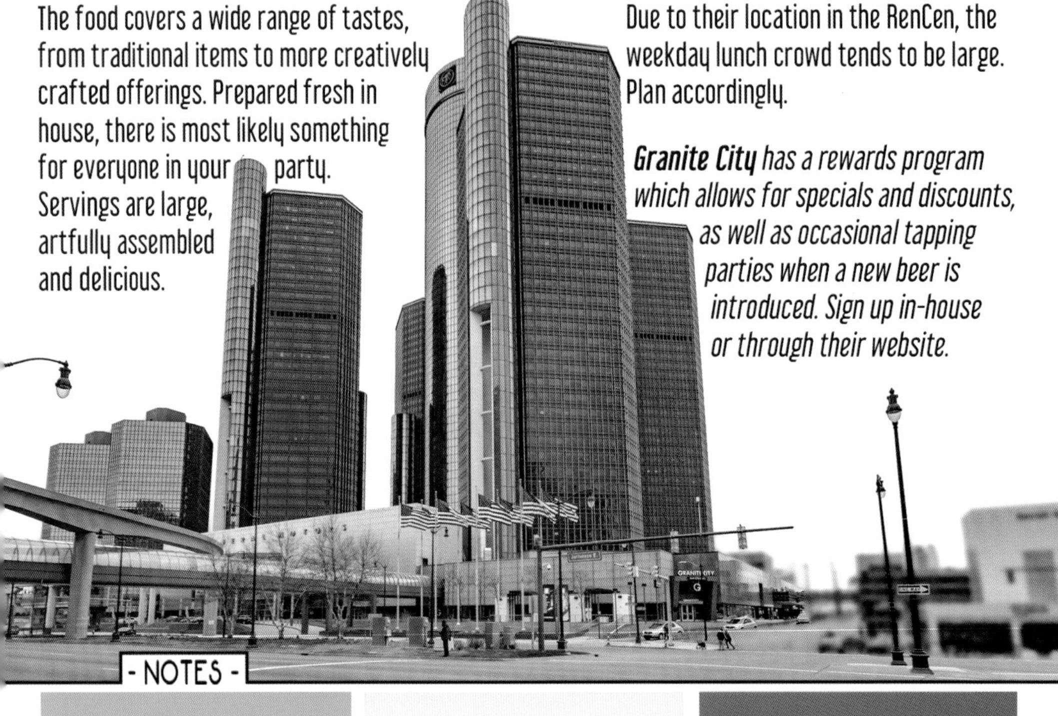

- NOTES -

**130 Cadillac Square**
**(313) 961-7885**

# Greenwich Time Pub

**Full bar:** ✓ **Draft beer:** ✓ **Full kitchen:** ✓ **Shuttle service:** ✗ **greenwichtimepub.wixsite.com/bargrill**

HOURS:
Mon - Thu: 11am - midnight
Fri - Sat: 11am - 2am
Sun: Closed

Just a block from the energy of Campus Martius, **Greenwich Time Pub** is a neighborhood bar where you'll find regulars and first-timers hanging out, enjoying a drink. Residing in a wedge shaped buiding, Greenwich Time can be entered from either Cadillac Square or Congress Street. There are two floors to the business. The first is divided in two, with the bar on one side, and the kitchen on the other. Upstairs is a large dining area with a service bar, often used for lunch (11am - 3pm) or for parties and overflow on busy days.

The bar area is not particularly large, but it is comfortable. When asked about happy hour, they said it's all the time. The prices are reasonable, and one of their mainstays is Miller High Life pints. They are always $2. **Greenwich Time** has three other beers on tap, more in bottles and cans, and a full selection of liquor.

The kitchen serves up a decent selection of sandwiches and burgers, a few appetizers, and soup and salads. The burgers and corned beef sandwiches are what they are most known for.

Greektown Casino and St. Andrew's Hall are nearby. Within a moderate walk or a ride on the People Mover or QLine, Ford Field, Comerica Park, the Fox and Fillmore theaters and the Detroit Opera House are within reach.

Parking is plentiful in this part of Detroit.

- NOTES -

Been there! ☐

Bricktown

# Jacoby's German Biergarten

624 Brush Street
(313) 962-7067
jacobysbar.com

Full bar: ✓ Draft beer: ✓ Full kitchen: ✓ Shuttle service: ✗

HOURS:
Mon - Sat: 11am - 2am
Sun: noon - 10pm

HAPPY HOUR:
Mon - Sun: 3pm - 7pm

**Jacoby's** is one of Detroit's oldest saloons, having been in business since 1904. This alone should put it on your list of places to visit. Once you step inside, you will find **Jacoby's** to be warm and inviting. The atmosphere is defined by the predominantly wood and brick interior, a throwback to historical architecture. If ever there was a place for the saying, "if these walls could talk," this is it. Jacoby's has been a constant for over a century as Detroit experienced highs, descended to some lows, and now, as the city is showing positive signs of rising once again.

**Jacoby's** has a full bar and bartenders capable of fulfilling your beverage needs and wants. They also have around 15 beers on tap, and an extensive beer list which leans heavily toward German beers. During the week-long happy hour, take advantage of ½ off appetizers, \$2 off beers, \$7 beer flights, and the "Detroit Special", a PBR or Tecate and a shot of Jack, Jägermeister, or Fireball for \$5.

The menu is dominated by German fare, although they offer a decent variety of other food as well, including burgers and sandwiches. The food, made in-house from scratch, has been featured on Destination America's food show; US of Bacon. The signature item they delved into? Rindfleisch Rouladen. It was modified a bit by the host of the show, however is still a crowd favorite.

*At the time of publishing, the upstairs was undergoing renovation.*

- NOTES -

140 Cadillac Square
(313) 223-2626

# The Keep

**Full bar:** ✓ **Draft beer:** ✓ **Full kitchen:** ✗ **Shuttle service:** ✗

HOURS:
Tue - Wed: 2pm - midnight
Thu - Sat: 2pm - 2am
Sun: noon - midnight
Mon: closed

HAPPY HOUR:
Mon - Fri: 4pm - 7pm

Author Favorite

This subterranean bar is amazingly cool. That's right, it is an underground bar. Sure, some would call it a basement, however when you walk into the space at the bottom of the stairs, the brick pillars and walls, combined with the lack of windows, reject the word basement. The ambiance is about as intimate as you can get, with a variety of private seating areas.

At the bar, which is where you must go to order and receive your drinks, you can get any number of creatively designed cocktails, which are clearly identified on the drink menu. A satisfying selection of beers, both craft and not, and basic house wines are also available.

There is no food here, so don't arrive hungry. **The Keep** is only a block away from Campus Martius, and not much more than a stone's throw away from Greektown. Ford Field, Comerica Park, Little Caesars Arena, and the Fox and Fillmore Theaters are just over a half mile away; walking distance for some.

Parking abounds in this area, with several parking structures and surface lots nearby, and limited metered parking on the streets. If you choose the latter, keep your meter fed unless you want to create revenue for the city. Once you have a spot, you can keep it by taking advantage of the nearby stops for the Detroit People Mover and the QLine to get around Detroit.

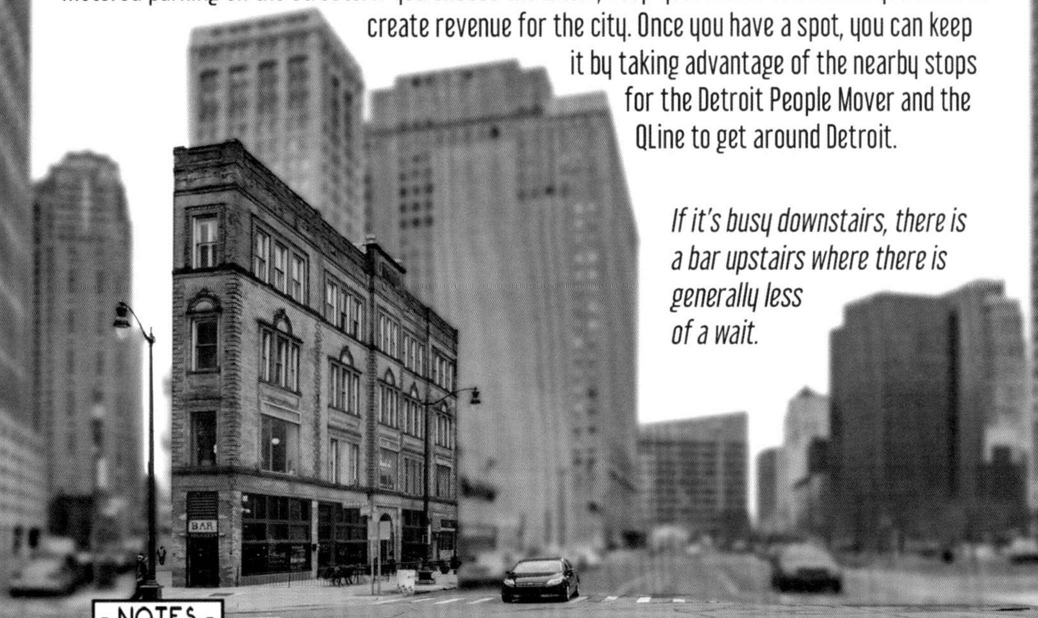


*If it's busy downstairs, there is a bar upstairs where there is generally less of a wait.*

- NOTES -

# M!X Bricktown

641 Beaubien Street
(313) 962-9548

**Full bar:** ✓ **Draft beer:** ✓ **Full kitchen:** ✓ **Shuttle service:** ✗ **mixbricktown.com**

HOURS:
Tue - Thu: 5pm - 1am
Fri - Sun: 5pm - 2am
Mon: closed

HAPPY HOUR:
Tue - Fri: 5pm - 9pm

**M!X** is a cross between a club and a lounge. There is a small bar at the entrance where drinks can be purchased prior to entering the main floor area. The main space is decorated such that it has a street/alley feel, with one wall covered in graffiti and another of solid brick. There is comfortable seating and room for dancing. The stage is also in this area, where music is played with frequency. Out back, weather permitting, there is a patio which allows the party to extend into the fresh night air.

The bar offers the standard fare when it comes to liquor, and a handful of beers on draft. Happy hour offers all beer, wine and wells for $3, Titos, Jack, Crown, and Jameson for $5, and Patron, Ciroc, Grey Goose, and Maker's Mark for $7. Every day from 5pm - midnight, Remy VSOP is $6 and 1738 is $9.

Food at **M!X** is prepared by Premium Taste Catering. The menu varies seasonally, however two items are permanent fixtures due to their popularity; Lamb Chops and Lobster Tails.

The entertainment includes karaoke, music driven by professional DJs, and live musical performances. Check their social media for the current schedule. **M!X** can get hopping, especially on the weekends, and is a good place to come with a group. Parking is plentiful in the area, and there is a Detroit People Mover station across the street.

- NOTES -

546 East Larned Street
(313) 262-6316

# Mo' Better Blues

**Full bar:** ✓ **Draft beer:** ✗ **Full kitchen:** ✓ **Shuttle service:** ✗

HOURS:

**Mo' Better Blues** is a clean, contemporary bar. The interior has a modern look and feel, with a dozen tables and a small bar. Altogether, the atmosphere is comfortable. An upstairs section is used for busier nights, private parties, and some of their events.

The bar features a list of recommended drinks, half of which are martinis. For beer drinkers, **Mo' Better Blues** offers a variety of brands in bottles and cans, however no drafts.

Food is available here. The style is classic American with a contemporary twist. The menu is filled with options, the most popular of which are the Philly Steak and Cheese, and the Chicken Philly, along with two signature offerings: The Mo' Better Burger and Mo' Better Wings.

CLOSED

There are several regular events at **Mo' Better Blues**. There is ballroom dancing on Wednesdays, Thursday specials which vary, open bar and food for a fixed price on Fridays, and Saturday nights are "Neo-soul nights" with live bands.

Parking is plentiful in the area. If you park in one of the neighboring surface lots, tell the attendant you are going to **Mo' Better Blues**, and the cost is only $5. **MBB** is close to St. Andrew's Hall, Greektown Casino, and Cobo Hall (somewhat). The Detroit People Mover can be caught at the nearby Millender Center, which brings more of downtown into reach.

*There are $5 lunch specials 11am-4pm, Mon - Fri.*

- NOTES -

# Ready Player One: Bar and Arcade

407 East Fort Street
(313) 395-3300
rpodetroit.com

Full bar: ✓ Draft beer: ✓ Full kitchen: ✓ Shuttle service: ✗

**Ready Player One** is located in the basement of the old Globe Tobacco Building (1888). Enter off Fort Street and head down a flight of stairs to reach a door that opens to a room where the walls are lined with an excellent selection of original arcade and pinball games. Down the middle of the space are tall wood-topped tables, most set up for community seating. At the far end of the room is the bar where a dozen or so metal stools provide patrons a place to sit and enjoy their drinks as they decide which game to play next.

HOURS:
Mon: closed
Tue - Fri: 5pm - 1am
Sat: 1pm - 2am
Sun: 11am - midnight

Featured on the drink menu are 7 craft cocktails; creative yet affordable, 8 beers on draft, and a score of others served by the can. On the food side of the menu, start with a list of a half dozen snacks ranging from garlic knots to crispy cauliflower glazed with a Rock 'n' Rye BBQ sauce. For the larger appetites, there are burgers, wings, BBQ chicken and brisket cheese steak sandwiches and more. As a reward for eating and drinking, you get four free tokens for every drink or food item ordered. Of course, more can be purchased as needed.

**Ready Player One** is practically surrounded by parking lots. There are a few parking structures in the area, and there is metered parking on the streets. To get to other parts of Detroit from here, the Detroit People Mover and QLine both have nearby stops.

21 and older after 9pm.
It is a bar after all.

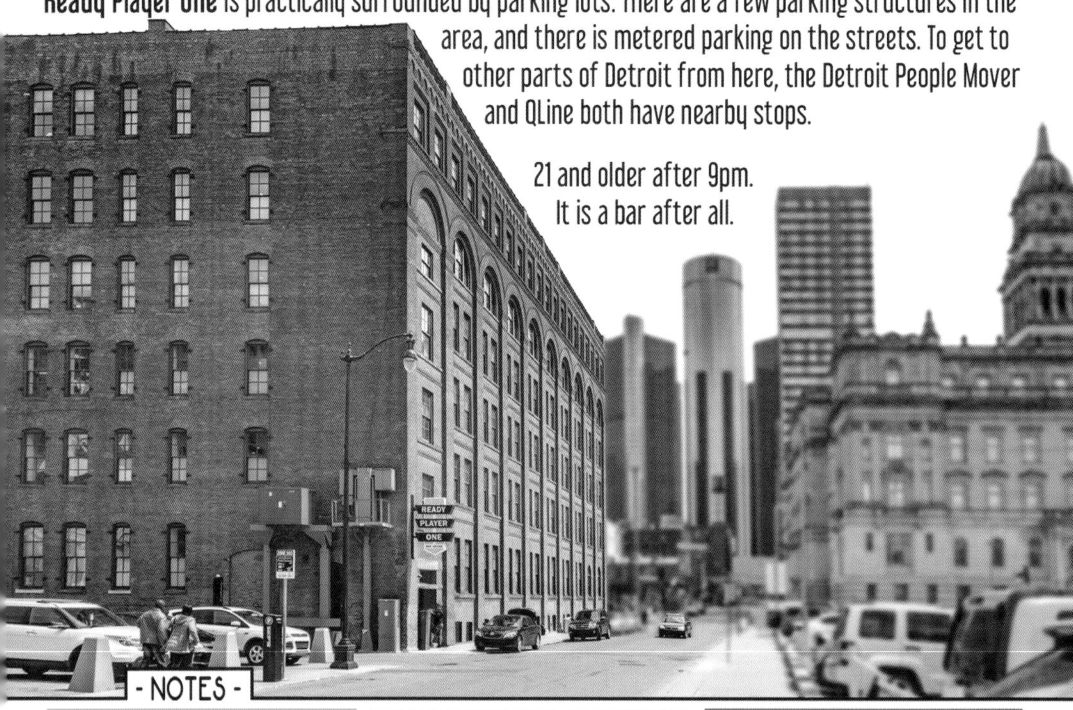


- NOTES -

400 E. Congress Street
(313) 962-2210

# Sweetwater Tavern

**Full bar:** ☑ **Draft beer:** ✗ **Full kitchen:** ☑ **Shuttle service:** ☑ **sweetwatertavern.net**

HOURS:
Mon - Sun: 11am - 2am

Housed in a beautiful old brick building built in the 1880s, **Sweetwater Tavern** has been a part of Detroit's Bricktown landscape for over thirty years. The inside of the tavern is a narrow layout, however stretches the length of the building. The bar area and limited seating is up front, and toward the back of the building is a space dedicated to diners. The way the rooms have been finished maintains the feel of being in a 19th century building, with the warm dark woods and the exposed brick walls.

The bar is on the smaller side, however is well-stocked. You'll find no draft beers here, but a good selection of regular and craft beers to choose from. They also have a selection of liquors more than sufficient to allow service of just about any standard mixed drink or shot order.

**Sweetwater Tavern** is best known for its chicken wings, and the house made sauce that coats them. How popular? They sell around 600 pounds of them every day. Besides wings, **Sweetwater** has a full menu of appetizers, entrees, and desserts.

Their Bricktown location makes them an easy walk to St. Andrew's Hall, the RenCen, Greektown, and a little further, to Comerica Park and Ford Field. They have several shuttle buses which run during every home game of the Lions, Tigers, and Red Wings and during major events in Detroit.

Parking is available in **Sweetwater's** lot, on the street, and in nearby structures.

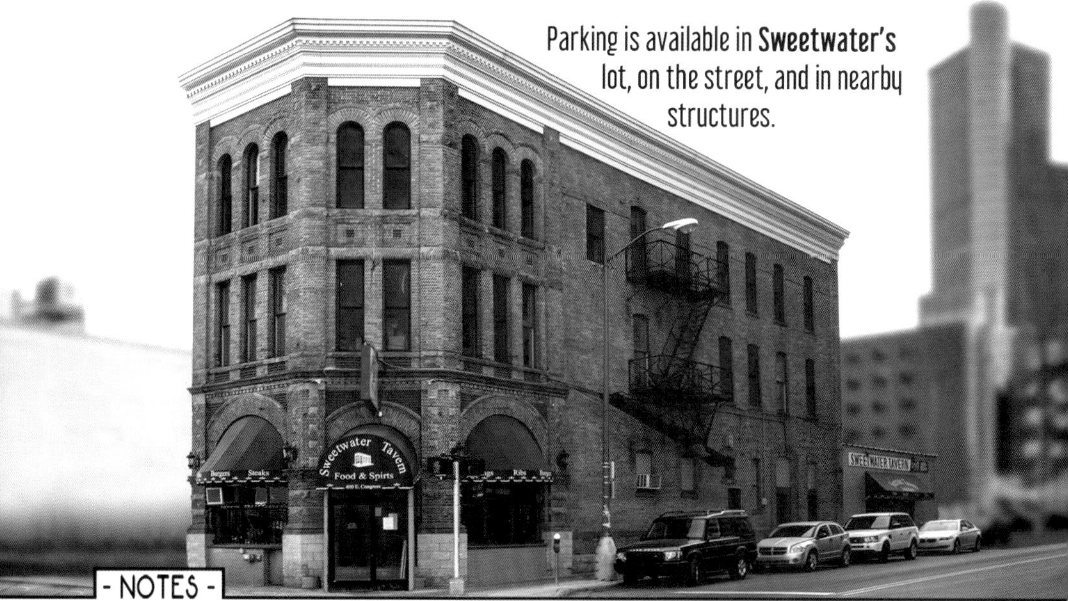


- NOTES -

# Corktown

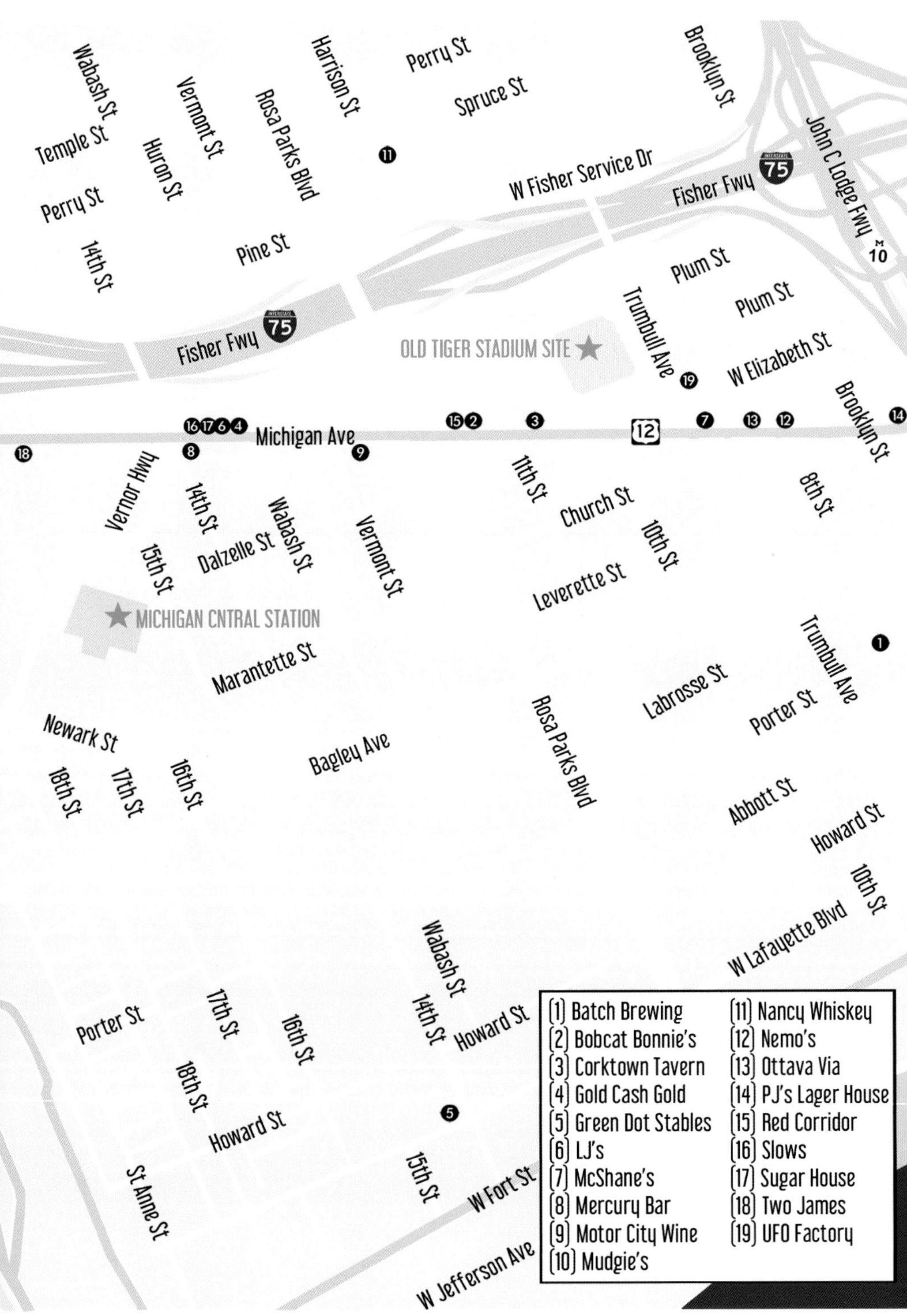

Wabash St
Temple St
Perry St
14th St
Huron St
Vermont St
Rosa Parks Blvd
Harrison St
Perry St
Spruce St
Pine St
Brooklyn St
W Fisher Service Dr
Fisher Fwy
75
John C Lodge Fwy
10
Plum St
Plum St
Trumbull Ave
W Elizabeth St
Fisher Fwy
75
OLD TIGER STADIUM SITE
Brooklyn St
Michigan Ave
12
Vernor Hwy
14th St
Wabash St
Vermont St
11th St
Church St
10th St
8th St
15th St
Dalzelle St
Leverette St
MICHIGAN CNTRAL STATION
Marantette St
Trumbull Ave
Labrosse St
Porter St
Newark St
Bagley Ave
Rosa Parks Blvd
18th St
17th St
16th St
Abbott St
Howard St
10th St
W Lafayette Blvd
Wabash St
Porter St
17th St
16th St
14th St
Howard St
18th St
Howard St
St Anne St
15th St
W Fort St
W Jefferson Ave
(1) Batch Brewing
(2) Bobcat Bonnie's
(3) Corktown Tavern
(4) Gold Cash Gold
(5) Green Dot Stables
(6) LJ's
(7) McShane's
(8) Mercury Bar
(9) Motor City Wine
(10) Mudgie's
(11) Nancy Whiskey
(12) Nemo's
(13) Ottava Via
(14) PJ's Lager House
(15) Red Corridor
(16) Slows
(17) Sugar House
(18) Two James
(19) UFO Factory

1400 Porter Street
(313) 338-8008

# Batch Brewing Company

**Full bar:** ✗ **Draft beer:** ✓ **Full kitchen:** ✓ **Shuttle service:** ✗ **batchbrewingcompany.com**

HOURS:
Sun - Thu: 11am - 10pm
Fri - Sat: 11am - midnight

Author Favorite

**Batch Brewing Company**, Detroit's first nano-brewery, is a small craft brewery in Corktown, the oldest neighborhood in Detroit. The outward appearance is a small, non-descript structure with an old rail car attached to it. Inside you will find a series of long picnic style tables for community seating. There are also a half dozen seats at the bar. The way it's set up encourages you to intermingle with people you might not know. Outside is a patio, set up in the same community seating fashion. The patio is open whenever the weather cooperates.

This is a brewery; although not a rule, they do not serve any alcohol besides beer. They do offer a few soft drinks, coffee, and water. The current beers are listed on the wall near the end of the bar.

Besides their fresh and excellent beer, they also have a small menu filled with creatively designed culinary delights. It is clear that **Batch Brewing Company** wants to be good at more than making beer. The prices are reasonable, and the food is wonderful.

If the conversation of your companions is not enough to keep you entertained, board games are available, which can be brought to the table for your enjoyment.

Once you settle in with your favorite beer, you have the option of purchasing some to go. **Batch** does not have growlers, however you can get 500ml, 750ml, or 40oz bottles.

Things to watch for at **Batch**: Octoberfest, new beer releases (4-6/yr), and their monthly feel good tap which benefits a worthy non-profit.

*Places like this exist because there can never be too much good beer in the world.*

- NOTES -

Been there! ☐

Corktown

# Bobcat Bonnie's

1800 Michigan Avenue
(313) 962-1383

**Full bar:** ☑ **Draft beer:** ☑ **Full kitchen:** ☑ **Shuttle service:** ☒ **bobcatbonnies.com**

HOURS:
Mon - Thu: 11am - midnight
Fri - Sat: 11am - 2am

HAPPY HOUR:
Mon - Fri: 4pm - 7pm
Thu: 4pm - close

BRUNCH:
Sat - Sun: 10am - 4pm

**Bobcat Bonnie's** in Corktown is one of those places with a lot of history. The building is over 150 years old, and has been home to several different bars going back over half a century. While creating their own presence, they maintain aspects from the past, most notably the rich brick walls that greet you from all sides. The accents added for the bar build-out are more modern-industrial, the end result being a warm, inviting atmosphere.

As a bar, **Bobcat Bonnie's** offers a full range of liquor, draft, bottled and canned beer, and wine. In addition, make sure to check out the full menu page of creative cocktails, both alcoholic and non-alcoholic. Their signature, "The Bonnie" is a mix of moonshine, bourbon, blackberry simple syrup, and lemon juice. Refreshing with a kick! During brunch, they have a build your own Bloody Mary bar.

Every weekday has a special to go with it. Monday is burger night, Tuesdays are for tacos, and you get trivia on Wednesday - round one at 7:30pm, round two at 8:30pm. On Thursday, happy hour runs from 4pm until closing, and on Friday there are wine specials to help you "wine down to the weekend". Finally, Saturday and Sunday have a special brunch menu and a build your own Bloody Mary or Mimosa bar. For more details visit their website.

Parking in Corktown is limited to surface lots and metered street parking. If you park in the spaces along Michigan Avenue, make sure you don't block any of the delineated bike lanes, unless you like to get parking tickets.

*Try some of their delicious, creative tots!*

- NOTES -

1716 Michigan Avenue
(313) 964-5103

# Corktown Tavern

Full bar: ✓ Draft beer: ✓ Full kitchen: ✓ Shuttle service: ✗ corktowntavern.com

HOURS:
Mon: closed
Tue - Thu: 11:30am - 10pm
Fri - Sat: 11:30am - 2am
Sun: TBD

**Corktown Tavern** is a hold-over from the past. To many, it would be considered a dive bar. To others, a traditional old school bar. However you look at it, the history is long and storied. **Corktown Tavern** has seen the who's who of not only the Detroit music scene, but also larger international artists walk through the doors. Many of them have graced the stage upstairs. There have also been scores of professional athletes holding seats down at the bar. Tigers, Red Wings, players from visiting teams. It's one of those kind of places. Much of the memorabilia is gone from the walls now, however the original bar remains. Through the clear surface of the bar top baseball cards can be seen, sealed in place for decades. The front rail for the bar has split Louisville Slugger baseball bats as a design feature. These are all throwbacks to when Tiger Stadium was in use, just next door.

The offerings at the bar are basic. This is not the place to come for something trendy. Beer, shots, and standard mixed drinks are the norm here. In the past, there was limited or no food, however with the change of ownership late in 2017, came the resurrection of the kitchen. Burgers, wraps, a variety of sandwiches, fried items and a handful of sides can now accompany your drinks.

Upstairs is another full bar and the entertainment venue. There's a stage for the performers, complete with a state of the art sound system. Not only is there music, but some nights **Corktown Tavern** hosts comedy shows. Check their website for details.

Park on the street in metered spots, or in the free lot next to the building. If it's a busy time, there are other lots along Michigan Avenue and in the neighborhoods.

*Past names: Stella's Steakhouse, The Stadium Bar, and The Batter's Box.*

- NOTES -

**Been there!** ☐ **Corktown**

# Gold Cash Gold

**2100 Michigan Avenue**
**(313) 242-0770**

**Full bar:** ☑ **Draft beer:** ☑ **Full kitchen:** ☑ **Shuttle service:** ☒ **goldcashgolddetroit.com**

HOURS:
Mon: Closed
Tue - Thu: 4pm - 10pm
Fri: 4pm - midnight
Sat: 10am - 3:30pm
4pm - midnight
Sun: 10am - 3:30pm
4pm - 10pm

HAPPY HOUR:
Tue - Sun: 4pm - 6pm

**Gold Cash Gold** is located in one of Corktown's more recognizable buildings, with the writing on the exterior and the Sam's Loans sign which still hangs on the front. The current owners have embraced the past, refreshing the old paint job and borrowing the name from the old pawn shop storefront; "***GOLD CASH GOLD***."

An eclectic yet comfortable decor awaits inside, starting with a colored glass enclosed vestibule just past the front door, followed by the ceiling and some walls covered with handmade wooden panels with multi-toned diagonal strips. The floor in the dining area is an old gym floor repurposed from a school in Detroit. To get to the dining area from the bar, you pass under painted brick arches, another unique feature of the architecture.

The bar offers delicious craft cocktails, many of them using house-made syrups and infusions. There is also a selection of beers, adult slushies, and a long list of liquors available in 2oz pours.

Food at **Gold Cash Gold** is Southern-inspired, and the recipes are unique and tantalizing. There is little that can be considered "standard" on the menu. For the true foodies out there, reserve the chef's table back by the kitchen, and see how your food is made.

***AUTHOR'S FAVORITE:*** *The Gold Rush is their signature drink, and one of the best I've had anywhere.*

*When the weather is nice (it does happen occasionally here in Michigan), the patio is a great place to hang out, perhaps while enjoying some adult slushies.*

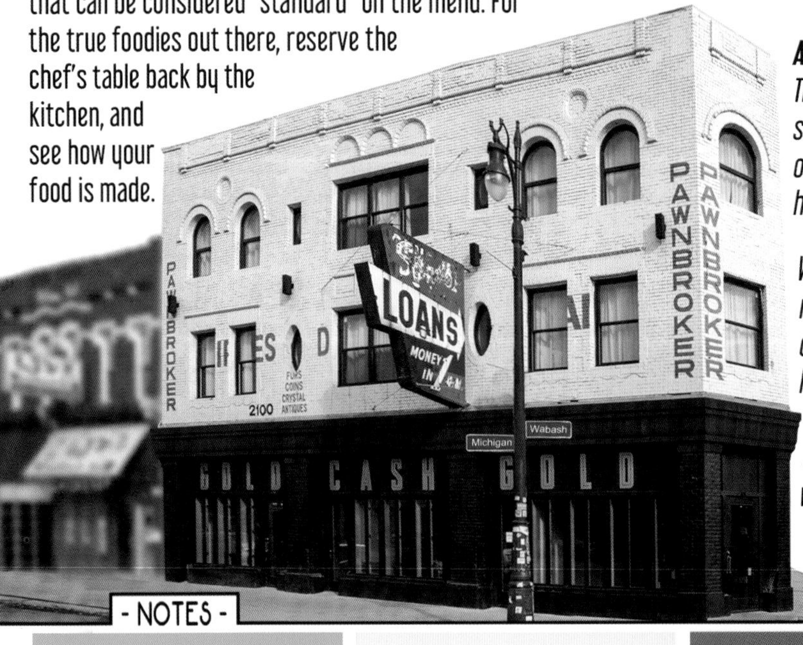


- NOTES -

Been there! ☐ Corktown

2200 W. Lafayette Boulevard
(313) 338-3760

# Green Dot Stables

Full bar: ☑ Draft beer: ☑ Full kitchen: ☑ Shuttle service: ✗ greendotstables.com

HOURS:
Mon - Wed: 11am - midnight
Thu - Sat: 11am - 1am
Sun: noon - 10pm

HAPPY HOUR:
*All the time!*

Author Favorite

**Green Dot Stables** is a bit off the beaten path, and the exterior is a disguise for what awaits within. Enter and find yourself in a cozy, warm, friendly environment. The interior has a lot of exposed woodwork finished with a dark stain, and the walls are decorated with horse-riding helmets. Patrons can belly up to the bar, sit in an elevated alcove at the end of the bar looking into the main room, or sit at tables.

At the bar, and from the kitchen, the prices are consistently low, providing great value. From a booze aspect, there is a list of $3 cocktails, encompassing a dozen items, with everything else being only a buck or two more. Beers are going to cost you $2 or $3, and the house wines are inexpensive, too. This is what you call "Happy Hour all the time."

The food fare is mainly sliders. Not the greasy fast food style sliders; really good sliders with fresh, creative ingredients. You can get appetizers, sides, soup, salad, and even dessert at the end if you haven't filled yourself up already.

**Green Dot Stables** is not conveniently close to anything in Detroit. The People Mover doesn't come out this far, the QLine is nowhere near, there's no shuttle, and it's really not practical to walk anywhere from here. Despite all of that, it is well worth it to find your way to their door. You will not regret it.

***AUTHOR'S FAVORITE**: My favorite slider is the Korean. It's a beef patty with Kimchi and peanut butter.*

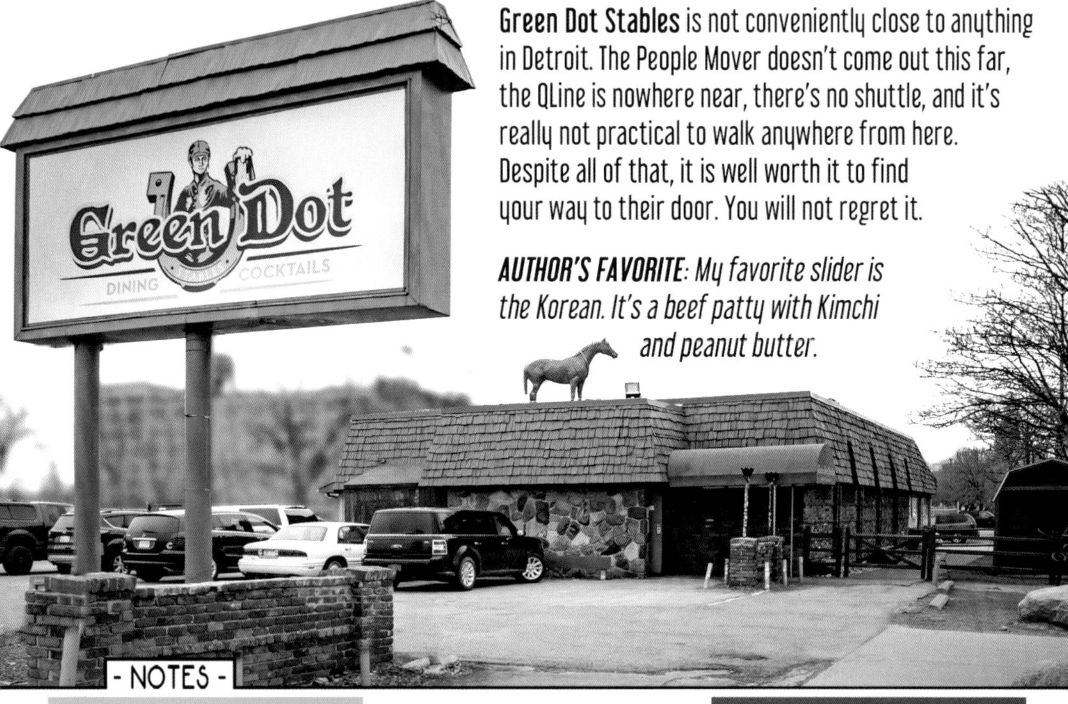


- NOTES -

# LJ's Sweetheart Bar

2114 Michigan Avenue
(313) 962-0013

**Full bar:** ✓ **Draft beer:** ✓ **Full kitchen:** ✗ **Shuttle service:** ✗

HOURS:
Sun - Thu: noon - close (depends on how busy)
Fri - Sat: noon - 2am

**LJ's Sweetheart Bar** is a small-town bar in a big city. It's on the smaller side, unassuming, and far from pretentious. The narrow building allows for regular bar activity in the front, and darts and Monday night comedy shows in the rear. **LJ's** has wood paneled walls and hardwood floors, with the bar running the length of the left side of the front room as you enter. Perhaps most eye-catching are the disco ball style, mirror-covered semicircular pillars over the bar. They are definitely unique. This also may very well be the only place in Detroit with a large fishtank behind the bar

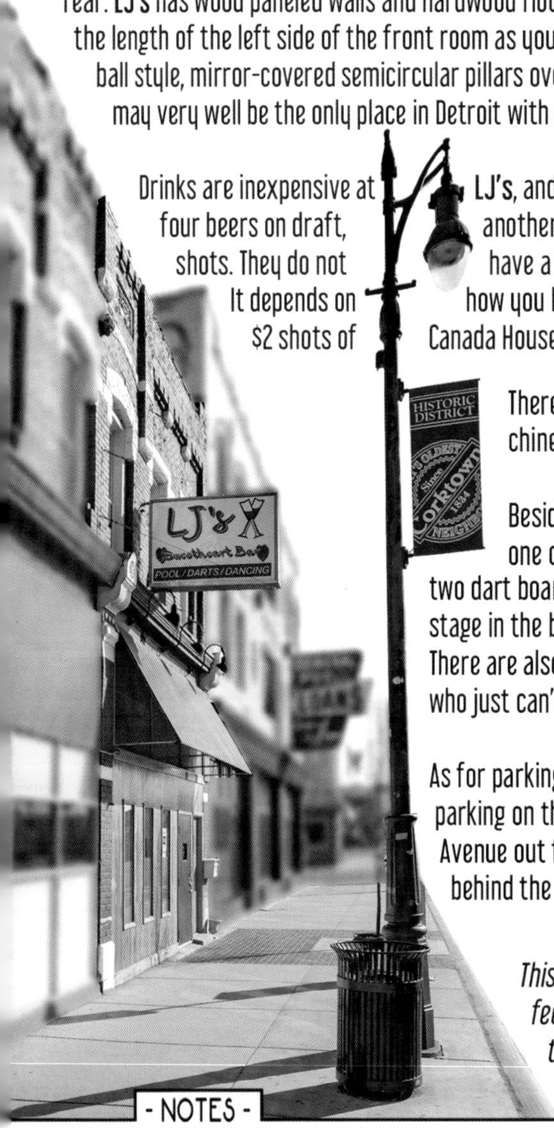

Drinks are inexpensive at **LJ's**, and you can choose from standard bar offerings, four beers on draft, another twenty or more in bottles and cans, and Jello shots. They do not have a happy hour, or they have happy hour all the time. It depends on how you look at it. They always have $2 PBR and Stroh's, $2 shots of Canada House, and $1 Jello shots.

There is no food at **LJ's**, aside from the vending machine stocked with chips, candy, and cigarettes.

Besides drinking, mingling, and watching a game on one of the TVs, **LJ's** has a pool table in the front room, two dart boards in the back room, and a comedy show on the stage in the back room every Monday night, starting at 8pm. There are also a couple of bar top video game units for those who just can't break free of their gaming addictions.

As for parking, there is a small lot out behind the bar, limited parking on the side streets, and metered parking on Michigan Avenue out front. If all of these are full, across the road behind the Mercury Bar is a secured parking lot.

*This is a no-frills kind of place where they make you feel welcome and at home, even if it's your first time there. Very relaxed.*

- NOTES -

Been there! ☐ Corktown

1460 Michigan Avenue
(313) 961-1960

# McShane's Irish Pub

Full bar: ☑ Draft beer: ☑ Full kitchen: ☑ Shuttle service: ☑ mcshanespub.com

HOURS:
Mon - Sat: 11am - 2am
Sun: 11am - midnight

HAPPY HOUR:
Mon - Sun: 3pm - 6pm

**McShane's** is, in a way, two bars in one. When you enter the building, you will be in the whiskey bar. With over 160 different whiskeys to choose from, if you are into whiskey, this is the place to be. In this space, there are a couple of pool tables and a few small tables.

Through a passageway and up a few steps, is the other bar. This one is more on the traditional side, with a row of beer taps and a full line of liquors on shelves along the wall. If you are there during happy hour (3-6pm every day), you will enjoy $2 domestic drafts, $3 well drinks, and $5 appetizers. **McShane's** offers daily drink specials, however they change frequently, so ask one of the staff. On game days for the Tigers, Lions, and Red Wings, there will be some sort of drink special as well.

Inside is spacious and on the dark side, with TVs scattered around on the walls to bring the games to the patrons. Behind the building is a rather large fenced in patio area where nice weather can be enjoyed without having to sit right by a busy road as is so often the case. For the nostalgic, from the patio you can look across Trumbull to the former site of Tiger Stadium.

Regarding parking, there is a secured lot behind the bar and limited metered parking on the street.

**McShane's** offers shuttle service to and from sporting events. For other events, check their website or call beforehand to determine availability. Something else to inquire about are their monthly pub crawls, road trips to select Mudhens games in Toledo, and road trips to select Tigers, Lions, and Red Wings away games. Every Thursday, **McShane's** hosts trivia night.

- NOTES -

# Mercury Burger & Bar

2163 Michigan Avenue
(313) 964-5000

**Full bar:** ✓ **Draft beer:** ✓ **Full kitchen:** ✓ **Shuttle service:** ✗ **mercuryburgerbar.com**

HOURS:
Mon - Thu: 11am - 11pm
Fri - Sat: 11am - 1am
Sun: 11am - midnight

Sitting in the shadow of one of Detroit's most iconic buildings, the abandoned Michigan Central Station, **Mercury Burger & Bar** provides a lively environment to gather with friends or stop in for good fresh food and a variety of drink options, including a wide selection of craft beers on tap.

Author Favorite

At first glance, it looks like a small place, however in addition to the seating at tables and the bar at street level, the basement is set up with tables, and provides more space for groups to gather. The decor in **Mercury** is fun, with a somewhat varied selection of items covering the walls. When Detroit is enjoying the warmer months, **Mercury Bar** opens its patio, expanding its capacity significantly.

**Mercury** is probably best known for their burgers, of which they offer a large variety, made fresh to order. There are fifteen different burgers listed on their menu, giving patrons a lot to choose from, and then there are 30+ toppings you can add to really personalize your choice. If you are not in the mood for a burger, there are also a slew of sandwiches, hot dogs, and salads .

There is limited parking on the surrounding streets, and a secured lot behind the bar for $5/car. If you park on the street, make sure you feed the meter (this can be done through an app), and do not park in the bike lane, lest you risk getting a hefty ticket.

The neighborhood, Corktown, is Detroit's oldest, founded in 1834. It is also enjoying one of the more aggressive comebacks in the city.

*They have Poutine and Poutine tater tots at* ***Mercury****. That's fries or tots, with gravy and cheese curds. Try them.*

- NOTES -

1949 Michigan Avenue
(313) 483-7283

# Motor City Wine

**Full bar:** ✓ **Draft beer:** ✗ **Full kitchen:** ✗ **Shuttle service:** ✗ **motorcitywine.com**

HOURS:
Mon: 4pm - midnight
Tue: closed
Wed - Thu: 2pm - 1am
Fri - Sat: 2pm - 2am
Sun: 4pm - 2am

Don't let the name fool you. This little non-descript wooden building on Michigan Avenue cleverly disguises a cool place that is much more than just a wine shop. Hardwood floors and a drop ceiling keep the decor on the simple side, but the racks of wine along the walls in the sitting room remind you that there is a retail side to this business.

The focus of the bar menu is wine, and the range is large. Since not everyone likes wine, there is a selection of beer, cider, and sipping spirits. There are no cocktails here.

There is food, but not a full kitchen. Basically there are some palette cleansing snacks and a couple of grilled cheese sandwiches on the menu.

Besides the friendly staff and shelves full of wine, there are several other things that bring in the crowds. Wednesday - Friday there is live jazz, and Saturday - Monday features house and techno DJ music, all without cover charges. The other gem about **Motor City Wine** is their large outdoor patio with a privacy fence to separate it from the rest of the world, creating a fun space for hanging with friends. Besides having drinks, music, and friends on the patio, there is also a bocce court for something just a little bit different.

Parking is available in the lot next to the building and along the street. If you park in the street, plug the meter and stay out of the bike lane.

Corktown is a cool neighborhood, however it is separated from downtown by a good distance, so plan accordingly if your visit to **Motor City Wine** is part of a larger schedule that involves an event in the city. Some of the bars in the area have shuttles, but not this one. Although, with the music, bocce ball, and a patio, why would you leave?

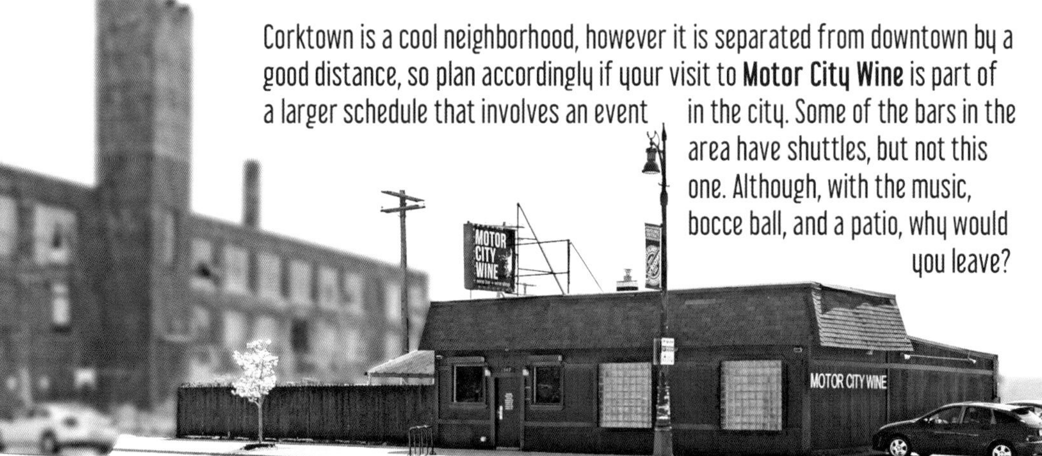


- NOTES -

# Mudgie's

1300 Porter Street
(313) 961-2000
mudgiesdeli.com

**Full bar:** ✓ **Draft beer:** ✓ **Full kitchen:** ✓ **Shuttle service:** ✗

Author Favorite

HOURS:
Mon - Wed: 11am - 9pm
Thu - Sat: 11am - 11pm
Sun: 10am - 3pm

HAPPY HOUR:
Mon - Fri: 4pm - 6pm

From the outside, it is a somewhat plain brick building. Go inside and find a store, a sit-down deli, a bar, and access to two patios.

You enter on the side, off Brooklyn Street, to the small store, where wine, some beer, and a few other things can be purchased. Head left into the bar, a small, cozy area with both bar seating and a couple of tables by the windows. It is safe to say **Mudgie's** has one of the largest beer lists in Detroit. They also have a good selection of cider, wine, and even mead. During happy hour, enjoy $3 shots of Jameson's and Frenet Branca, $2 rotating beer, and to-go pricing on wine and large format beers. All day, every day, there is a list of deli-drinks, special to **Mudgie's**.

The Deli part of the business is what put **Mudgie's** on the map, and it shows from their menu. The pre-designed offerings of sandwiches and wraps is a couple of pages long, and then there's the build your own part. The list of ingredients you can use takes up a whole page, allowing you to get as creative as you want.

Located in the historic Corktown neighborhood, there is free parking on along the streets, and a private lot behind the building. It's not really close enough to reasonably consider walking to any of Detroit's arenas or theaters, but then, those are not the only reasons to be in Detroit.

*Aside from the deli, this is a beer lovers version of heaven. So many choices!*

- NOTES -

2264 Harrison Street
(313) 962-4247

# Nancy Whiskey

Full bar: ✓ Draft beer: ✓ Full kitchen: ✓ Shuttle service: ✗ nancywhiskeydetroit.com

HOURS:
Mon - Sun: 11am - 2am

HAPPY HOUR:
Mon - Fri: 3pm - 6pm

**Nancy Whiskey** is a little off the beaten path, but worth the trip. Established in 1902, they've seen more than a few people come through the doors, and now it's your turn.

The outside looks more like a big old house than a bar, but all of that goes away once inside. Most of the room is taken up by the long wooden bartop, and the rest by tables and chairs. At the very back is a small stage, where bands perform most Fridays and Saturdays. Besides the place itself, the hidden gem is the large outdoor patio enclosed by a wooden privacy fence. That's where it all happens in the summertime.

The bar serves up just a couple of beers on tap, one of them being Guinness. Always. There are more to choose from in bottles and cans, and during happy hour domestics are just $2. Since it's an Irish bar, in addition to a standard range of booze, Irish whiskey flows with regularity. Above the bar are a line-up of fire hats, and on the coolers there are stickers from fire departments and unions of all types. Both are part of the proud heritage of **Nancy Whiskey**.

Food is good and fresh, with a range of choices of bar sides, sandwiches, and burgers. From September through June, there is a fish-fry every Friday.

Parking is on the streets, and that can be hard to come by on any given weekend. If you are in the city on the 4th of July, St. Patrick's Day, or for Santarchy, **Nancy Whiskey** is a great place to go for the festivities. They are, after all, "***Detroit's Oldest Party***", according to the sign on the building.

*On Wednesdays it is free to operate the jukebox.*

*There's a two drink minimum when the bands are playing.*

- NOTES -

**Been there!** ☐

**Corktown**

# Nemo's Bar

**1384 Michigan Avenue**
**(313) 965-3180**

**Full bar:** ☑ **Draft beer:** ☑ **Full kitchen:** ☒ **Shuttle service:** ☑

**nemosdetroit.com**

HOURS:
Mon - Sun: 11am - 2am

**Nemo's** has been in operation since 1965. They are, and always have been, a sports bar. In fact, in 2005, Sports Illustrated named them the #3 sports bar in the country. In 1997, Mike Ilitch, owner of the Red Wings, brought the Stanley Cup to Nemo's after their win. It's that kind of place, and it has that kind of history.

The inside of **Nemo's** has two rooms. The front has the long bar and the burger grill, along with a couple of tables. The back room is about the same size, and is filled with tables. The walls on both sides are covered with framed front pages documenting some of the greatest Michigan sports moments. Behind the frames, the walls roll into the coved tin ceiling, a carry over from the historic past of this building, which was built in 1883.

**Nemo's** offers a breakfast buffet from 9-11am when the Lions have a home game. Aside from that, their kitchen is open from 11:00am - 2:30pm for lunch, during which their menu contains multiple options. Anytime beyond that, they offer burgers, chips, and nuts. They are known for their burgers.

**Nemo's** has plenty of parking behind their building, and offers a $3 shuttle to games and events.

*Huge days: Parade day, St. Patrick's, and opening day (Tigers).*

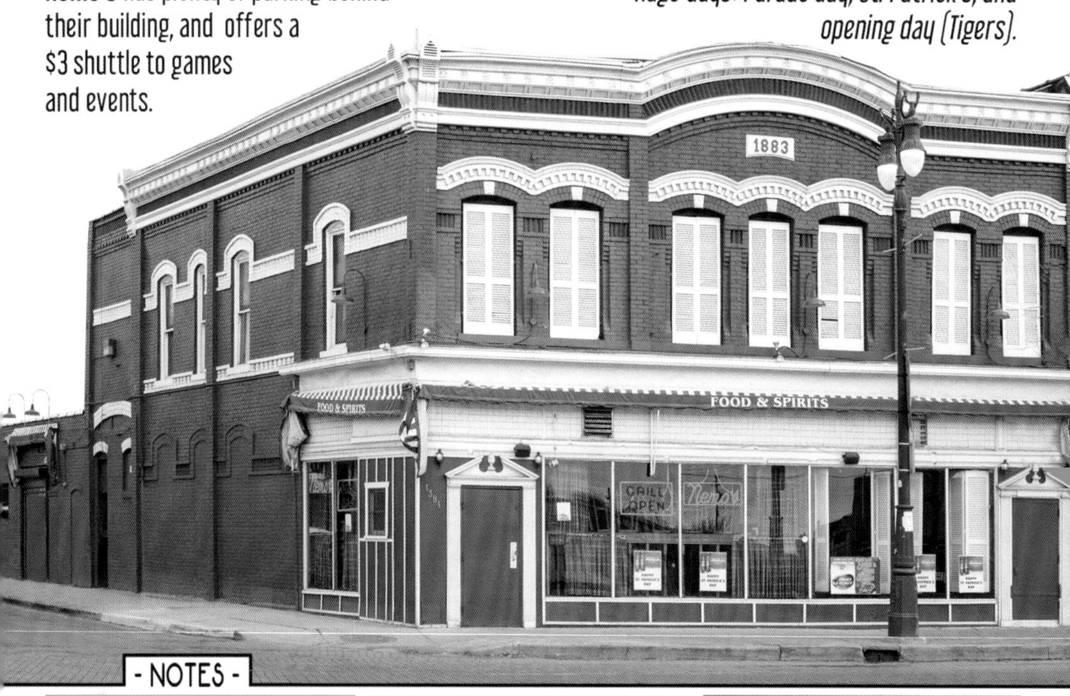


- NOTES -

# Ottava Via

1400 Michigan Avenue
(313) 962-5500

**Full bar:** ✓ **Draft beer:** ✓ **Full kitchen:** ✓ **Shuttle service:** ➡ (Use Nemo's - same owner)

HOURS:
Mon - Thu: 11am - 10pm
Fri - Sat: 11am - 11pm
Sun: 11am - 9pm

BRUNCH:
Sat - Sun: 11am - 3pm

**Ottava Via** is an elegant Italian restaurant and bar, a pleasant outlier when compared to its neighbors in Corktown. Pass through the old vestibule and enter into a large open floorplan with high ceilings. The aromas wafting from the open-view kitchen at the rear, along with the decor, are warm, delicious, and inviting.

Sit at the long bar and enjoy one of their seasonal drinks, a cold draft, a mixed drink, or choose a wine from their extensive list, sold both by the glass and by the bottle.

In addition to traditional Italian dishes, **Ottava Via** has a selection of small plates and pizzas, the latter prepared in an authentic brick pizza oven brought over from Italy. If you are dining with a group, it is suggested to order several different things and share them around the table family style. During lunch, there is a small selection of sandwiches, and on Saturday and Sunday, they offer a brunch menu.

When the weather is cooperating, there is a wonderful large back patio, complete with two bocce courts and an outdoor fireplace. Definitely one of the nicer patios in the city.

There are several options for parking at **Ottava Via**. They have a free, secure, private lot behind the patio, free parking along 8th Street, and metered parking along Michigan Avenue. Having an owner in common, the Nemo's shuttle can be used to go from **Ottava Via** to sporting and other major events in the city. Check ahead for availability, and don't forget to tip the driver.

- NOTES -

Been there! ☐ Corktown

# PJ's Lager House

1254 Michigan Avenue
(313) 961-4668

**Full bar:** ☑ **Draft beer:** ☑ **Full kitchen:** ☑ **Shuttle service:** ☒ **pjslagerhouse.com**

HOURS:
Mon - Tue: 1pm - 2am
Wed - Fri: 11am - 2am
Sat - Sun: 10:30am - 2am

HAPPY HOUR:
Mon - Wed: 3pm - 6pm
Thu - Fri: 11am - 6pm

BRUNCH:
Sat - Sun: 10:30am - 3pm

**PJ's** has been around in one form or another since 1914, and it is still going strong. They have bands most evenings, so be prepared to be entertained. The history of this building is long and interesting, from the days when numbers were run out of the basement, to the big name artists who have played on the stage in the back room over the years. History is visible in the restored tin ceilings, the pictures on the wall, and the reclaimed wood from old Detroit buildings used for table tops and the stage surface.

After you see the bar for the first time, it will remain in your memory. Set into the surface are over 6,000 guitar picks. Behind this musically inspired bar is a full stock of liquor, a dozen drafts, and a selection of around forty other varieties of beer. During happy hour, you get $1 off bottled and canned beer, and $4 pints of Guinness.

Author Favorite

From the kitchen, in addition to standard menu items you would expect in a bar, **PJ's Lager House** offers a respectable vegetarian menu including veggie burgers made from house-made falafel. Fortunately for the patrons, the owner, PJ, has been influenced by the food of New Orleans. There is a tasty selection of po'boys on the menu, **PJ's** famous Detroit Gumbo, and several other items where Cajun flavors come into play. Come for brunch on Saturday or Sunday (10:30am - 3pm), and enjoy vegan biscuits and gravy, shrimp and grits, or any of the other wonderful offerings.

Live music is a normality at **PJ's**, sometimes as often as 7 days a week. The upcoming schedule can be found on their website. If you have the time, make sure to check out Underground Vinyl, the record store located in the basement.

- NOTES -

**1830 Michigan Avenue**
**(313) 285-8591**

# Red Corridor

**Full bar:** ☑ **Draft beer:** ☑ **Full kitchen:** ☑ **Shuttle service:** ☑

HOURS:

**Red Corridor** is a self-proclaimed "*Upscale Dive Bar*" in Corktown, occupying the space formerly known as Casey's Pub. Outside, the charm comes from the brick and faded wood facade. Inside, the old tin ceilings help to maintain a cozy feel in a throw-back environment.

There are two floors to the establishment. The first has more of the typical bar feel, with a long wooden bartop running the length of the room on the left, while the upstairs is the "Game Cave". Aptly named, the 2nd floor has air hockey, a pool table, darts, a juke box, and a video game console with arcade games from the 80s. Both upstairs and down have TVs where you can catch whatever game might be on at the time. During the warmer months, another option is the patio.

Red Corridor has all day happy hour every day, and a brunch on Saturdays and Sundays from 10am-4pm. During brunch, Bloody Marys and mimosas are $5 for the first, and $1 for each subsequent one. The food fare is primarily burgers and sandwiches, however they also have a variety of loaded fries, their signature culinary calling.

There is free parking in the rear, and metered parking out front. If you choose the metered parking, make sure you stay out of the bike lane or you may receive a hefty ticket.

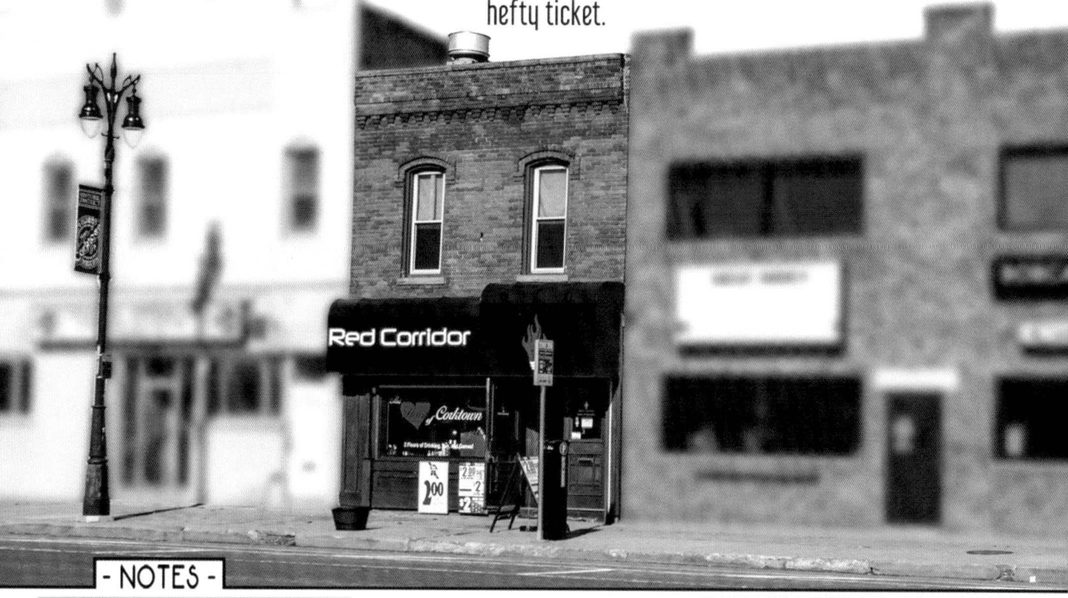


- NOTES -

**Been there!** ☐

**Corktown**

# Slows Bar B Q

**2138 Michigan Avenue**
**(313) 962-9828**

**Full bar:** ☑ **Draft beer:** ☑ **Full kitchen:** ☑ **Shuttle service:** ☒ **slowsbarbq.com**

HOURS:
Sun - Wed: 11am - 10pm
Thu - Fri: 11am - 11pm
Sat: 11am - midnight
*Bar is open one hour longer*

**Slows** is located on Michigan Avenue across the street from one of the most iconic abandoned buildings, Michigan Central Station. **Slows** has received a lot of publicity for their barbeque, and is a popular place. If you are heading there during prime lunch or dinner time, or if there is a major event in Detroit, be prepared for a wait.

The ambiance of **Slows** is old-Detroit comfort. Warm woods and brick dominate the design features of both the interior and the exterior of the building. The bar in the center of it all features 20 beers on tap, some of which can be taken to go in growlers, a wide variety of liquors, and everything needed to make both basic and complex drinks.

The barbecue is the claim to fame here, made from Michigan sourced meat, and smoked fresh on site. Once you are in the area your nose will start guiding your brain to go in and eat. It's hard to resist the permeating odor of the smokers. **Slows** offers the standards; ribs, brisket, chicken, pulled pork, smoked sausage and TVP, as well as a wide variety of sides and appetizers. If you are not in the mood for a huge meal, **Slows** has a rather extensive sandwich menu, built around their smoked meats.

There is limited metered parking on the street, and a guarded pay lot across Michigan Avenue, behind Mercury Bar.

*When the weather is warm, **Slows** opens their patio.*

- NOTES -

Been there! ☐

2130 Michigan Avenue
(313) 962-0123

# Sugar House

Full bar: ✓ Draft beer: ✗ Full kitchen: ✗ (small plates) Shuttle service: ✗ sugarhousedetroit.com

Author Favorite

HOURS:
Mon - Tue: 5pm - midnight
Wed - Fri: 5pm - 2am
Sat - Sun: 3pm - 2am

HAPPY HOUR:
Sat - Sun: 3pm - 5pm

When you enter **Sugar House** from the often bustling activity that is Michigan Avenue, the dark interior breathes a calm and intimate feeling into your soul. Always full, never crowded, a seat at the bar will provide a show of watching the mixologists creating the drinks for which they are so well known. Of course, if you would rather, there are tables in the remaining space, including a couple with a view of the outside. Finally, up on the walls overlooking everything are a variety of large animal mounts that somehow fit well with the decor.

The cocktail menu consists of 101 selections, however you are not limited to those. Any one of the experts behind the bar is willing and able to mix something you choose, or come up with something new for you based on flavors you are seeking. Beyond the cocktails are a large selection of rare and vintage pours, a dozen or so beers, and many choices of whiskey. If you are there during happy hour, enjoy 20% off cocktails, spirits on the back bar, and beer. For food, there is a menu of small plates.

Being in Corktown makes **Sugar House** a fair distance from downtown Detroit. The only place to walk to from here are other bars and restaurants along Michigan Ave. Parking is metered Monday through Saturday until 10pm on the street. There is also a paid lot behind Mercury Bar across the street, and for $5 per car on the street behind **Sugar House**.

- NOTES -

# Two James Spirits

2445 Michigan Avenue
(313) 964-4800
twojames.com

Full bar: ☑ Draft beer: ☒ Full kitchen: ☒ Shuttle service: ☒

HOURS:
Mon - Wed: 1pm - 11pm
Thu: 1pm - midnight
Fri: 1pm - 1am
Sat: noon - 1am
Sun: 1pm - 8pm

Author Favorite

**Two James** is a drinking destination. They are a tasting room located inside a distillery. The bartenders are willing and able to mix up some tasty concoctions using the **Two James** line of spirits.

Located in Corktown, **Two James** is within sight of the old train station, one of Detroit's most recognizable and still beautiful abandoned buildings. It is also easy walking distance to the restaurants in Corktown in case you want to have a meal before or after a visit to **Two James**. Tours of the distillery are offered on Friday, Saturday and Sunday afternoons. Reserve your space through their website.

When you step inside the building, you are faced with a modern bar, the centerpiece of the room. The wall on the distillery side of the building is made up of old barrell halves, appropriate decor for a distillery. The rest of the walls in the taproom are usually covered with framed art from a local artist. A new artist is chosen every three months or so.

**Two James** does not have a kitchen, and thus, does not offer food. In the past they have made arrangements with a food truck, however at the time of publishing, there was nothing permanent in place.

Parking is available on the street out front, and there is a secured lot behind the building.

*Did you know? **Two James** is the first licensed distillery in Detroit since prohibition. They make three kinds of whiskey, two different bourbons, two types of gin, absinthe, and even their own mezcal, which is distilled in Oaxaca, Mexico.*

TWO JAMES

- NOTES -

## UFO Factory

2110 Trumbull Street
(313) 610-6216

Full bar: ☑ Draft beer: ☑ Full kitchen: ✘ Shuttle service: ✘ ufofactory.com

HOURS:

CLOSED

Planning on re-opening sometime in 2018.

The **UFO Factory** is a smallish bar located on Trumbull, across from the old Tiger Stadium site. It's a nice, somewhat dark, divey bar where fun and privacy can be had.

They have a small stage and put it to use with double feature movies on Tuesdays, DJs, and live bands. Sundays are Karaoke nights. To see what is coming up, check their website. Other entertainment in the bar can be had by way of a couple of video games, a pinball game, and a photo booth.

The **UFO Factory** has a full bar, and a handful of draft beer options. During their happy hour, you get $1 off well drinks and domestic bottled beer.

The food they serve is provided by Laika Dog, and features some of the more unique hot dogs around, with creative flavor combinations, as well as affording you the ability to design/build your own dog. Vegans and vegetarians will be happy to know that they also offer vegan options. In fact, everything on the menu, besides the hotdogs, is vegan.

On Wednesdays, all food is 1/2 off from 4pm - 10pm. On Saturday and Sunday, they offer a brunch menu from 11am -3pm.

*What other bar do you know of where you can go for some drinks and catch an old Godzilla movie?*

*On August 2, 2017 the building was severly damaged during construction on the neighboring property. The plan is to open back up in 2018.*

\- NOTES -

# Downtown

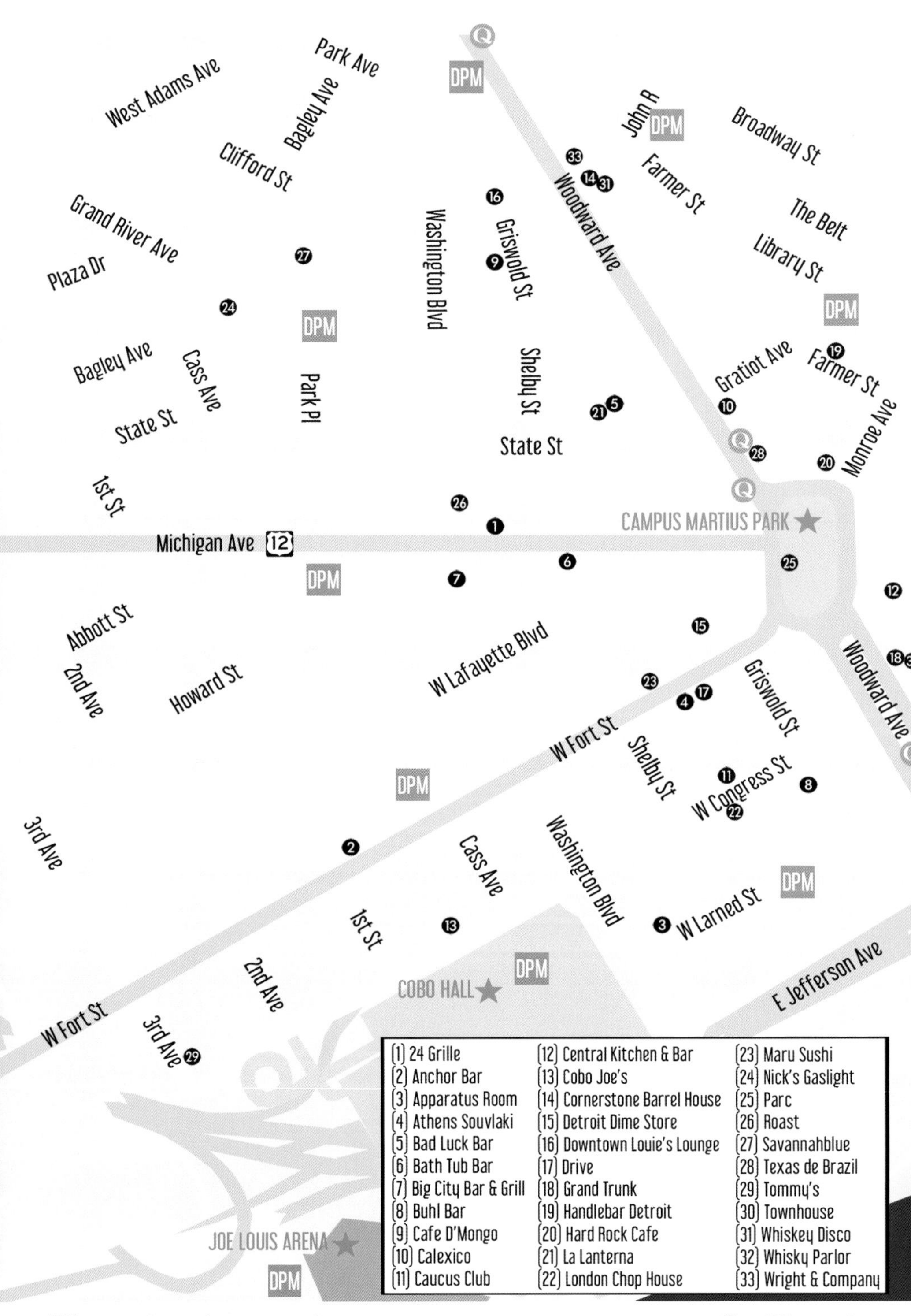


| | | |
|---|---|---|
| (1) 24 Grille | (12) Central Kitchen & Bar | (23) Maru Sushi |
| (2) Anchor Bar | (13) Cobo Joe's | (24) Nick's Gaslight |
| (3) Apparatus Room | (14) Cornerstone Barrel House | (25) Parc |
| (4) Athens Souvlaki | (15) Detroit Dime Store | (26) Roast |
| (5) Bad Luck Bar | (16) Downtown Louie's Lounge | (27) Savannahblue |
| (6) Bath Tub Bar | (17) Drive | (28) Texas de Brazil |
| (7) Big City Bar & Grill | (18) Grand Trunk | (29) Tommy's |
| (8) Buhl Bar | (19) Handlebar Detroit | (30) Townhouse |
| (9) Cafe D'Mongo | (20) Hard Rock Cafe | (31) Whiskey Disco |
| (10) Calexico | (21) La Lanterna | (32) Whisky Parlor |
| (11) Caucus Club | (22) London Chop House | (33) Wright & Company |

DPM = Detroit People Mover station

Q = QLine station

Been there! ☐ **Downtown**

**204 Michigan Avenue**
**(313) 964-3821**

# 24 Grille

**Full bar:** ☑ **Draft beer:** ☑ **Full kitchen:** ☑ **Shuttle service:** ☒

**24grille.com**

**24 Grille** finds its home in the magnificent Westin Book Cadillac Hotel. The building, built in 1924, exudes elegance. The inside of 24 Grille has been finished with an industrial flare. Black painted exposed ductwork and pillars complete the scene. Those sitting at tables enjoy the large windows which face out to Michigan Avenue.

HOURS:
Mon - Thu: 11am - 10pm
Fri - Sat: 11am - midnight

BRUNCH:
Sun: 10am - 3pm

HAPPY HOUR:
Mon - Fri: 4pm - 6:30pm

A wooden topped bar meanders around in the back of the space, with a TV hanging over the display of liquor bottles. They offer a large wine menu, 20+ beers, and a list of cocktails. During happy hour, there are some discounted small plates, as well as $5 house wines and well pours, $6 drafts, and $7 specialty cocktails.

Foodwise, **24 Grille** offers a little bit of everything. Whenever possible, the ingredients are Michigan sourced, and the dishes are prepared fresh to order.

The location allows for a variety of parking options, including the valet service offered (for a fee) by the Westin. There are also metered spots and parking garages in the area.

*Another option in the Westin is **Motor Bar**, upstairs from **24 Grille**. **Motor Bar** is a casual location with open floorplan seating, large windows facing out to Michigan Ave, and all of the elegance of the hotel.*

- NOTES -

Been there! ☐ | Downtown

# Anchor Bar

450 West Fort Street
(313) 964-9127

**Full bar:** ☑ **Draft beer:** ☑ **Full kitchen:** ☑ **Shuttle service:** ☑

HOURS:
Mon - Sat: 7am - 2am
Sun: noon - 2am

**Anchor Bar** is one of Detroit's long-standing, traditional sports dive bars. While this is the third location for the bar, it has been family owned for more than 50 years. The current location provides a comfortable, casual setting with high ceilings, tables, booths, and some bar space. At the front of the bar there are two pool tables, and play is free. This area is popular for groups to comingle, play some pool, and enjoy food and drinks.

The bar, as with many places in Detroit, is an old wooden masterpiece, preserving some of the history that is all-too-often lost. You'll find the drink selection to be satisfactory, and the prices low. Domestic draft beers and well drinks start at $3, crafts beers at $5, allowing patrons to enjoy an afternoon without breaking the bank. **Anchor** has a couple of video games and a juke box for more entertainment.

The menu at **Anchor Bar** revolves around their selection of burgers and sandwiches, as well as a list of bar-style appetizers. Feeling hungry? Try the totchos - tater tots smothered in chili, cheddar cheese, sour cream, and salsa. It's their signature appetizer. There are also daily and game day food specials.

Parking is plentiful in the area, and **Anchor Bar** provides shuttle service to Detroit sporting events as well as other large, local events. Check with them directly for availability.

- NOTES -

250 West Larned Street
(313) 800-5600

# The Apparatus Room

**Full bar:** ✓ **Draft beer:** ✓ **Full kitchen:** ✓ **Shuttle service:** ✗ **detroitfoundationhotel.com/apparatus-room**

One of the newest bars in this book, **The Apparatus Room** is located in the Foundation Hotel, also a new addition in Detroit. The building, on the other hand, has been around since 1929, and was formerly the Detroit Fire Department Headquarters. Fortunately, much of the beauty of the old structure has been preserved. The front and side have the old red fire-house doors set into large stone arches, and the inside carries forward many of the old architectural and design touches.

HOURS:
Mon - Sun: 11am - midnight

HAPPY HOUR:
*Coming soon, but not yet in place at time of printing.*

The bar is to the left, and while part of the larger restaurant, could stand on its own. The large, rectangular wooden bar top is complimented with leather bar chairs. Above the bar is one of the most unique features; hundreds of hanging lights. Not only functional, but also beautiful. The bar serves up beers in draft, cans, and bottles, has a large selection of wines, and an extensive list of whiskey, rye, and bourbon. There are a respectable number of Michigan brands represented, and a special cocktail menu offers a half dozen cocktails, all with a Detroit twist.

The Foundation Hotel is located across Washington Boulevard from Cobo Hall. There is limited parking on the street, several surface lots, and multiple parking garages in the vicinity. If parking elsewhere, or doing something somewhere else in the city, the Detoit People Mover's Financial District station is just a block down Larned. Woodward Avenue and the QLine is three blocks over, and that will get you up to the sports venues and theaters.

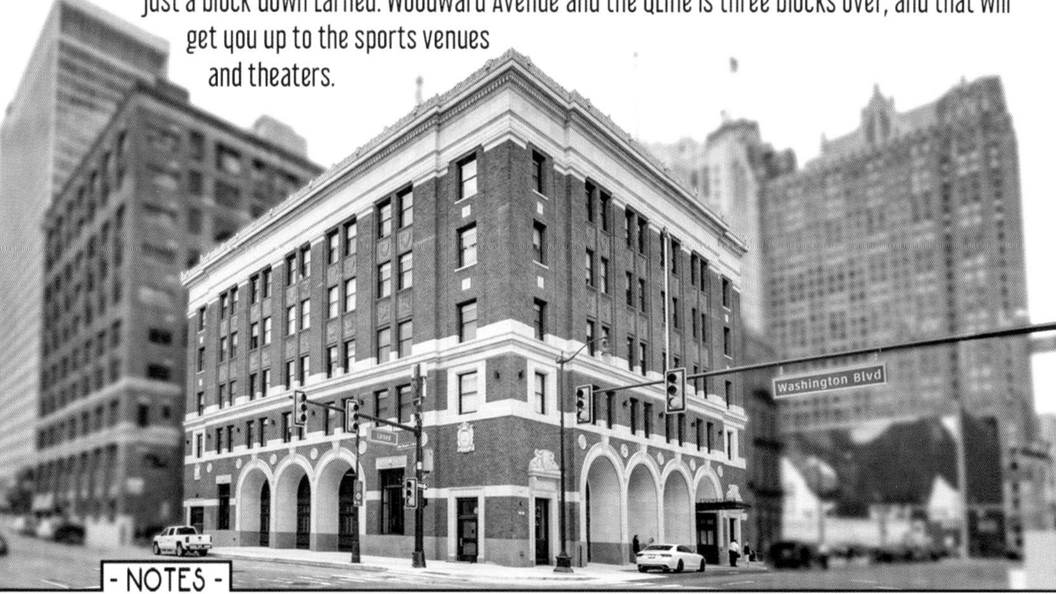


- NOTES -

Been there! ☐

Downtown

# Athens Souvlaki

645 Griswold Street
(313) 265-3178

Full bar: ✓ Draft beer: ✓ Full kitchen: ✓ Shuttle service: ✗ athenssouvlaki.com

HOURS:
Mon - Fri: 8am - 11pm
Sat - Sun: closed

There are two entrances to **Athens Souvlaki**. One is through the front of the Penobscot Building, on Griswold Street, and the other, off Fort Street, takes you directly into the restaurant. The bar is at the back of the restaurant, while the dining area faces out to Griswold.

The bar is relatively small, with a half dozen or so stools at the bartop, and a few cozy bar tables. Despite the somewhat compact space, it is a full bar, with over 30 different beers, and a full line of liquor. Every day has its own drink special. You get $1 off drafts on Monday, $1 off tequila shots on Tuesday, and $1 off whiskey shots on Wednesday. On Thursday, they have "The Jack" - Greek Mythos beer and a shot of Jameson. End the week on Friday with $1 off flavored vodka shots.

Greek food is the name of the game from the kitchen. The menu is absolutely massive, with dozens of choices. The restaurant space is set up diner style, and is comfortable, bright and clean.

This downtown location is a block from Woodward Avenue and Campus Martius. The QLine has a station there, and the train can get you easily to Comerica Park, Ford Field, The Fox and Fillmore theaters, Little Caesars Arena, MOCAD, the DIA, and more. There are several parking structures in the area, and metered parking on the streets.

- NOTES -

Been there! ☐ Downtown

1218 Griswold
(313) 657-9177

# Bad Luck Bar

Full bar: ✓ Draft beer: ✗ Full kitchen: ✗ Shuttle service: ✗ badluckbar.com

HOURS:
Wed - Sat: 5pm - 2am

Perhaps the strangest location of any of the bars in Detroit, **Bad Luck Bar** can only be accessed by going down the alley behind the Albert Hotel. To top it off, it's a true city alley. The contrast comes when you get to the door about 75 yards down the alley. There are red lights behind glass block next to the door, letting you know you are in the right place. Pass through the door into a small vestibule with a black-out curtain and a host stand. On the other side of the curtain is a dim and intimate space with a soaring ceiling and a handful of small tables.

At the very back of the room, a tall shelving system holds the bottles for the bar, and stretches up to the ceiling. Soft backlighting creates a glow on and around the bottles, while at the same time providing some of the minimal interior light. Cocktails are the name of the game here, and a menu filled with über creative craft cocktails, gives patrons a hint as to what to expect. The staff's mixology skills are virtually unmatched. For the beer drinkers out there, **Bad Luck Bar** has one choice for you: Miller High Life.

There is no kitchen here, so do not arrive with an appetite. There are nuts and small snacks.

Park out on Griswold or in a nearby garage, and make your way to the **Bad Luck Bar**. It's an experience you won't likely find anywhere else. It's a small place, so don't come here with a large group. Also, fair warning, the prices are among the highest in the city. Nevertheless, this is a popular bar.

- NOTES -

**Been there!** ☐

**Downtown**

# St. Brigid's Bath Tub Pub

**129 Michigan Avenue**
**(313) 962-0700**

**Full bar:** ✓ **Draft beer:** ✓ **Full kitchen:** ✗ **Shuttle service:** ✗

HOURS:
Mon - Sun: noon- 2am

HAPPY HOUR:
Mon - Fri: 4pm - 6pm

Located next to two of Detroit's iconic Coney Island restaurants, **Bath Tub Pub** carves out the end spot on the block. Inside it is a bit dark and worn, the narrow main room stretching from Michigan Avenue to Lafayette Boulevard. A small open kitchen area sits at the front end of the long wooden bar. A few booths fill the remaining space along the other wall. There is a very large upstairs area which is slated to be used for music and dancing.

The bar serves up the basics when it comes to shots and mixed drinks, and stocks around ten different beers in bottles and cans. During happy hour everything is $1 off the already low prices.

Food from the kitchen is limited to just a handful of items, of which burgers and wings are the most commonly ordered plates.

**Bath Tub Pub** is a no-frills kind of place. A jukebox and one large TV provide the entertainment in the main bar area, and although not in place at the time of publication, the owner is trying to gain access to some of the garden area outside for additional seating options.

- NOTES -

Been there! ☐

**Downtown**

1020 Washington Boulevard
(313) 963-8808

# Big City Bar & Grill

**Full bar:** ☑ **Draft beer:** ☑ **Full kitchen:** ☑ **Shuttle service:** ☑

HOURS:
Mon - Fri: 11am - 2am
Sat: 4pm - 2am
Sun: 4pm - midnight

HAPPY HOUR:
Mon - Fri: 11am - 6pm

Located inside the Holiday Inn Express - Detroit, **Big City Bar & Grill** is bright, clean, and modern. It presents well as a sports bar, with several TVs allowing viewing from just about anywhere in the bar, a pool table, darts, a juke box, and a bartop video game unit.

The bar itself occupies about a third of the space, with the bartop wrapping around the serving area. In addition to a good selection of beer in bottles and cans, there are 15 taps to choose from. During their extensive happy hour, **Big City** offers $3 domestic beers, $4 imports, and $5 premium beers, house wines, and special shots. When one of the Detroit teams are playing, they offer additional drink and food specials.

From the kitchen, guests can order American style food, with a selection of a dozen entrees, along with sandwiches, burgers, wraps, stone oven pizzas, and salads. During lunch, there is an abbreviated menu with a balanced selection of the same.

Located in the inner part of Detroit, **Big City** is close to Cobo Hall and Campus Martius, and not terribly far from the sports arenas and the downtown theaters. **Big City** provides a shuttle for games and major events.

- NOTES -

Been there! ☐

DOWNTOWN

# Buhl Bar

535 Griswold Street
(313) 963-6118

Full bar: ✓ Draft beer: ✗ Full kitchen: ✗ Shuttle service: ✗ buhlbardetroit.com

HOURS:
Mon - Fri: 4:00pm - 7:30 pm
Sat - Sun: closed

The **Buhl Bar** is located on the first floor of the 26-floor Buhl Building, which has graced the skyline of Detroit since 1925. The elegant style of the exterior smoothly extends to the inside. As you cross the threshold, you enter a space befitting a Rat Pack era movie. A sense of unforced coolness permeates the air, and it's clear the expected clientele is business-professional.

It is a small space with comfortable seating on the perimeter and a few seats at the bar itself. Bourbon is the drink of preference, and there are many varieties to choose from. Not to worry, if that is not your thing, there are other options.

Food is not offered other than small bowls of nuts or chips. Only open during the work week, most of the patrons are here for a little unwinding before heading home.

Located in the Financial District of Detroit, the **Buhl Bar** is close to everything downtown. It's just a block from Woodward and the QLine, and there is a Detroit People Mover station nearby, making both viable options to get to the Fox or Fillmore theaters, as well as to the Detroit sports arenas.

While there is curbside parking on many of the streets in the area, for the time period **Buhl** is open, it is often difficult to find an open spot. Neighborhood parking structures are your best bet.

*The proprietors of **Buhl Bar** are protective of their image and their clientele. This is not a bar for grabbing a few beers. If you are not dressed appropriately, you likely will be turned away. In a world where almost everything has become über-casual, this is nice.*

- NOTES -

1439 Griswold Street
(313) 961-2543

# Cafe D'Mongo's Speakeasy

**Full bar:** ✓ **Draft beer:** ✗ **Full kitchen:** ✗ **Shuttle service:** ✗

Author Favorite

HOURS:
Thu: 5:30pm - 10:30pm
Fri: 5pm - 1:30am
Sat: 7pm - 1:30am
Sun - Wed: closed

**Cafe D'Mongo** is a museum as much as it is a bar. The entrance is a time portal, and on the other side is a slice of the past. Almost every square inch of the walls is covered with historic items, from a framed newspaper reporting Marilyn Monroe's death to pictures of the Purple Gang, the notorious mob of bootleggers and hijackers who operated out of Detroit in the 20s. The artifacts and memorabilia throughout **Cafe D'Mongo** would take days to study thoroughly, and every minute of it would be interesting.

The bar itself only seats a handful of people, however there are small tables set up throughout this wonderful space, and even a sitting area outside on the sidewalk. **Cafe D'Mongo** has three signature drinks, one of which incorporates Faygo's Rock & Rye, and one which uses Vernors, both famous Detroit brands. Besides those, there is a good selection of liquors and a few beers. There is a two drink minimum here, although that's not a stretch with so much atmosphere to take in.

Food is limited to grilled cheeses, and they are not your run of the mill, American white bread style. These have a gourmet lean, and the flavor offerings change from time to time.

*You owe it to yourself to come here at least once while in Detroit.*

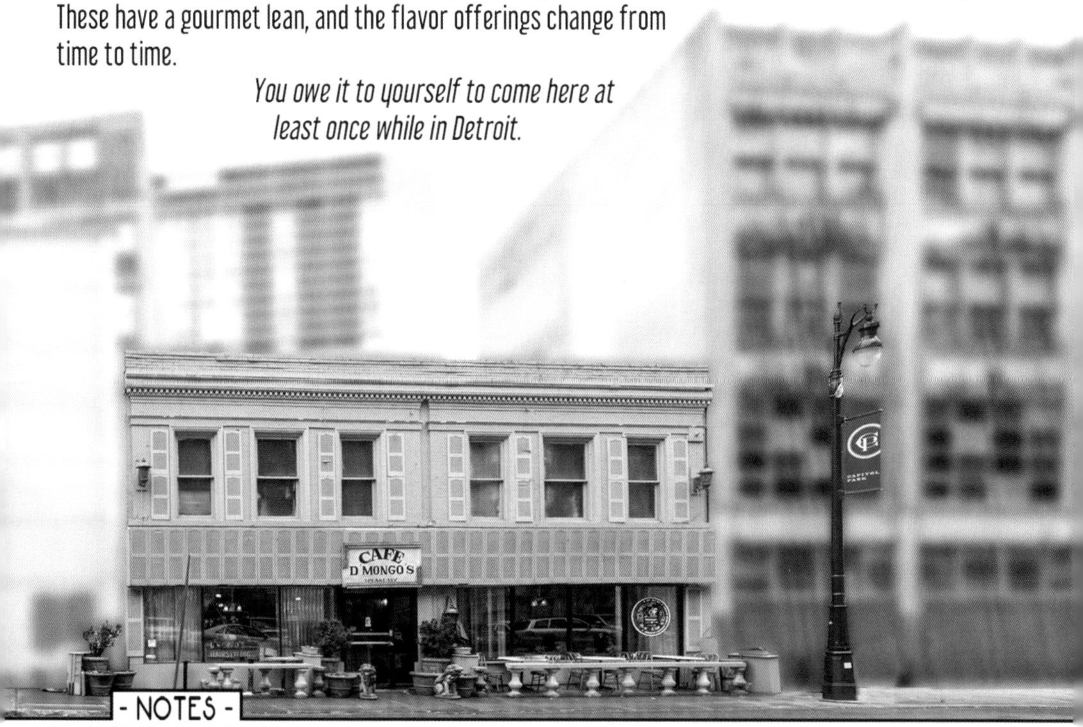

- NOTES -

**Been there!** ☐

**Downtown**

# Calexico

**1040 Woodward Avenue**
**(313) 262-6361**

**Full bar:** ✓ **Draft beer:** ✓ **Full kitchen:** ✓ **Shuttle service:** ✗

**calexico.net**

HOURS:
Mon - Thu: 10:30am - 11pm
Fri - Sat: 10:30am - 1am
Sun: 10:30am - 9pm

HAPPY HOUR:
Mon - Thu: 3pm - 7pm
Fri: 3pm - 6pm
Sun: 10:30am - 9pm

On the 1st floor of One Campus Martius in the heart of downtown Detroit, **Calexico** has established itself as a goto for California influenced Mexican food. The business was already well established in New York, and this is the first location outside of the Big Apple.

**Calexico** is finished in a modern fashion, with natural colored wood and exposed brick being the predominant theme. About a third of the interior is the bar, complete with liquor shelves hanging from the ceiling. The bar menu is filled with cocktails that have a Mexican twist, a range of margaritas, and a couple of Micheladas - beer based mixed drinks. Beyond the standard liquors, **Calexico** has a Tequila list 35 deep. During happy hour you get $3 beers, $4 well drinks, $5 house margaritas, and $1 off tacos.

The kitchen is open to the restaurant, which allows the wonderful smells to pour out into the dining room. When the front of the dining area is open to the street, this feature certainly must bring in new business. They offer eight varieties of tacos along with burritos, enchiladas, fajitas, and quesadillas.

One of the more central locations in downtown Detroit, Campus Martius, Greektown, and St. Andrew's Hall are a short distance away, and while the sports arenas aren't too far up Woodward, there is a QLine stop out front and a People Mover station in the parking garage.

*The sidewalk seating area is a fun place to have a drink and watch the people go by. Ball games and events at Campus Martius are good days for this activity.*

- NOTES -

Been there! ☐ Downtown

150 West Congress
(313) 965-4970

# Caucus Club

Full bar: ✓ Draft beer: ✓ Full kitchen: ✓ Shuttle service: ✗ caucusclubdetroit.com

**Caucus Club** occupies a prime space in the first floor of the historic Penobscot Building. Following 60 years of operation, it had been closed since 2012. Freshly reinvented, it's back on the scene in Detroit.

HOURS:
Mon - Thu: 11am - 10pm
Fri: 11am - 11pm
Sat: 5pm - 11pm
Sun: 4:30pm - 9pm

HAPPY HOUR:
Mon - Fri: 3pm - 6pm

Keeping with the elegant style of the building, the dining area greets you with linen covered tables, comfortable seating, and visual assurances that you are in a fine-dining establishment. In order to provide some privacy, the space is segmented into multiple rooms, with the bar occupying the area in the back.

In addition to the stools at the long bartop, multiple high-top booths and cozy bar tables provide sitting options. Drink-wise, **Caucus Club** has a massive list of wines, and a few dozen cocktails featured on their extensive bar menu. Their signature drink is the Bullshot - beef consomé, gin, balsamic bitters, and lime. When it comes down to it, if you want it, they probably have it. Get here for happy hour and save on wine, cocktails, one of the drafts, and a selection of small plates.

For the foodies out there, this is a destination for high-end steaks that have been dry aged in house. Beyond the beef, there is a focus on seafood and a raw bar. In an effort to keep everyone happy, you can also get soups, salads, and a variety of sandwiches and appetizers.

**Caucus Club** has a valet service, or you can find a spot on the street, in a surface lot, or in one of the many parking garages in the area.

To get around town without having to get in and out of your car or walk everywhere, catch the QLine on Woodward, or the People Mover at a nearby stop.

- NOTES -

**Been there!** ☐

**Downtown**

# Central Kitchen & Bar

**660 Woodward Avenue**
**(313) 963-9000**
**centraldetroit.com**

**Full bar:** ☑ **Draft beer:** ☑ **Full kitchen:** ☑ **Shuttle service:** ☒

HOURS:
Mon - Thu: 11am - 10pm
Fri - Sat: 11am - midnight
*(bar open one hour later)*

HAPPY HOUR:
Mon - Fri: 3pm - 6pm

BRUNCH:
Sat: 10am - 2pm
Sun: 10am - 3pm

**Central Kitchen & Bar** can be found in the renovated First National Bank Building on Woodward, just across from Campus Martius. While most of the decorative touches are modern, one large wall is covered with a scene from historic Detroit, and much of the old ceiling shows above the ductwork and lights. In addition to the comfortable padded booths and table seating, there is a large year-round patio area out front that can be opened up for good weather.

The bar in the middle of the interior space is uncluttered and contemporary. Along with a list of craft cocktails and a wide selection of wines, **Central Kitchen & Bar** offers a dozen craft beers, often showcasing hard to get releases. During happy hour, beers and mixed drinks are $1 off, wine by the glass is $3 off, and free seasoned popcorn is served.

The kitchen provides three menus; brunch on the weekend - complete with a complementing cocktail menu, a menu for lunch, which leans toward burgers, sandwiches, tacos, and salads, and a dinner menu which mirrors the lunch menu, with the addition of a selection of entrees. All of the offerings are a step up from "basic" with inventive, quality ingredients.

***AUTHOR'S FAVORITE:*** *I have a hard time ordering anything but the Cuban sandwich. It's delicious!*

Walking to the theaters and arenas is possible, however the QLine, with a stop at Campus Martius, makes it easier to get there.

- NOTES -

**Been there!** ☐

**Downtown**

**422 W. Congress Street**
**(313) 965-0840**

# Cobo Joe's Bar and BBQ

**Full bar:** ☑ **Draft beer:** ☑ **Full kitchen:** ☑ **Shuttle service:** ☑

**cobojoes.com**

HOURS:
Mon - Sat: 10:30am - 6pm
when there are no events.
Mon - Sun: 10:30am - 1 or 2am
when there are events in town

**Cobo Joe's** is located just up from Cobo Hall on West Congress Street. It's unassuming from the outside, but once you walk in, it is immediately clear you are in a sports bar. The walls are covered in sports themed beer mirrors, pictures, banners, and other sporting memorabilia. Several large TVs provide the opportunity to watch from just about any seat in the facility.

The bar serves a full range of liquor, mixed to your liking, and puts forth a small selection of draft beers which you can get in 16oz or 22oz servings. The beer selection expands when you get into the bottled portion of the beer list.

The menu is dominated by barbecue dishes, however they do offer a good selection of traditional bar style appetizers, burgers, sandwiches, salads, and pizzas. Most of the meats, even the burger patties, are smoked, and all of the smoking is done in-house. They've got a good handle on the process. Their food is tasty!

Keep in mind that the business hours at **Cobo Joe's** will vary greatly depending on what is going on in downtown Detroit. If you plan to visit in the evening, it's probably a good idea to call ahead to make sure they will be open.

Parking garages abound in this area, and there is limited metered parking on the street. Cobo Joe's will have their shuttle running for games in town, so despite Comerica Park, Ford Field, and Little Caesars Arena being across town, this is still a good place to go for food and drinks before and after a game. The distance from the parks may be to your advantage, allowing you to avoid some of the traffic.

***AUTHOR'S FAVORITE:*** *CANDIED BACON!*
*Literally sweet candied bacon on a stick. You won't regret it. It's a good start for any meal.*

\- NOTES -

Been there! ☐

Downtown

# Cornerstone Barrel House

1456 Woodward Avenue
(313) 338-3238

Full bar: ☑ Draft beer: ☑ Full kitchen: ☑ Shuttle service: ☒ cornerstonedetroit.com

Occupying the first floor of an old eight story building on Woodward Avenue, the interior of **Cornerstone** has tall ceilings and a comfortable ambiance. Darkened windows allow light from the outside without being blinding. Seating along the windows allows the opportunity to do some people watching while relaxing with a drink and some food. When it's warm, seating is available outside, too.

HOURS:
Mon: 4pm - 11pm
Tue - Thu: 11:30am - midnight
Fri - Sat: 11:30am - 2am
Sun: 11am - 10pm

HAPPY HOUR:
Mon - Fri: 3pm - 6pm

A long wooden bar fills more than a third of the space, and the offerings range from draft craft beers to an impressive list of bourbon, rye, scotch, and whiskey, and a host of creative craft cocktails. The friendly bar staff can also serve you up any type of traditional cocktail with a smile. During happy hour, enjoy $3 domestic bottled beer, $4 craft drafts, $5 house wines, $6 Detroit mules, $4 bourbon shot of the day, and a decent selection of $3 minis and sides.

For the hungry crowd, the kitchen prepares a selection of soups, salads, sandwiches and entrees, made fresh, in view, in the open kitchen at the end of the bar. Good food is one of their calling cards, accompanied by cheerful service.

Their location is conveniently within walking distance of all of Detroit's sports facilities, as well as the Detroit Opera House and Campus Martius. In lieu of walking, the QLine serves Woodward, and the Detroit People Mover has several stations nearby. Parking is limited on the streets, however there are parking garages in the area.

***Whiskey Disco** is located in the basement. Check their page in this guide for more details.*

- NOTES -

Been there! ☐

719 Griswold Street, suite 180
(313) 962-9106

Downtown

# Dime Store

Full bar: ☑ Draft beer: ☑ Full kitchen: ☑ Shuttle service: ☒

eatdimestore.com

HOURS:
Mon - Fri: 8am - 4pm
Sat - Sun: 8am - 3pm

**Dime Store** is, in their words, an "American Brunch Bar". They make their home in the 23 story Chrysler House, AKA The Dime Building, one of the oldest skyscrapers in Detroit (1912). Their choice location on the first floor allows the whole front wall to be windows facing out to Griswold Street.

Inside, the space is finished in a modern industrial manner and the walls adorned with large paintings of an old dime, and a Mercury head. It is a relatively small space, with bar and counter seating enough to accommodate around a dozen people, and table seating for another 40.

The bar has about 10 beers, two on draft, a limited wine list, and basic liquors. On the menu four drinks are highlighted on their "Day Drinking List": Bloody Mary, Peach Mimosa, Beermosa, and Irish Coffee.

**Dime Store** is a breakfast and brunch place, thus the menu is filled with omelets, breakfast sandwiches, hash, and the like. For those looking for other than breakfast options, there are also sandwiches, burgers, soups, and mac 'n' cheese. Any sandwich on the menu can be made into a salad, placing the sandwich fillings on a bed of greens for the same price.

This location is right in the middle of downtown. Parking is often tough to find on the street, however **Dime Store** validates parking for the Financial District Garage (enter off Lafayette).

If you need to get to other parts of the city after visiting **Dime Store**, the QLine can be caught on Woodward, or the People Mover can be utilized, although the nearest station is a couple of blocks away.

***Dime Store** is a popular place. Anticipate there will be a wait. It's worth it.*

- NOTES -

**Been there!** ☐

**Downtown**
**30 Clifford**
**(313) 961-1600**

# Downtown Louie's Lounge

**Full bar:** ✓ **Draft beer:** ✓ **Full kitchen:** ✓ **Shuttle service:** ✗ **downtownlouieslounge.com**

HOURS:
Mon - Thu: 11am - 11pm
Fri: 11am - midnight
Sat: 4pm - midnight
Sun: closed

HAPPY HOUR:
Mon - Fri: 3pm - 6pm

Sitting all clean and proper amongst a collection of much larger buildings, one would think **Downtown Louie's** Lounge has been here forever. Such is not the case. While there is a lot of history in the building itself, **Louie's** opened its doors in 2014.

The interior is beautiful, with rich wood in all directions, carefully thought out table and booth positioning, a grand, tall bar on the left side complete with an underlit stone bartop, and a large mezzanine overlooking the first floor.

From the bar, there is a good selection of both draft and bottled beers, a full line-up of liquor, and one of the largest wine lists in Detroit. In fact, some of their wine storage is in a walk-in with glass walls, custom built above the bar, accessible from the mezzanine. During happy hour, enjoy $2 domestic beers and $5 house wines and well drinks.

The food menu is extensive, and the items are made fresh in house. This is a wonderful place to go for a relaxing, fancier meal. Perfect for a date, special occassion, or "just because."

Reservations are a good idea on weekends and during Detroit events.

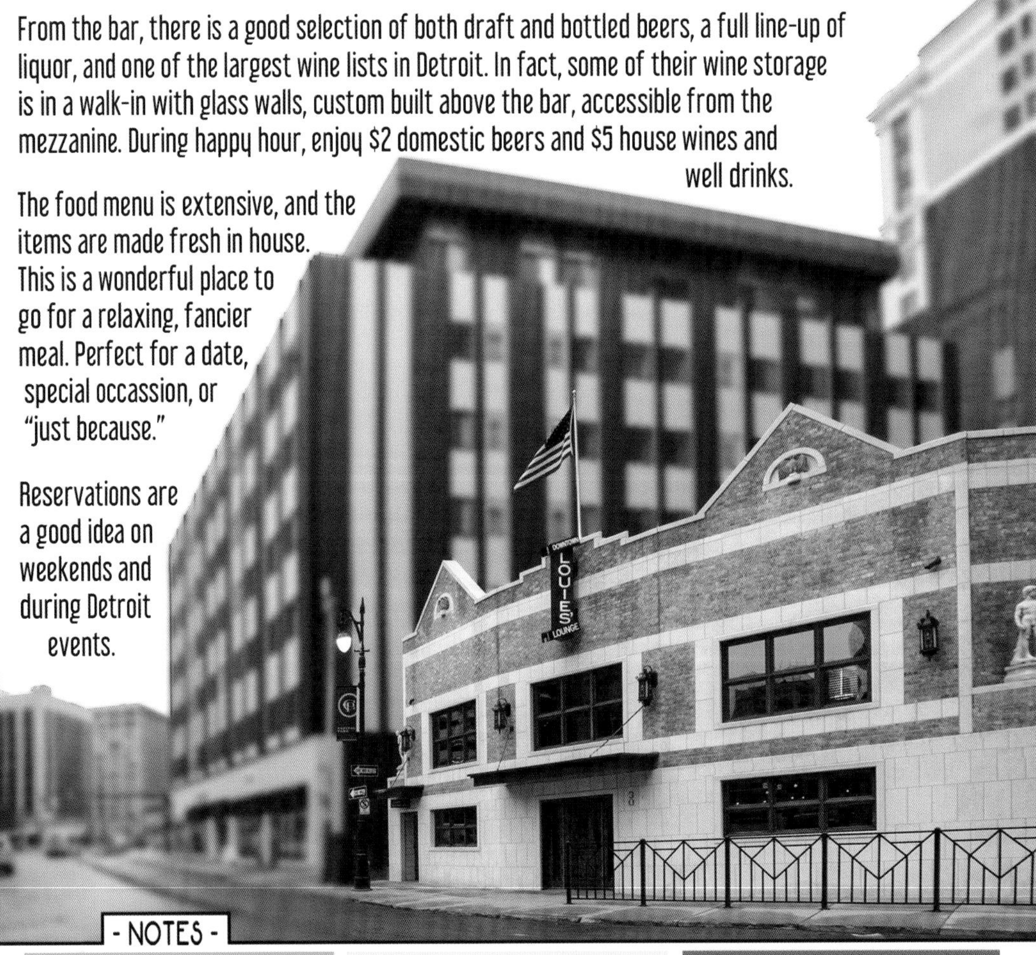


\- NOTES -

645 Griswold Street
(313) 962-1830

# Drive - Table Tennis Social Club

Full bar: ✓ Draft beer: ✗ Full kitchen: ✓ Shuttle service: ✗ drive-detroit.com

Just when you think you've seen everything in the bar scene, there's **Drive - Table Tennis Social Club**. Ping Pong! Located in the Penobscot building, this space is filled with a bar, a restaurant, and five ping pong tables. The setting is open and modern with seating for diners in the front, the bar in the middle, and the ping pong tables in the back.

HOURS:
Mon - Thu: 11am - 10pm
Fri: 11am - midnight or 2am
Sat: 2pm - midnight or 2am
Sun: closed

HAPPY HOUR:
Mon - Fri: 3pm - 7pm

The bar is set up to handle all of the basics with a somewhat standard selection of liquor, 20+ different beers, and a variety of house wines. During happy hour (M-F, 3pm-7pm), enjoy $2 off any drink.

Come with an appetite and enjoy fresh made pizzas, burgers, craft sandwiches, and gourmet hot dogs. There are also appetizers and salads. The food here is available for dine in, carry-out, or can be catered to your location.

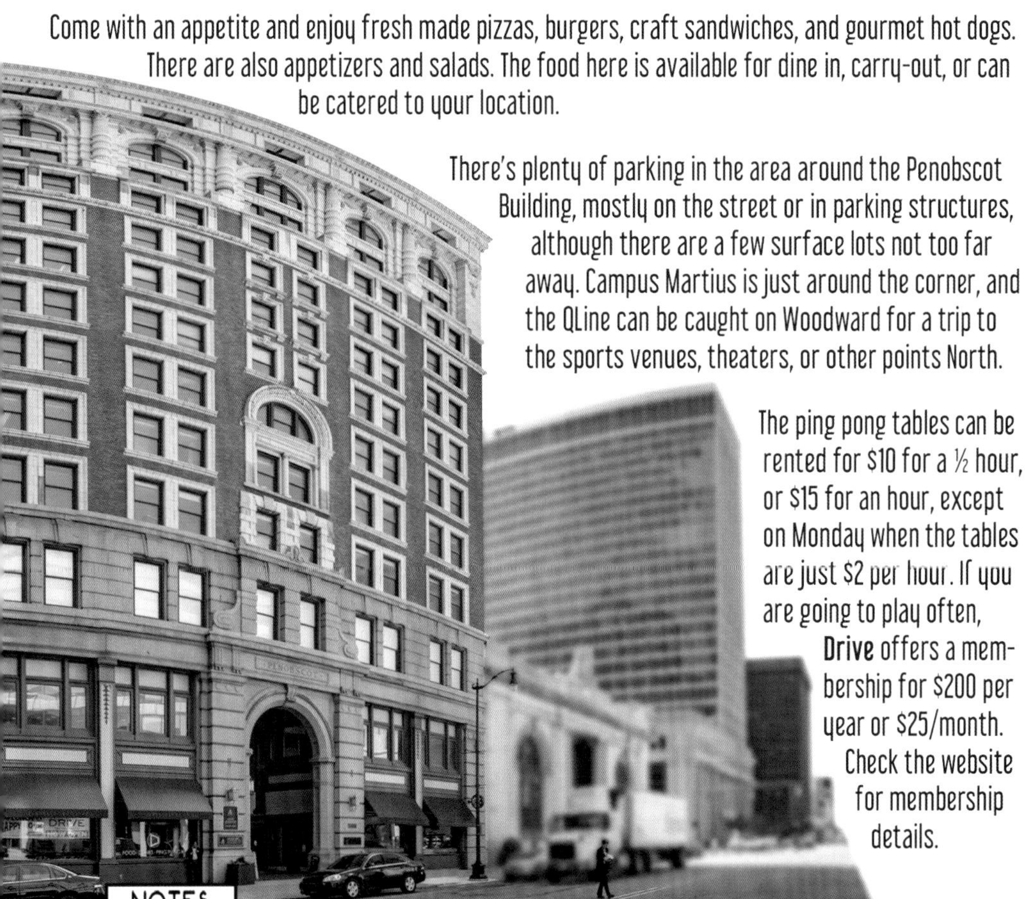


There's plenty of parking in the area around the Penobscot Building, mostly on the street or in parking structures, although there are a few surface lots not too far away. Campus Martius is just around the corner, and the QLine can be caught on Woodward for a trip to the sports venues, theaters, or other points North.

The ping pong tables can be rented for $10 for a ½ hour, or $15 for an hour, except on Monday when the tables are just $2 per hour. If you are going to play often, **Drive** offers a membership for $200 per year or $25/month. Check the website for membership details.

- NOTES -

**Been there!** ☐

**Downtown**

# Grand Trunk Pub

**612 Woodward Avenue**
**(313) 961-3043**

**Full bar:** ☑ **Draft beer:** ☑ **Full kitchen:** ☑ **Shuttle service:** ✘ **grandtrunkpub.com**

HOURS:
Mon - Fri: 11am - 2am
Sat - Sun: 10am - 2am

HAPPIEST HOUR:
Mon: 11pm - 2am

**Grand Trunk Pub** is one of those places, that when you step inside, you feel like you have been transported back in time. The inside of this historic building (1879) is filled with old wood trim, hardwood floors, warm brick, and eclectic decorations. This building has been a bar since 1935. Located on Woodward, just up from Jefferson Avenue, **Grand Trunk** is within easy walking distance of Campus Martius, Hart Plaza, and the RenCen. With minimal effort, it is within wandering distance of Cobo Hall.

The bar is a long wooden beauty running all the way down the left side of the main room. Since **Grand Trunk** is often packed, it's a squeeze to make your way between the barstools and the tables. Aside from a broad selection of draft beers, there are more in cans and bottles, mixed drinks, shots, wine, and hard ciders. Check out their brunch cocktails, Sat-Sun 10am-3pm, 24 oz heavily garnished My Bloody Valentines or 24oz Hair of the Dog. Come in on Tuesdays and enjoy Michigan drafts for just $3.

This is a comfortable place to gather with friends, enjoy a cold draft or cocktail, and have a meal. The menu, beyond a pleasant variety of appetizers, is mostly sandwiches and burgers, however they they do delve into a few main dishes, too.

There are numerous parking garages in the area, street parking and surface lots nearby. The QLine can be caught right out on Woodward, bringing points north into range.

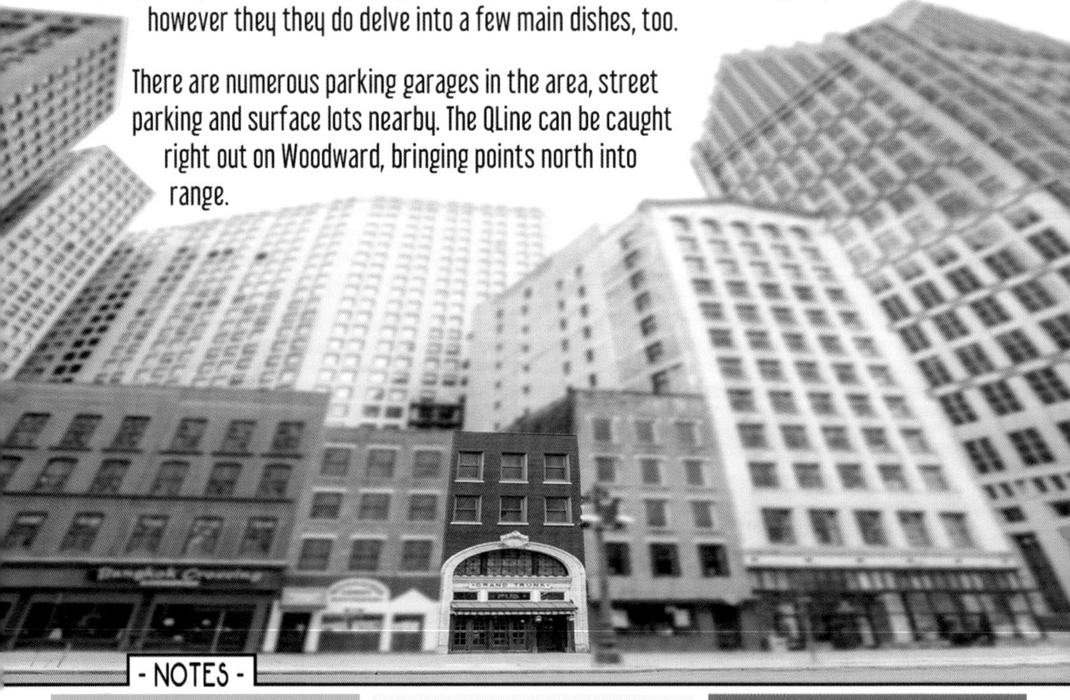


- NOTES -

**Been there!** ☐ **Downtown**

**190 Gratiot Avenue**
**info@handlebardetroit.com**

# The Handlebar Detroit

**Full bar:✗ Draft beer:✗ Full kitchen:✗ Shuttle service:✗ handlebardetroit.com**

HOURS:
Mon - Fri: 12:30pm - 10pm
Sat - Sun: 10am - 10pm

**The Handlebar Detroit** is one of Detroit's bicycle pubs. Each of the vehicles can hold 16 people plus the driver. Your group will have 10 people at the pedals, 2 on bar seats without pedals, and four on a bench. Sorry, the driver is a pro, and comes with your rental. There is a stereo on board, but you are responsible for your own drinks. You can bring beer, wine, and canned beverages, just no hard alcohol, and nothing in glass containers. Once you start your tour, no alcohol can be purchased and brought on the pub. However, you can drink at the bars where you stop along the way.

You must be at least 18 to ride on **The Handlebar Detroit**, and 21 or older to drink. Your driver has a few recommended routes, although they can be customized ahead of time if you have somewhere particular in mind. Even though you might have 16 people, there is only one renter, and that is the only person the driver will answer to. You'll have to figure that out before you start.

The tour starts and ends at 190 Gratiot. The bar only moves under pedal power, so your speed depends upon the effort you put in, typically 5-7 mph. Small coolers, coats, snacks and other things you may have with you can be stored in the overhead racks.

There are quite a few rules and legalities that you will need to be familiar with, so make sure to review them on their website. They are the final authority about what you can and can't do.

Prices for the tours are $300 for a 2hour tour Sunday-Thursday and $400 for a 2hour tour on Friday or Saturday. Tipping your bar handler is certainly a nice thing to do if you feel they did a good job.
Having seen these bars around town often, they are about having fun.
Go pedal. Drink. Laugh. Enjoy!

- NOTES -

Been there! ☐ Downtown

# Hard Rock Cafe

45 Monroe Avenue
(313) 964-7625

Full bar: ✓ Draft beer: ✓ Full kitchen: ✓ Shuttle service: ✓ hardrock.com/cafes/detroit

HOURS:
Sun - Thu: 11am - 11pm
Fri - Sat: 11am - midnight

*Bar open 1 extra hour*

**Hard Rock Cafe**. Sure, it is a worldwide chain restaurant. Putting that aside, the atmosphere is fun, with music and videos playing and the occasional live show. It also has the advantage of being clean and consistent. If you enjoy a good craft beer, this is probably not the place for you, as they tend toward mainstream, national brand beers.

Metered parking is available on many of the streets in the area, however your best bet might be the parking garage at Farmer and Monroe. **Hard Rock** will validate your ticket, saving you a few bucks.

**Hard Rock** offers a free shuttle service to events around Detroit, increasing their convenience. In addition to the shuttle, the Detroit People Mover has its Cadillac Center stop in the aforementioned parking structure. This brings most of the downtown area into reach for a mere 75c. Finally, the QLine runs up and down Woodward, offering another solution for commuting around the city.

The menu at **Hard Rock Cafe** is pretty typical American style food. Burgers, sandwiches, salads... Generally decent food, pretty mainstream and consistent. There is also enough variety on the menu to have something for everyone.

They have a room that is separate from the main dining area that can be reserved for parties, and there is a seating area in the courtyard area of One Campus Martius.

As with any of the other **Hard Rock Cafes** across the world, this one has a Rock Shop where you can buy shirts, jackets, jewelry, and of course, for all you pin-heads out there, **Hard Rock** pins.

- NOTES -

1214 Griswold Street
(313) 962-8821

# La Lanterna

Full bar: ☑ Draft beer: ✗ Full kitchen: ☑ Shuttle service: ✗ daedoardo.net/lalanterna

HOURS:
Mon - Thu: 11am - 10pm
Fri - Sat: 11am - 11pm
Sun: 11am - 9pm

HAPPY HOUR:
Mon - Fri: 3pm - 6pm

**La Lanterna** occupies a portion of the first floor of the Albert Hotel, an Albert Kahn design built in 1924. The exterior presents as one of Detroit's beautiful old buildings. Inside **La Lanterna** you will find a clean, modern space with a rectangular marble-topped bar in the front, and tables for dining leading to the back, where the open kitchen is located.

At the bar, there is a large TV for patrons to enjoy and a line-up of liquors which include some Italian brands. There are a dozen or so beers to choose from, although there are no draft offerings. There is a wine list which is approximately 20 deep, and in line with the Northern Italian style of food, **La Lanterna's** bar provides a cocktail list filled with Italian concoctions. During happy hour, non-craft domestic beers, house wines and the Margherita pizza are ½ off, and the house made meatball appetizer is only $3.

**La Lanterna's** location puts them comfortably in the center of downtown, a short walk to Woodward and Campus Martius. From there, the QLine or the Detroit People Mover can take you to just about all of the sights and events in and around Detroit. Parking along the streets can be a little tricky in this area, so be prepared for the possibility of some walking once you find a spot.

- NOTES -

Been there! ☐ | Downtown

# London Chop House

155 W Congress Street
(313) 962-0277

Full bar: ☑ Draft beer: ☑ Full kitchen: ☑ Shuttle service: ☒ thelondonchophouse.com

HOURS:
Mon - Wed: 11am - 11pm
Thu: 11am - midnight
Fri: 11am - 1am
Sat: 4pm - 1am
*Sun: private events*

HAPPY HOUR:
Mon - Fri: 3:30pm - 6:30pm

The entrance takes you immediately to a set of stairs leading down to this Detroit icon. **London Chop House** has been a prime destination in the city since 1938. It is unmistakably elegant with dark wood surfaces, dim lights, soft music, and chandeliers over the bar.

It takes four pages of the menu to share the wine list, and there are classic cocktails, wine and champagne mixed drinks, matinis, 24 different beers, a dozen types of cognac, port and dessert wines, frozen drinks, coffee drinks, and over 20 whiskeys to choose from. All of these are served up either at the beautiful antique bar, with your meal at one of the tables, or in the cigar lounge, which is one floor up, has billiards tables, and opens at 4:30pm. The happy hour menu has a much smaller offering of discounted drinks, and includes some food.

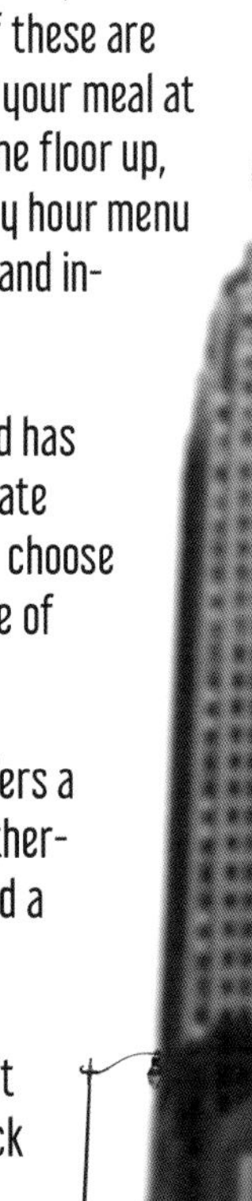

**London Chop House** is renowned for its steaks and has a few tantalizing cuts to choose from. To accomodate those not wanting beef, there are other options to choose from. If you come during lunch, you can enjoy some of the same menu items at a slightly lower price.

Parking can be tricky in this area, however **LCH** offers a valet service which can save you a lot of hassle. Otherwise, there is limited metered parking, pay lots, and a couple of parking garages.

Cobo Hall is just a block and a half away, the Detroit People Mover's Financial District station is one block toward the river, and the QLine rail can be caught a couple of blocks over, on Woodward Avenue.

Been there! ☐ Downtown

160 West Fort Street
(313) 315-3100

# Maru Sushi

Full bar: ☑ Draft beer: ☑ Full kitchen: ☑ Shuttle service: ☒ marurestaurant.com/detroit/

HOURS:
Mon - Thu: 11am - 10pm
Fri: 11am - 11pm
Sat: noon - 11pm
Sun: noon - 8pm

HAPPY HOUR:
Mon - Fri: 2:30pm - 6:30pm
Sat - Sun: noon - 4pm

In a large space on the first floor of Detroit's old Federal Reserve Building, **Maru Sushi** has soaring ceilings with long dangling lights, and seating areas equipped with elegant tables and chairs. Huge windows along the front flood the dining area with natural light, and a large marble topped bar provides a comfortable place for patrons to enjoy a cocktail. In front of the open kitchen, bar style seating allowing diners to observe the chefs as they skillfully make the food.

The bar has many offerings of wine and sake, 15 beers on draft, a large selection of whiskeys, and a respectable array of spirits. Happy hour at **Maru Sushi** is one of the longest in the city - four hours each day, every day, including the weekend.

Consistent with the name, the selection of sushi is impressive. For those not wanting sushi, there are other dishes available - all of Asian persuasion. With five other locations across Michigan, **Maru Sushi** has a proven track record of excellence.

Parking is plentiful in this area, and it's a short walk to Campus Martius, Hart Plaza, and the Riverfront. Nearby, on Woodward, the QLine can be caught, and there are four Detroit People Mover stations within a couple of blocks. Basically, the rest of the city is within range thanks to these public transportation solutions.

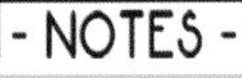

**Been there!** ☐ **Downtown**

# Nick's Gaslight Restaurant

**441 Grand River Avenue**
**(313) 963-9191**

**Full bar:** ☑ **Draft beer:** ☒ **Full kitchen:** ☑ **Shuttle service:** ☒

HOURS:
Mon - Sun: 11am - 2am

A single story structure with a slate roof, **Nick's Gaslight Restaurant** stands out as unique among the other buildings in downtown Detroit. Enter and find a large space. Brick covered pillars break up the room and time seems to have been frozen decades ago when it comes to the decor. Most of the space is taken up by tables set for dining, arranged in a way to give everyone a good view of the stage at the back. A large tile bartop to the right surrounds the bar service area. Dated but comfortable, **Nick's Gaslight** serves as both a bar and a restaurant, with the capability of entertaining large groups.

The bar handles the basics: beer, booze, and a few choices of wine. There are no beers on draft, and trendy cocktails will not likely be poured here. There are, however, low prices and daily drink specials.

Known for good food, the kitchen serves up a variety of burgers and sandwiches, as well as a line-up of dinner entrees. The menu is mostly American style food, although several items have a Greek influence.

The stage at the back is home to comedy shows on the 2nd Saturday of each month. There is generally a cover for the comedy. **Nick's Gaslight** also hosts DJ nights, though not on a regular schedule. If this is of interest, watch their Facebook page for dates. There are also a few video games and a dart board for your entertainment.

Parking is plentiful, with surface lots and metered street spots in the area.

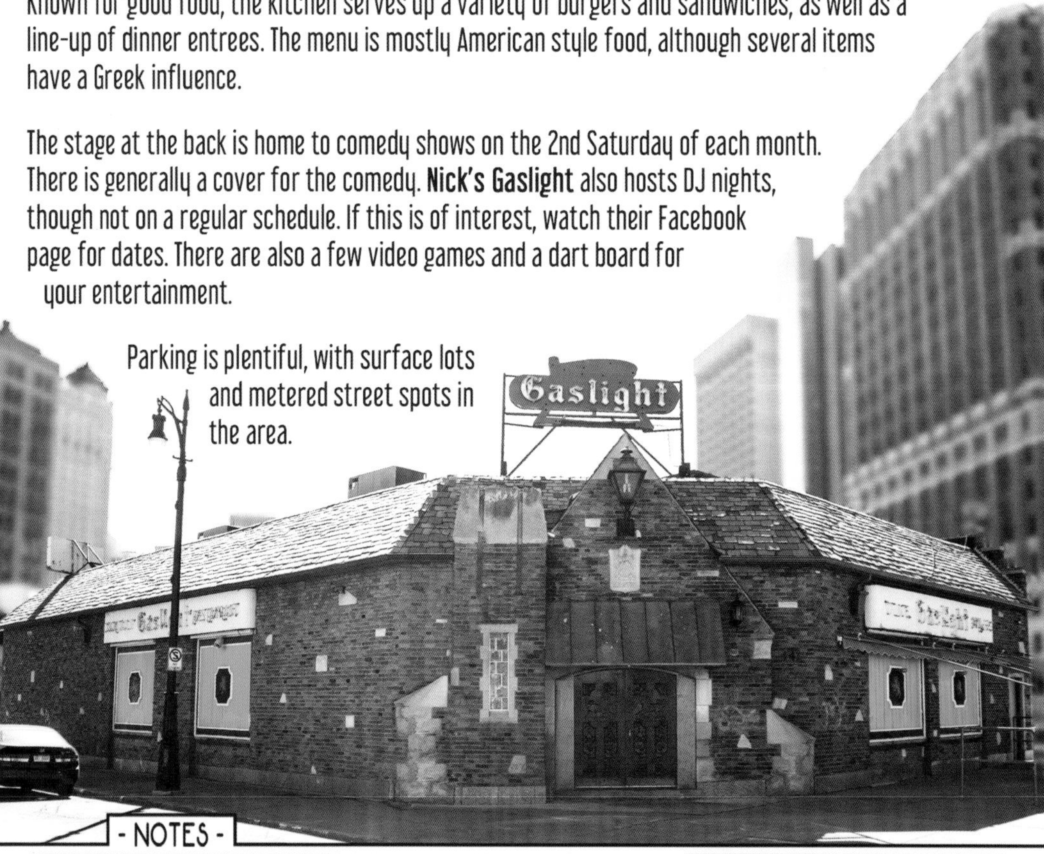


- NOTES -

**Been there!** ☐ **Downtown**

**800 Woodward Avenue**
**(313) 922-PARC**

# Parc

**Full bar:** ☑ **Draft beer:** ☑ **Full kitchen:** ☑ **Shuttle service:** ☒ **parcdetroit.com**

HOURS:
Mon - Wed: 11am - 11pm
Thu - Sat: 11am - 1am
Sun: 11am - 9pm

HAPPY HOUR:
Mon - Fri: 3pm - 6pm

**Parc** is conveniently located at Campus Martius Park, making it a popular spot on weekends and when the park is hosting one of its many events. This is a modern, upscale venue with a creative menu and a top shelf bar. It is a good location to bring a date, or if you just feel like having a wonderful meal and perhaps a bottle of fine wine.

Because of its location, parking is readily available. There are metered spots along the streets, surface parking lots, and nearby parking structures. From **Parc**, it's an easy walk to Greektown, and with a little more effort, Comerica Park, The Fox, Ford Field, and the Fillmore Theater. Another option is to ride the QLine, which has a station nearby on Woodward.

Happy hour offerings include \$5 beers,\$6 and \$8 glasses of wine, and \$7 cocktails along with a selection of small bites for \$7 each. **Parc** boasts one of the larger wine lists in Detroit.

Lunch is served from 11am-3pm, and the dinner menu starts at 5pm. The variety of food offered will excite people looking for gourmet meals, and for the connoisseurs, ask for the list of off menu reserved steaks. The selection varies based on availability.

- NOTES -

Been there! ☐

# Roast

Downtown
1128 Washington Boulevard
(313) 961-2500
roastdetroit.com

**Full bar:** ✓ **Draft beer:** ✓ **Full kitchen:** ✓ **Shuttle service:** ✗

HOURS:
Mon - Thu: 5pm - 10pm
Fri - Sat: 5pm - 11pm
Sun: 5pm - 9pm
*(Bar service starts at 4pm daily).*

HAPPY HOUR:
Mon - Fri: 4:30pm - 6:30pm

Owned by Food Network's Iron Chef Michael Symon, **Roast** has received high reviews since opening in 2008. Notably, Detroit's "Restaurant of the Year" in 2009 by the Detroit Free Press, and "Best Steakhouse" by Hour Magazine. It makes its home in the beautiful Westin Book Cadillac Hotel, and the elegance of the building flows smoothly into the restaurant.

The stone-topped bar wraps around a central glass enclosed wine room. An extensive wine list shows exactly what is available. Rows of liquor demonstrate a wide variety of offerings, enhanced by a lengthy spirits menu and a list of new and trendy cocktails. Of the 40 beers offered at **Roast**, 10 are drafts. During happy hour the food on the bar menu is half off, house white, red, and rosé by the glass are $5, one of the draft beers will be $4, and simple mixed drinks are $5.

Renowned for its food, especially the steaks, the menu at **Roast** is relatively small. What is offered is well crafted, fresh, delicious, and masterfully presented. Besides the steaks, most of which are dry-aged, there is a seasonal pasta dish, two fish meals, short ribs, chicken, and lamb.

There is an expectation of decorum at **Roast**. The dining area has a sophisticated, modern design, with leather wrapped chairs and booths, and as would be expected, table linens. Leather clad pillars break up the space.

While this location is on the far side for a stroll to the arenas and theaters on Woodward, the nearest QLine station is just two blocks away.

- NOTES -

1431 Times Square
(313) 926-0783

# Savannahblue

**Full bar:** ✓ **Draft beer:** ✗ **Full kitchen:** ✓ **Shuttle service:** ✗ **savannahbluedetroit.com**

HOURS:
Mon - Thu: 4pm - 11pm
Fri - Sat: 4pm - midnight
Sun: *closed*

HAPPY HOUR:
Mon - Fri: 4pm - 7pm

**Savannahblue** is an elegant oasis tucked away on the second floor of an old slate-grey painted brick building in the heart of downtown Detroit. This uniquely inspired space has not only a dining room, but also a living room where patrons can enjoy some drinks, conversation, and music all while sitting in a comfortable chair. Choose the dining room and sit at a table to enjoy some fine-dining.

Author Favorite

The bar presence matches the ambiance, with a select wine list, top-shelf alcohol, creative and inventive cocktails made with fresh squeezed juices, and a selection of bottled beer. During happy hour, take advantage of discounted drinks and appetizers.

The culinary offerings are impressive in their appearance as well as their quality. The kitchen serves masterfully crafted dishes, many with a soul food influence. Each course is well represented, from starters through dessert. If you appreciate good food, want to entertain someone special, or want to be pampered and escape the hustle of the city, **Savannahblue** is a good destination.

There are secured parking lots and metered parking on the street and **Savannahblue** offers valet parking to their guests. If you plan on going to a show or event in the city after visiting **Savannahblue**, the Detroit People Mover's Times Square stop is at the corner, and the QLine can be caught over on Woodward, just a few blocks away. Both of these options bring most of the rest of the city into reach.

*Enjoy live piano music in* ***Savannahblue's*** *living room.*

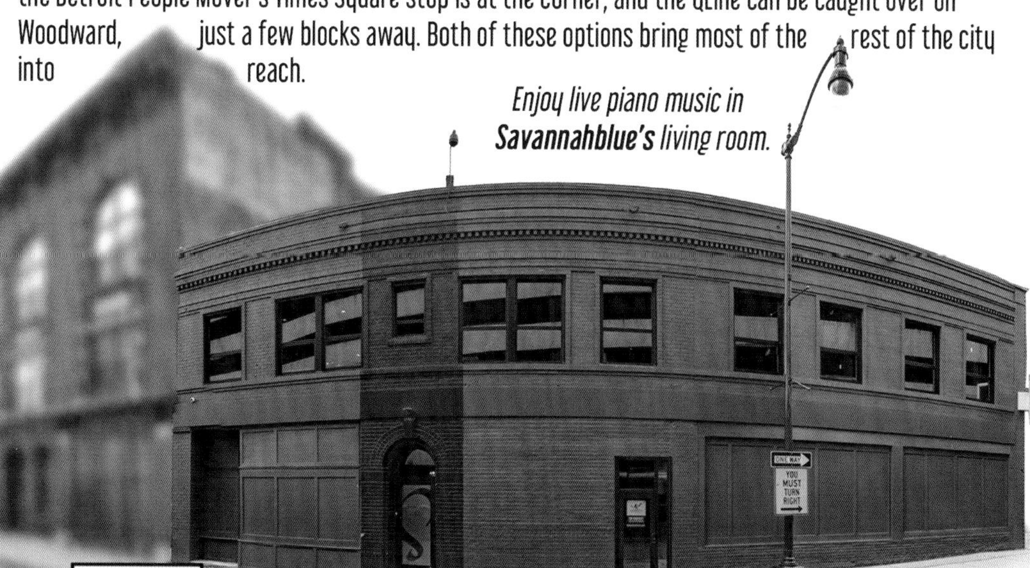


- NOTES -

Been there! ☐ | Downtown

# Texas de Brazil

1000 Woodward Avenue
(313) 964-4333
texasdebrazil.com

**Full bar:** ✓ **Draft beer:** ✗ **Full kitchen:** ✓ **Shuttle service:** ✗

Taking residence inside One Campus Martius, one of Detroit's newest office buildings, **Texas de Brazil** has established itself as a dining destination. The dark woods and soft music give the place a comfortable feel.

The bar area is relatively small, however the offerings are large. The wine racks above the bar display only a small portion of what can be ordered. Beyond the large wine list is an impressive selection of Brazilian cocktails and different types of liquor. There are around a dozen beers to choose from in bottles, dessert martinis, and dessert wines, truly an impressive breadth of coverage. During happy hour domestic beers are $3, caiparinhas are $5 as are select wines and simple mixed drinks, and martinis are $7.

HOURS:
LUNCH:
Wed - Fri: 11am - 2:30pm

DINNER
Mon - Thu: 5pm - 9:30pm
Fri: 5pm - 10pm
Sat: 4pm - 10pm
Sun: 4pm - 9pm

HAPPY HOUR:
Mon - Fri: 4:30pm - 7pm

**Texas de Brazil** is a churascaria, which is a Brazilian steakhouse. There is a buffet with 50-60 items; sides, salads, cheeses, and soups. The main meal consists of meat. Carvers work their way through the dining room cutting and serving a variety of meats to the guests. Everything here is all you can eat, so you can try everything without risk. There is an option to order only the salad bar, or you can go with the whole experience. Either way, it's a fixed price menu.

It would be difficult to find a more central location in Detroit. From here, it's not much of a walk to most venues.

There is a parking garage behind the building, and another, the Z Lot, across Gratiot.

- NOTES -

**Been there!** ☐ **Downtown**

**624 3rd Street**
**(313) 965-2269**

# Tommy's Bar & Grill

**Full bar:** ✓ **Draft beer:** ✓ **Full kitchen:** ✓ **Shuttle service:** ✓ **tommysdetroit.com**

HOURS:
Mon - Sat: 11am - 2am
Sun: closed

HAPPY HOUR:
Mon - Fri: 4pm - 8pm

**Tommy's Bar & Grill** occupies an old brick building (1840) down by Cobo Hall. Inside, the wood paneled walls hide some of this history, although the pictures that cover them bring it back with decades of Detroit sports and city history being displayed. The main part of the building is dominated by the bar, which takes up half of the room. Another room at the back of the bar has tables and chairs, more TVs, and a dart board. This is a true Detroit sports bar. It is comfortable, appropriately loud, and divey with a lot of personality.

The bar is stocked as one would expect - booze, beers, including a dozen or so draft offerings, and a small selection of house wines. During happy hour, drafts and domestic bottled beers are $1 off their already low prices, and well drinks and wine are just $3. On game days, there is generally a drink special running, the details of which can be found on a board at the end of the bar.

The kitchen kicks out a steady flow of burgers, sandwiches, and traditional bar-style appetizers. There are daily lunch specials between 11am - 3pm, and carry-out orders are available.

While the proximity to Joe Louis Arena gave **Tommy's** a steady stream of customers during hockey season for nearly four decades, it survived as a bar for decades prior, and should carry forward even as the Wings move across town. They are close to Cobo Hall and WCCC, and offer a free shuttle bus to all Lions, Red Wings, and Tigers games, as well as most major events and concerts in the city.

Parking is available on the street, in paid lots, and in several nearby parking structures.

*For some cool history on the building and its role during prohibition look up the following on YouTube:*
"Digging Detroit - Episode 1: Tommy's - Inside a Detroit Speakeasy"

- NOTES -

Been there! ☐

Downtown

# Townhouse

500 Woodward Avenue
(313) 723-1000

Full bar: ☑ Draft beer: ☑ Full kitchen: ☑ Shuttle service: ☒ eatattownhouse.com

**Townhouse** is located on the 1st floor of the One Detroit Center building, a recognizable piece of the Detroit skyline.

The decor and ambiance is fun and a bit on the fancy side of things. Leather barstools and chairs provide a comfortable place to sit at the beautifully crafted hardwood tables.

HOURS:
Mon - Thu: 11am - midnight
Fri: 11am - 2am
Sat: 10am - 2am
Sun: 10am - midnight

BRUNCH:
Sat - Sun: 10am - 3:30pm

HAPPY HOUR:
Mon - Fri: 3pm - 6pm

There are two bars at **Townhouse**. At the main entrance, a large marble topped bar faces you as you come in. Tall shelves of liquor display prominently, and the service area is lined with house made syrups, infusions, and fresh garnishes. The second bar is in the sizeable greenhouse style outdoor seating area. The depth of offerings between the two is impressive, including an extensive selection of whiskey, bourbon, and rye, plus a list of hard-to-get / rare bottles ranging from $110 - $950. All can be reviewed in the leather bound bar menus.

The selection of food on the menu is varied, from burgers to elk tenderloin, and from sushi to a build-your-own salad menu. There are separate menus for brunch, lunch, dinner, and happy hour. There is even a kid's menu, which seems to be a rarity at many places these days.

Located on Woodward Avenue, **Townhouse** is close to Cobo Hall, the Riverfront, and Campus Martius. The QLine can be used to get to Detroit's sports venues, the Fox and Fillmore theaters, as well as many other attractions along Woodward. The Detroit People Mover has two nearby stations and provides options in the downtown area. There are several parking garages nearby and some metered street parking.

- NOTES -

Been there! ☐



2 John R Street / 1456 Woodward Ave
(313) 473-9401

# Whiskey Disco

Full bar: ☑ Draft beer: ☒ Full kitchen: ☒ Shuttle service: ☒ cornerstonedetroit.com
(see information below regarding draft beer and food)

HOURS:
Fri - Sat: 9pm - 2am

**Whiskey Disco** is located in the basement of the Cornerstone Barrell House on the corner of John R and Woodward. Don't allow the word basement to put you off. The space has been artfully finished, with black slatted walls and ceiling, comfortable chairs around the perimeter, and room to dance.

Only open to the public on weekends, or as an overflow when there are large events in Detroit such as opening day for the Tigers, DJs pump out the music for all to enjoy. The space can also be rented for corporate or special events. This is a very popular place during Detroit's Electronic Music Festival.

There is a full bar at **Whiskey Disco**, and drinks can also be brought down from Cornerstone, which is under the same ownership. While food can also be brought down, they encourage you to eat upstairs. Drinks of all sorts, and a selection of beers and craft cocktails are on the menu shared with Cornerstone, as is their amazing selection of bourbon, rye, scotch, and whiskey. If you want draft beer, those can only be purchased upstairs.

*There is limited metered parking on the streets in this area, although there several parking structures close by. The QLine has a station nearby, as does the Detroit People Mover.*

This is a fun place for drinks, music, and dancing.

- NOTES -

Been there! ☐

Downtown

# The Whisky Parlor

608 Woodward Avenue
(313) 961-3043

**Full bar:** ✓ **Draft beer:** ✗ **Full kitchen:** ✗ **Shuttle service:** ✗ whiskyparlor.com

**The Whisky Parlor** is hidden in plain view. It is located upstairs from the Grand Trunk Pub. At the back of the bar, the stairs to **The Whisky Parlor** are by the restrooms. They also have their own entrance from the street.

HOURS:
Sun - Thu: 5pm - midnight
Fri - Sat: 5pm - 2am

At the top of the stairs, the busy, vibrant energy of Grand Trunk and Detroit itself melts away to the calm, sophisticated air of **The Whisky Parlor**. It's a dark and intimate atmosphere, a long room with a lot of comfortable sitting areas, and a small bar at one end. This is a speakeasy lounge, of sorts.

The bar menu will demonstrate an impressive whisky selection, a cocktail list that includes their award winning drink, "The Detroit," a few beers, and a small wine list. In addition to the whisky, they are known for their spirits knowledge and mixology.

There is a limited food menu, mostly palate cleansing snack items. On Thursday and Saturday nights there is live jazz, and Friday nights are vinyl nights, with an assortment of records being spun.

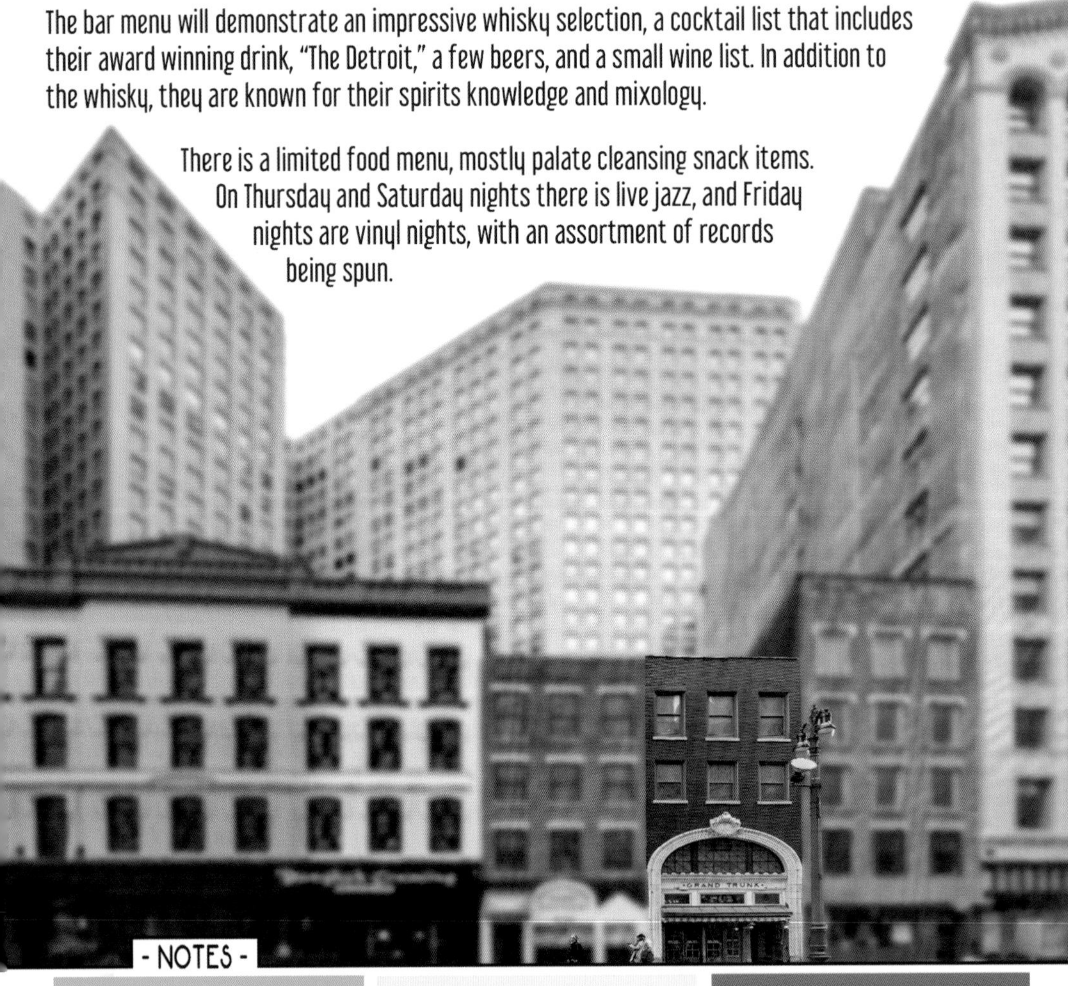


- NOTES -

Been there! ☐



1500 Woodward Avenue
(313) 962-7711

# Wright & Company

Full bar: ✓ Draft beer: ✓ Full kitchen: ✓ Shuttle service: ✗ wrightdetroit.com

HOURS:
Mon - Thu: 4pm - midnight
Fri - Sat: 4pm - 2am
Sun: 10:30am - 2pm

An elegant place, **Wright & Company** is located above John Varvatos in the amazingly beautiful Wright-Kay Building, once known as the Schwankovsky Temple of Music. Built in 1891, it is one of the oldest buildings in Detroit.

The space they occupy is graced with high celiings covered in old ornate pressed tin, a long marble bar, and hardwood floors.

From the bar, you can expect skillfully mixed cocktails, many using syrups and infusions made in house, as well as fresh herbs and fruit. They offer a large selection of bottled beer and a wide range of wines and champagne.

The food leaving the kitchen is as impressive as the building in which it is served. The variety of offerings is enough to entice patrons with a range of tastes, yet limited enough to not be overwhelming.

With its Woodward Avenue location, **Wright & Company** is conveniently close to just about anything happening in downtown Detroit. If a destination is not within walking distance, the QLine has a nearby station, as does the Detroit People Mover.

There is ample parking in the area, with nearby parking structures, and metered parking along many of the streets.

*While the address says Woodward Avenue, the entrance is on the side, off John R Street.*

- NOTES -

# Eastern Market

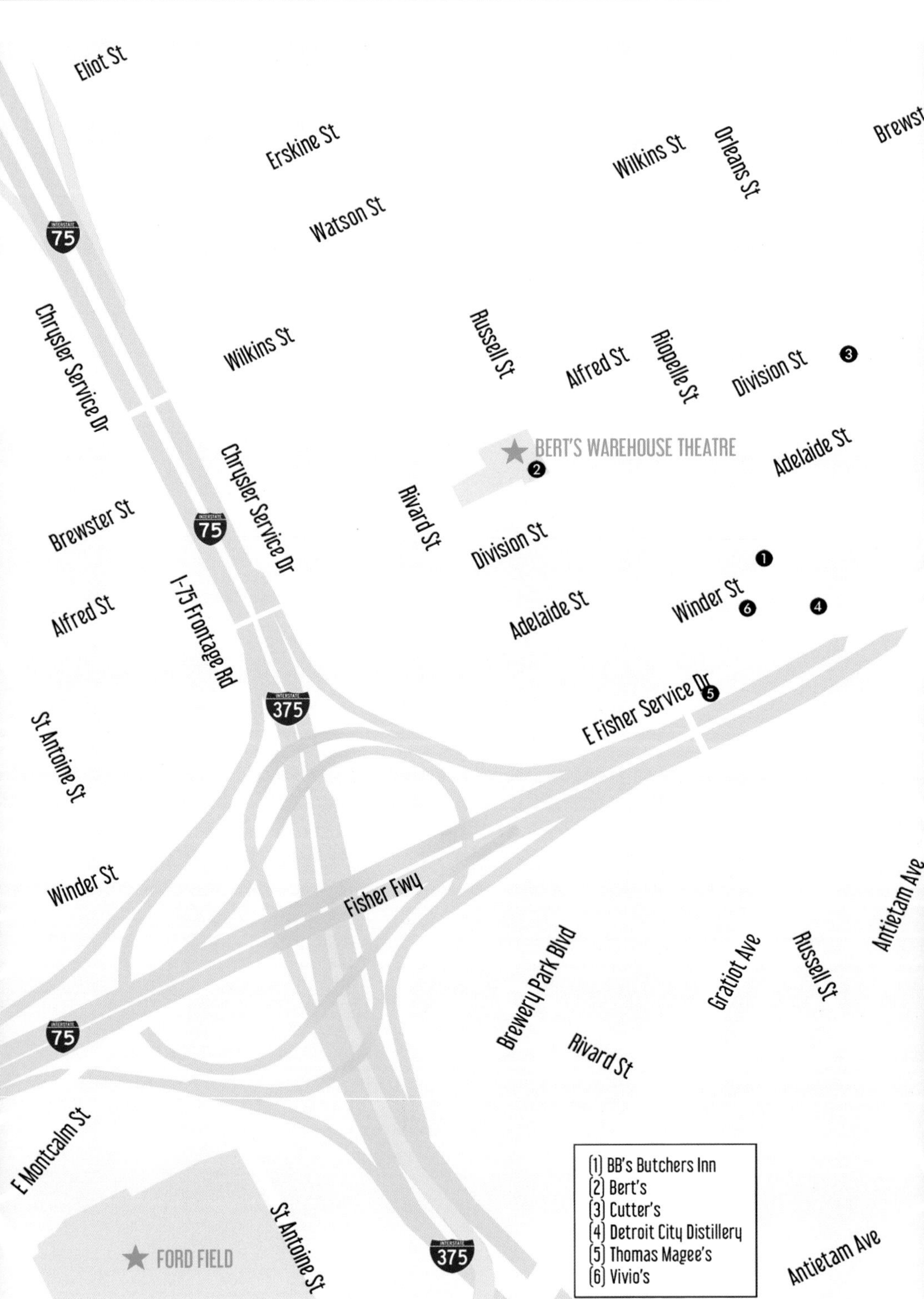

1489 Winder Street
(313) 818-0200

# BB's Butchers Inn

**Full bar:** ☑ **Draft beer:** ☑ **Full kitchen:** ☑ **Shuttle service:** ☒

Located in Detroit's historic Eastern Market, **BB's Butchers Inn** stands out from its surroundings with a vividly colorful exterior. The inside is almost a polar opposite. Two stories tall, with seating upstairs and down, the eye-catching fature of the interior is the large, exposed wood-beam construction.

HOURS:
Mon - Sun: 7am - 2am

HAPPY HOUR:
Mon - Fri: 3pm - 6pm

**BB's** has a full bar, complete with a selection of both draft and bottled beers. Drink specials are always changing, so your best bet is to check the board behind the bar. Happy Hour runs from 3pm-6pm on weekdays, during which you can get a burger and a domestic beer for $8. Finally, for those who are up for the challenge, you can get a 1/2 yard of beer for $10. That's an 18 inch tall glass that holds 32 ounces of beer.

The kitchen offers a wide range of food from breakfast through dinner, seven days a week. Each menu is rather large, however **BB's** is most known for its Gumbo and as the home of Steak & Shrimp. Make sure to ask about the daily specials. They cover every meal and change frequently.

Being in Eastern Market makes this a conveniently close place when the markets are open, and during Detroit Lion's football games. Parking is plentiful in the lots and along the streets in the area. All of Eastern Market is within a short stroll of **BB's**, and Ford Field and Comerica Park are also within walking distance.

*Like what you had here? **BB's** caters. Follow **BB's** on Facebook or Instagram: @east7bbs*

- NOTES -

Been there! ☐ Eastern Market

# Bert's Entertainment Complex

2727 Russell Street
(313) 567-2030

**Full bar:** ✓ **Draft beer:** ✓ **Full kitchen:** ✓ **Shuttle service:** ✗ **bertsentertainmentcomplex.com**

HOURS (Jazz Club):
Mon - Sun: 10am - 2am

HOURS (Motown Bistro):
Mon - Fri: noon - 11pm
Sat - Sun: noon - 1am

**Bert's Entertainment Complex** is all that and more. There are two large bars, one a jazz club, the other Motown, a food market, fresh BBQ, huge venues that can be rented for parties and events, and so much more. This has been a hot spot in Eastern Market for years.

The **Jazz Club**, at the left end of the complex, is a restaurant, bar, and venue for live musical acts. As you enter, the stage is to the right, and seating is in the front and to the left, set in a way that everyone will have a good view of the performances. The walls are decorated with jazz themed art and pictures of jazz musicians. Dangling chandelier-like lights complete the look. Food comes from the marketplace, with burgers, sandwiches and BBQ being the main fare. The bar serves a full range of options, from beers to cocktails to wine.

---

To the right of the marketplace is the **Motown Bistro**, a quietly elegant bar and dining space decorated with old vinyl records, music industry memorabilia, and pictures of Motown greats. Comfortable semi-private booths around the perimeter of the room provide guests with some privacy while still being able to enjoy the live music performed on the weekends.

The bar service at the **Motown Bistro** is complete, including a fine assortment of top shelf offerings. The food is a mix of seafood, with oysters and a variety of fish offerings, as well as steaks and other entrees.

*Parking is plentiful in the area except during Lions home games. All of the Detroit sports complexes are within walking distance.*

- NOTES -

2638 Orleans Street
(313) 393-0960

# Cutter's Bar & Grill

**Full bar:** ✓ **Draft beer:** ✗ **Full kitchen:** ✓ **Shuttle service:** ✗ **cuttersdetroit.com**

Hidden away on a back street in Eastern Market, **Cutter's Bar & Grill** could easily go unseen. It leans toward being a dive bar, but it's clean and cozy. With no windows and a lot of black surfaces inside, it has a dark, relaxing atmosphere. The interior is divided into two parts, with the bar dominating one side, the other filled with small tables, and on Fridays, a DJ. Both rooms have their share of televisions, good for game days.

HOURS:
Mon - Thu: 10am - 10pm
Fri - Sat: 10am - 2am
Sun: Football days only

HAPPY HOUR:
Mon - Sat: 10am - 6pm

The bar is no-frills. No draft beer, and only a small selection of beer at all. In spite of that, they have a special that runs all day, every day: buy five beers and your sixth is free. The wine selection is also small. The focus here is liquor, and it reflects in happy hour, with $5 Margaritas and Long Island iced tea, and $2 Altos shooters. **Cutter's** also carries a full line-up of Detroit's own Faygo pops.

The kitchen serves up a selection of American style food, made fresh to order. In addition to bar sides, sandwiches and burgers, there are also several varieties of loaded baked potatoes, and what may be their claim to fame, multiple choices of stuffed burgers. Make sure you look through these. It's good to have something different.

Parking in Eastern Market is plentiful on some days, scarce on others. Much of this disparity comes from whether the outdoor market is open, or if the Detroit Lions have a home game, so keep that in mind. There are garages and surface lots as well as curbside spots. It is a short walk over to Ford Field and Comerica Park.

***AUTHOR'S FAVORITE**: Consider the Greek stuffed burger. It's a fresh patty filled with Feta cheese and red onion.*

- NOTES -

Been there! ☐

Eastern Market
2462 Riopelle
(313) 338-3760

# Detroit City Distillery

**Full bar:** ✓ **Draft beer:** ✗ **Full kitchen:** ✗ **Shuttle service:** ✗ **detroitcitydistillery.com**

Author Favorite

HOURS:
Tue - Thu: 4pm - 10pm
Fri: 4pm - midnight
Sat: 10am - midnight
Sun: noon - 6pm

*Closed Mondays*

**Detroit City Distillery** is not really a bar, and is definitely not a restaurant. It is more along the lines of a tasting room for the distillery.

The interior is on the small side, yet is not a cramped space. Most of the seating is at the bar itself, and there are a few small tables for those seeking a little more intimacy. The ceilings are high, the walls predominately brick, and the mood comfortably casual.

At the bar, all of the drinks are made from the spirits created by **Detroit City Distillery**. This means every cocktail features either their gin, vodka, rye whiskey, or bourbon. To call the people behind the bar "bartenders" would be a misnomer. They are mixologists. House made syrups and infusions are on hand, as are fresh herbs and fruit.

Although there is no kitchen here, they do offer a small handful of food items to help balance out the drinks. However, you are better off coming here thirsty rather than hungry.

Parking in Eastern Market is available along the streets, and in lots around the area.

*Follow them on Facebook to find out about special events. Occasionally they have a food pop-up.*

- NOTES -

1408 E Fisher Freeway
(313) 263-4342

# Thomas Magee's Sporting House Whiskey Bar

**Full bar:** ✓ **Draft beer:** ✓ **Full kitchen:** ✗ **Shuttle service:** ✓ **thomasmagees.com**

Located just across the Fisher Freeway from Eastern Market, **Thomas Magee's** is a popular bar for sports, and we're not talking just Detroit sports. They show every televised English Premier League, Spanish League, and US Soccer game. They also favor big boxing matches.

The interior of the bar is mostly dark-stained wooden surfaces, with a few half-casks, mirrors, and signs to complete the decoration. High tables and a high bar make it comfortable for people in the same group to sit or stand.

HOURS:
Mon: 4pm - 2am
Tue - Fri: 1pm - 2am
Sat: 9am - 2am
Sun: 11am - 2am

HAPPY HOUR:
Mon - Fri: 4pm - 7pm

This soulful Irish pub has a deep selection of whiskey, and professes to have the largest selection of Irish whiskey and Irish beer in the city. They offer a pay-to-join whiskey club that gets you discounts on drinks from specially procured barrels, invites to barrel release parties, and other events. Ask at the bar for details. Whiskey is not the only drink here. There are over a dozen drafts, a wide selection of beer in cans and bottles, their signature Irish coffee, and their award winning Bloody Marys. You can get a Bloody Mary anytime, however on the weekends they come loaded. For happy hour, you get $2 domestic beers, $3 wells, and $4 glasses of wine.

Besides the games on the TVs, there is a hockey foosball table, Golden Tee, and a juke box. There is also a stage for live entertainment. The first and third Wednesdays of the month are comedy nights, Tuesdays are acoustic sexy soul time, and many of the other days have performances booked. Check the website for showtimes and details.

Other than the garnishes for the loaded Bloody Marys, there is no food at **Thomas Magee's**.

Parking is plentiful in the area, and **Thomas Magee's** will shuttle you to games.

- NOTES -

Been there! ☐ **Eastern Market**

# Vivio's Food & Spirits

**2460 Market Street**
**(313) 393-1711**
**viviosdetroit.com**

**Full bar:** ☑ **Draft beer:** ☑ **Full kitchen:** ☑ **Shuttle service:** ☑

HOURS:
Mon - Thu: 11am - 8pm
Fri: 11am - 9pm
Sat: 8am - 7pm
Sun: 11am - 5pm

HAPPY HOUR:
Mon - Fri: 3pm - 7pm

**Vivio's** is located in the heart of Eastern Market of Detroit. Although **Vivio's** was opened in 1967, the first floor of the historic Meyfarth's Hall building, where **Vivio's** is located, has been a bar since the building opened in 1892. In addition to the space on the first floor, **Vivio's** occupies the second floor, complete with another bar set-up. Much of the wall surfaces are covered with an eclectic assortment of advertising, pictures, and unique items.

The highlight of the bar is a large stained glass awning running the full length, hanging over the bottles and service area. While they have bottled booze, 8 beers on tap, and more in bottles and cans, the bar is known for its Bloody Marys. In fact, Vivio's has won "Best Bloody Mary in Detroit" so many times, they decided to bottle and sell their namesake mix.

From the kitchen comes an assortment of sandwiches, burgers, appetizers, salads, and what they are perhaps most known for, mussels. **Vivio's** offers seven different varieties of mussels, and they are very popular.

There are many places to park in Eastern Market, including the lot in front of **Vivio's**. For major events in Detroit, **Vivio's** provides a free shuttle. Check for availability if this is part of your plans.

When the Detroit Lions have a home game, this is one of the busiest places in Eastern Market.

- NOTES -

# Foxtown

Charlotte St
Temple St
MASONIC TEMPLE THEATER
Sproat St
Woodward Ave
Adelaide St
John R St
Brush St
Cass Ave
Winder St
Leduard St
LITTLE CAESARS ARENA
E Fisher Service Dr
75
E Montcalm St
FORD FIELD
2nd Ave
Fisher Freeway
COMERICA PARK
Henry St
W Fisher Service Dr
FOX THEATER
Witherell St
E Adams Ave
Beacon St
Clifford St
THE FILLMORE DETROIT
Madison St
W Columbia St
W Elizabeth St
MUSIC HALL
Brush St
DETROIT OPERA HOUSE
Cass Ave
W Adams Ave
Park Ave
DPM
John R St
Centre St
Broadway St
3rd Ave
Plum St
Grand River Ave
Gratiot Ave
W Elizabeth St
The Belt
Woodward Ave
Library St
Plaza Dr
Bagley Ave
Beech St
Grand River Ave
MGM GRAND
Griswold St
Monroe Ave
Bagley Ave
State St
Michigan Ave
12
Michigan Ave
CAMPUS MARTIUS
3rd Ave
1st St
Cass Ave
W Lafayette Blvd
10
Abbott St
2nd Ave
Howard St
W Fort St
W Congress St
Washington Blvd
Griswold St
Larned St
10
COBO CENTER
(1) Bookies
(2) Brass Rail Pizzeria
(3) Broderick Grille
(4) Centaur
(5) Centre Park Bar
(6) Cheli's
(7) Cliff Bell's
(8) Coaches Corner
(9) Colors
(10) Detroit Beer Company
(11) Detroit Rolling Pub
(12) Ellwood, The
(13) Foxtown Grille
(14) Harry's
(15) Hockeytown Cafe
(16) La Casa Cigars
(17) MGM Casino
(18) Michgan Pedaler
(19) Park Bar
(20) Punch Bowl Social
(21) PV Ultra Lounge
(22) Queens Bar
(23) Republic Tavern
(24) Royce, The
(25) Rockefellers
(26) Rusted Crow
(27) Skip, The
(28) Small Plates
(29) Standby
(30) State Bar
(31) Town Pump, The
(32) Truth
(33) Vertical
(34) WXYZ
DPM = Detroit People Mover station
Q = QLine station

Been there! ☐

Foxtown

# Bookies Bar & Grille

2208 Cass Avenue
(313) 962-0319
bookiesbar.com

**Full bar:** ✓ **Draft beer:** ✓ **Full kitchen:** ✓ **Shuttle service:** ✓

HOURS:
Tue - Sat: 11am - 2am
Sun: 11am - 8pm
Mon: closed

HAPPY HOUR:
Tue - Fri : 5pm - 7pm

**Bookies** is a spacious, clean, and impressive bar located close enough to the Detroit sports arenas to hear the cheers when our teams score. There are three levels to the bar. The first is a substantial room with high ceilings, a large bar, and ample seating. The 2nd floor overlooks the first, has more seating, and a service bar. The third, and perhaps the most fun, is the roof-top patio which has both open air and enclosed seating, and another full bar. If you can't be at the game, this might be the next best thing.

The bars can meet just about any desire, with large varieties of booze, more than 15 different beers on tap, and more in bottles and cans, a menu full of seasonal cocktails, happy hour specials from 5-7pm Tuesday-Friday, and gameday specials including a pitcher and 4 shots for $15.

The kitchen pumps out a steady stream of delicious burgers, wraps, sandwiches, soups, salads, and appetizers.

Proximity to the arenas and the Fox and Fillmore theaters make parking plentiful in the area, and **Bookies** will even shuttle you to the events if you don't feel like walking.

For more entertainment, there is a pool table, Golden Tee, TVs everywhere, and a juke box.

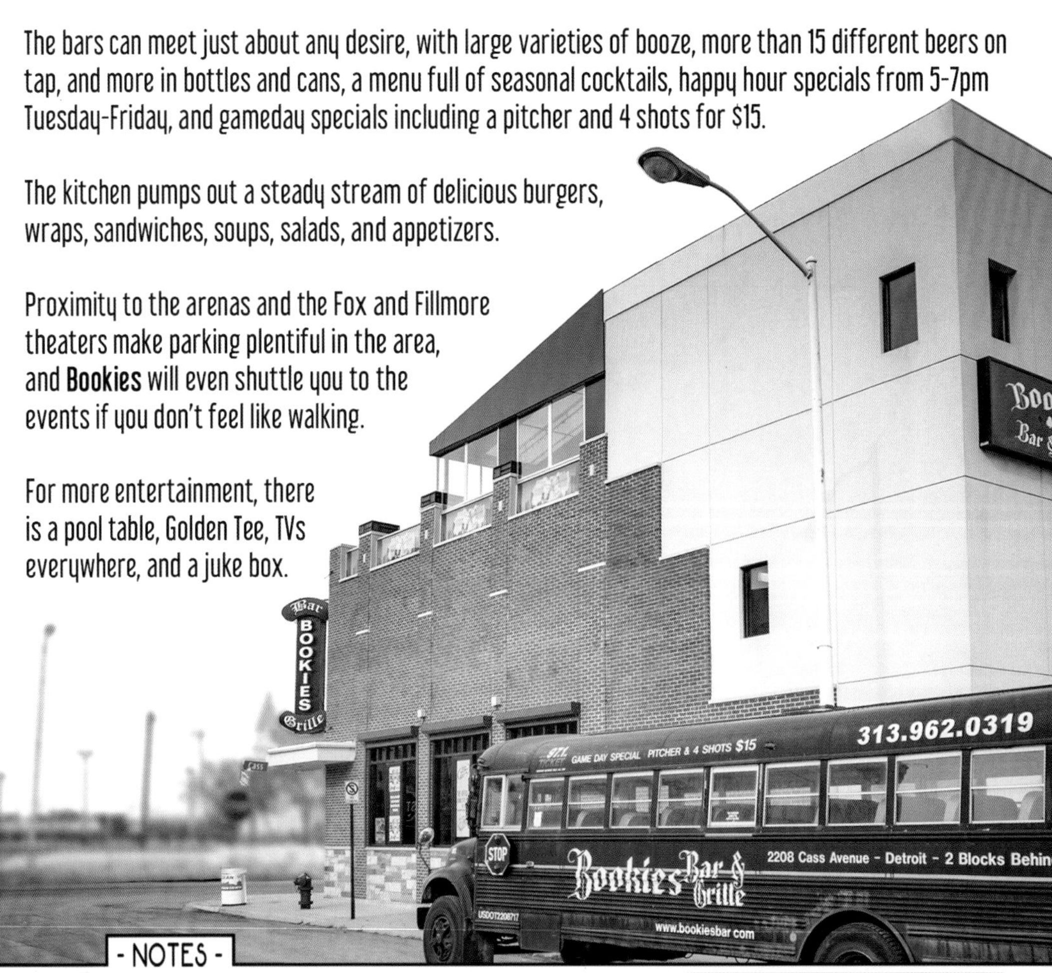


- NOTES -

Been there! ☐ Foxtown

18 West Adams Avenue
(313) 964-0782

# Brass Rail Pizza Bar

Full bar: ✓ Draft beer: ✓ Full kitchen: ✓ Shuttle service: ✗ brassraildetroit.com

The space housing the **Brass Rail Pizza Bar** is quite large and most of the dining space boasts soaring ceilings. There are three parts to the interior. Closest to the entrance is the main dining room, set to handle the basic food crowd. The next space is dominated by the large bar, and also has tables for dining. The front windowed wall can be opened like a garage door, joining inside to outside. Finally, there is the mezzanine, another dining space that overlooks the bar. Overall, the ambiance is comfortable and inviting.

HOURS:
Sun - Thu: 11am - 11pm
Fri - Sat: 11am - 1:30am

HAPPY HOUR:
Mon - Fri: 4pm - 6pm
Sun: 11am - 11pm
(No happy hour on game days)

With 52 draft pulls, three tall rows of backlit shelving filled with all varieties of liquor, and glass-fronted coolers beneath the bar, the drinking scene is impressive. Check the chalkboard for the draft list, or peruse the menu for all their draft, wine and specialty cocktail options. Several large TVs make it possible for bar patrons to keep up with the day's games.

Pizza is the star on the menu which also lists sandwiches, sliders, and pasta. On Wednesdays from 5-10pm, burgers are just five bucks. That price is hard to beat in Detroit.

If the **Brass Rail** was any closer to the sports arenas, it would be in the way of the players. Because of this, there are plenty of places to park in the area.

***HISTORICAL NOTE:*** *This location was once home to a burlesque show called the **Brass Rail**.*

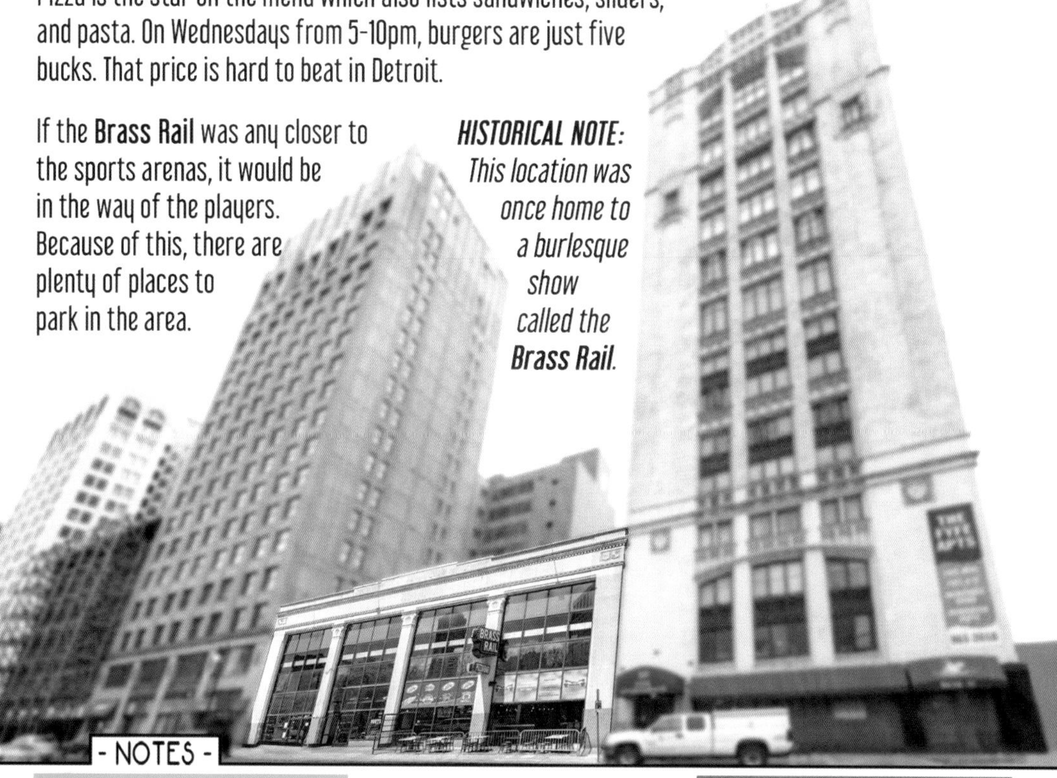

- NOTES -

Been there! ☐ Foxtown

# Broderick Grille

1570 Woodward Avenue
(313) 672-2073

**Full bar:** ☑ **Draft beer:** ☑ **Full kitchen:** ☑ **Shuttle service:** ☒ broderickgrilledetroit.com

HOURS:
Mon - Fri: 11am - close
Sat-Sun: 10am - close

HAPPY HOUR:
Mon - Fri: 3pm - 6pm

Located inside the wonderfully restored Broderick Tower, **Broderick Grille** is a clean and modern bar-restaurant. Inside you will find a cozy back-lit bar near the entrance and a large restaurant space complete with a 2nd level that overlooks the lower.

At the bar, all of the standard fare is available, including ten different beer taps, with many more available in bottles, and a small wine list. During happy hour, patrons enjoy $1 off any beverage. During **Broderick Grille's** brunch, the bar serves up eight accompanying drinks, including mimosas.

The kitchen offers three different menus - brunch, lunch, and dinner. For brunch, there are breakfast items plus some burgers and sandwiches. The lunch menu expands from the burgers and sandwiches to include salads, and the dinner menu steps up the offerings with full entrees. The food here is typically American fare, and burgers are what most people come in for. Their version of the Big Mac is a hot seller.

**Broderick Grille** has a prime location in regard to Detroit sports, as Ford Field, Comerica Park, and the new Little Caesars Arena are all within view. The Fox Theater, Fillmore Theater, and the Detroit Opera House are also very close. To reach the other popular sites in Detroit, the Detroit People Mover has a stop nearby, and the QLine runs on Woodward Avenue, with a stop right at Grand Circus Park.

Parking is abundant in this part of town, with numerous parking structures supporting the sporting arenas. There are also surface lots and limited metered spots on the street.

- NOTES -

2233 Park Avenue
(313) 963-4040

# Centaur Bar

Full bar: ✓ Draft beer: ✓ Full kitchen: ✗ Shuttle service: ✗

centaurbar.com

HOURS:
Mon - Sun: 4pm - 2am

HAPPY HOUR:
Mon - Sun: 4pm - 7pm

Located in the historic 1920s Iodent Building, formerly a toothpaste factory, **Centaur Bar** carries forward the Art Deco style of the structure. Visually impressive, the interior has two floors with a large mezzanine in between. Every piece of furniture has a unique, elegant look, from the tall bar stools to the leather sofas. Elegance without pretentiousness.

As one would expect, the bar is stocked, and the bartenders knowledgable, able to mix up traditional cocktails accurately and swiftly. If you've come to know **Centaur** for their martinis, that's changing, as they are reducing the focus there. The wine list is quite large, and between the handful of beers on tap with more in bottles and cans, most if not all drink wishes should be able to be granted.

When it comes to food, **Centaur** is a tapas bar. This means appetizers and small plates. There's plenty to balance out a few drinks, and for the lighter eaters may even constitute a meal. During happy hour select appetizers are just $5.

The mezzanine is a great place to sit to either get away from the crowd, or to people watch those at the bar below, all from the comfort of a relaxing couch.

Two pool tables upstairs offer additional entertainment while hanging out with friends.

Parking is plentiful, thanks to its proximity to Ford Field, Comerica Park, The Fox and Fillmore, and Little Caesars Arena.

***AUTHOR'S NOTE:*** *It's a nice place to take a date, or for something a little fancier than the average bar.*

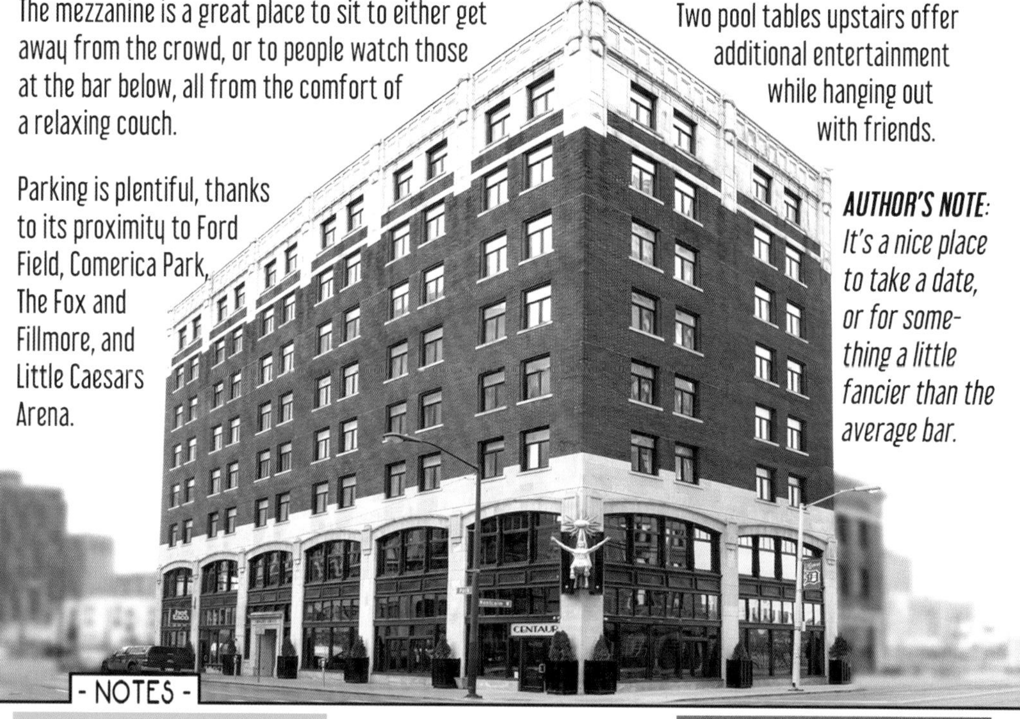


- NOTES -

Been there! ☐

Foxtown

# Centre Park Bar

1407 Randolph Street
(313) 962-4999

**Full bar:** ✓ **Draft beer:** ✓ **Full kitchen:** ✓ **Shuttle service:** ✗

HOURS:
Tue - Sat: 5pm - 2am
Sun: 7pm - 2am
Mon: closed

HAPPY HOUR:
Mon - Fri: 4pm - 7pm

This bar often takes the party out to the courtyard in front of the building. Inside, a long curving bar lit from underneath, paired with the colorfully lit walls behind the bar, set the tone for the atmosphere. The colored lights, in sync with the music, and changing frequently, are most dramatic in the evening. The front of the bar opens to the street, and to a small park with ample seating which is also part of the bar. Drinks and food are allowed to be ordered to this area, and the music from the bar easily reaches.

The bar offers a relatively standard selection of liquors, wines, and beers, and there is a bottle service option available for those interested. During happy hour, weekdays from 4pm - 7pm, drink specials get the party started.

The kitchen pushes out a combination of common bar fare as well as a few items with a Mediterranean flare such as stuffed grape leaves, falafel, and shawarma. The food can be enjoyed both inside and out in the courtyard.

The location puts **Centre Park Bar** within walking distance of all of Detroit's sports venues, the Detroit Opera House, Music Hall, the Fox and Fillmore Theaters, and Greektown Casino. Close proximity to the Detroit People Mover's Broadway station brings the rest of downtown into reach, and the QLine over on Woodward to bring points north into play.

There are numerous parking garages in the area, as well as limited metered parking on the streets.

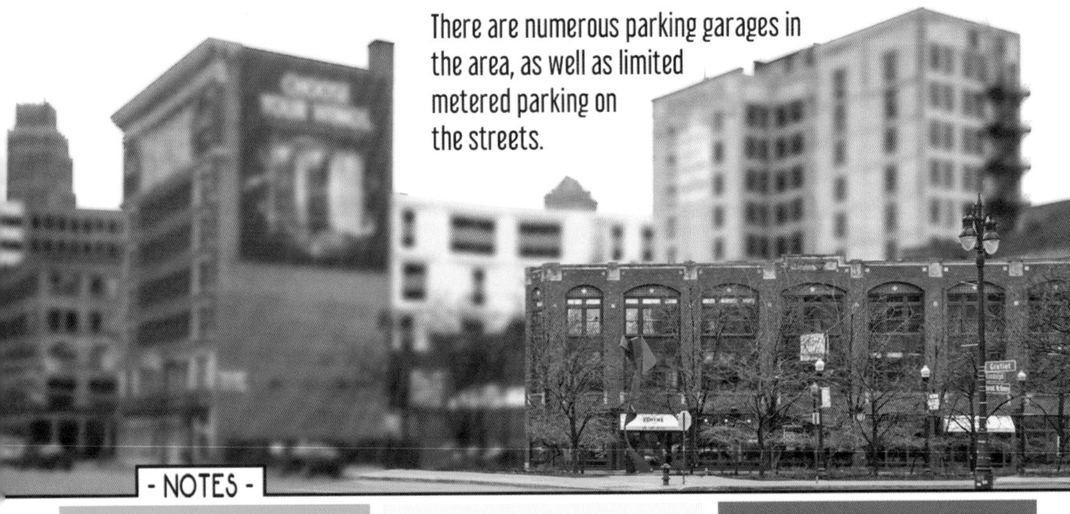

- NOTES -

47 E. Adams Avenue
(313) 961-1700

# Cheli's Chili Bar

**Full bar:** ✓ **Draft beer:** ✓ **Full kitchen:** ✓ **Shuttle service:** ✓ **chelischilibar.com**

HOURS:
Mon - Sun: 11am - 2am
*open at 10am for 1pm games*
*open early for home Lions games.*
*- for game days, verify on Facebook or Twitter.*

**Cheli's Chili Bar** is located basically in the parking lot out front of Comerica Park, and is owned by former Detroit Red Wings defenseman, Chris Chelios. There are over 30 flatscreen TVs throughout the three floors and rooftop patio, and live music on game days. High ceilings, magnificent woodwork, and tons of memorabilia and pictures throughout create a welcoming vibe, and solidify **Cheli's** reputation as a sports bar. The rooftop patio is a very popular party spot on warm game days, with food, drinks, music, and the sounds from Comerica Park. For larger events, **Cheli's** also sets up huge party tents in the parking lot.

The bars inside offer up more than 30 choices of draft beers, and can handle just about any drink request you might have. The offerings from the kitchen vary seasonally, but always bring at least the basics with chili, burgers, sandwiches, and a selection of sides. During the peak seasons, the menu is significantly expanded.

Parking in the area can be difficult when there is a game, so plan ahead. Surface lots and parking structures are in the area, and the QLine runs on Woodward, which expands the area of parking possibilities.

*This place is a party on game days!*

- NOTES -

Been there! ☐

Foxtown

# Cliff Bell's

2030 Park Avenue
(313) 961-2543
cliffbells.com

**Full bar:** ✓ **Draft beer:** ✓ **Full kitchen:** ✓ **Shuttle service:** ✗

HOURS:
Tue - Thu: 4pm - midnight
Fri: 4pm - 1am
Sat: 5pm - 1:30am
Sun: 11am - 10pm

HAPPY HOUR:
Tue- Fri: 5pm - 7pm

BRUNCH:
Sun: 11am - 3pm

Enter **Cliff Bell's** and instantly be teleported back 100 years. This is a one-of-a-kind location. Art Deco themed with brass and mahogany accents, you know you're in a jazz club when you walk through the door. Elegance oozes from every corner.

**Cliff Bell's** has a full bar, including draft and bottled beers, and an extensive wine list. Perfectly crafted cocktails are just a request away, and can be enjoyed in the dining area or at the long, beautiful mahogany bar, one of the nicest in Detroit.

For those intending to dine, reservations are required, and a full meal must be ordered. **Cliff Bell's** is a fine dining establishment, and the menu reflects the same. The menu items and kitchen are overseen by Chef Joe Susko.

Entertainment is the central theme at **Cliff Bell's**, with a steady flow of perfomers coming through. Check the website to find out who will be performing, as well as how much the cover will be. On Sundays during brunch, there is always live entertainment and no cover charge.

Parking is plentiful and **Cliff Bell's** offers valet service.

***Cliff Bell's** has a long history. Read about it here:*
*cliffbells.com/the-story/*

- NOTES -

220 Bagley Avenue
(313) 963-4000

# Coaches Corner Bar & Grill

**Full bar:** ✓ **Draft beer:** ✓ **Full kitchen:** ✓ **Shuttle service:** ✗ **coachescornerdetroit.com**

**Coaches Corner** is a large sports bar located just a couple of blocks from Comerica Park. The space is big, the walls are dotted with large flat screen TVs, and there is even a cornhole game (beanbag toss) set up inside most of the time. When the game isn't on, there's a jukebox which provides music not only for everyone inside, but also those in the sidwealk seating area.

HOURS:
*Open only on the days when the Tigers play at home. Doors open 3 hours ahead of the first pitch.*

Sixteen cold beers on draft, more in bottles and cans, and a full bar await thirsty game-day patrons. The buckets of beer and pint specials are popular, as are shots and mixed drinks. Liquid libations are complemented with a focused selection of bar style food. Also worthy of note are the reasonable prices.

**Coaches Corner** has their own parking lot, and there are other surface lots and some limited curbside metered parking in this neighborhood. They are close enough to Comerica Park that you can probably be sitting at the bar and hear the crowd cheer a Tiger home run, therefore an easy enough walk for most.

*This is a good place to go with a group. They can handle the volume.*

*There are rumors that the bar may be open for more than just Tiger games in the future.*

- NOTES -

Been there! ☐ Foxtown

# Colors

311 East Grand River Avenue
(313) 496-1212

**Full bar:** ☑ **Draft beer:** ☒ **Full kitchen:** ☑ **Shuttle service:** ☒ **colorsrestaurantdet.com**

HOURS:
Tue - Wed: 11am - 3pm
Thu - Fri: 11am - 3pm
5pm - 10pm
Sat: 5pm - 10pm
Sun - Mon: closed

Located beneath the Carr Center in the historical Harmonie Club Building built in 1895, **Colors** is an interesting space. The dining and bar areas have a clean, modern finish, while the tile floors and domed tile ceiling add a unique look and feel.

**Colors** is a place of learning. The restaurant and bar are working classrooms, where students spend four weeks in classes then six weeks on the floor, providing them the opportunity to not only learn, but also gain important experience.

The bar provides a decent selection of beer, wine, and liquor. Nothing over-the-top, but likely enough to meet most wants, and their prices are reasonable. There are drink specials, and they change from time to time. Ask your server for the current offerings.

From the kitchen comes a small menu of mostly American-style dishes. **Colors** serves up both a lunch and a dinner menu.

With its central location, **Colors** is easily within walking distance of the Opera House, all of Detroit's sports arenas, the Detroit Music Hall, the Fox and Fillmore theaters, and the heart of the city. Parking is also plentiful in the area, with metered street spaces, surface lots, and several large parking structures.

*While the food is prepared by students, they are overseen by a chef to ensure quality and consistency.*

- NOTES -

1529 Broadway Street
(313) 962-1529

# Detroit Beer Company

Full bar: ✓ Draft beer: ✓ Full kitchen: ✓ Shuttle service: ✗ detroitbeerco.com

Not only does **Detroit Beer Company** make their own beer, they do it well. Right when you enter the establishment, you come face to face with the large, shiny brewing vats. At any given time they will have a half dozen or more of their products on tap, offering a consistent cold and flavorful draft. If you are not a beer person, you'll be OK. **Detroit Beer Company** has liquor at their bar, too.

HOURS:
Mon - Thu: 11am - midnight
Fri - Sat: 11am - 2am
Sun: noon - midnight

Author Favorite

HAPPY HOUR:
Mon - Fri: 4pm - 6pm

In business since 2003, **Detroit Beer Company** has a full menu filled with tasty, fresh made offerings. There's everything from soups, salads and a decent selection of sandwiches and burgers to fresh made brick oven pizzas. During their happy hour from 4pm - 6pm, M-F, appetizers are half off, and drinks are 75c off.

There are two floors of seating, as well as limited seating at the bar itself. This is a good place to go with small to medium-sized groups. With anything more than eight people, it's probably best to call ahead.

Located across from the Detroit Opera House on Broadway, they are easy walking distance to Comerica Park, Little Caesars Arena, Ford Field, the Fox, and the Fillmore. Parking is plentiful, with several parking garages nearby. There is also very limited metered street parking available.

If you join their birthday club online, you get a free meal during your birthday month, as well as other special offers and information about events at the **Detroit Beer Company**.

*A personal favorite of mine is the "Hair of the Dog" burger with a side of sweet potato fries. Despite the name, a hangover is not a pre-requisite to order this. The burger patty is a full half pound, so bring your appetite.*

- NOTES -

**Been there!** ☐ **Foxtown**

# Detroit Rolling Pub

**1331 Broadway Street**
**(231) 286-5257**

**Full bar: X Draft beer: X Full kitchen: X Shuttle service: X detroitrollingpub.com**

HOURS:
Mon - Sun: 10am - 10pm

All year long, even in the winter!

So here's the deal: This bar moves. It gets its power from you and your friends pedaling. Some may ask why anyone would want to work while drinking. Because it is fun! With the **Detroit Rolling Pub**, you move through the streets of Detroit with drinks, music, and your friends. If you get tired of pedaling, stop at another bar and go in for a drink. **Detroit Rolling Pub** can either provide you with a route around downtown Detroit, or you can work with them to design a custom route tailored to your group's style and taste.

This is a rolling bar, and part of the deal is that you bring your own alcohol. There are a few rules to follow: no glass, no liquor, and you cannot stop to buy alcohol during the ride, other than what you drink in the bars along the way. Because of legalities, it is imperative that you review the rules and guidelines as written on **Detroit Rolling Pub's** website. ( http://detroitrollingpub.com/faq/ )

You can bring your own snacks or arrange for them to cater. There are speakers you can plug into so you can listen to the music of your choice. For other guidelines, again, refer to their website.

Rentals are in two hour blocks:
Mon - Thu, 6-15 people, $250/hr
Fri - Sun, 6-15 people, $320/hr

*This is a fun way to experience Detroit in a different way!*

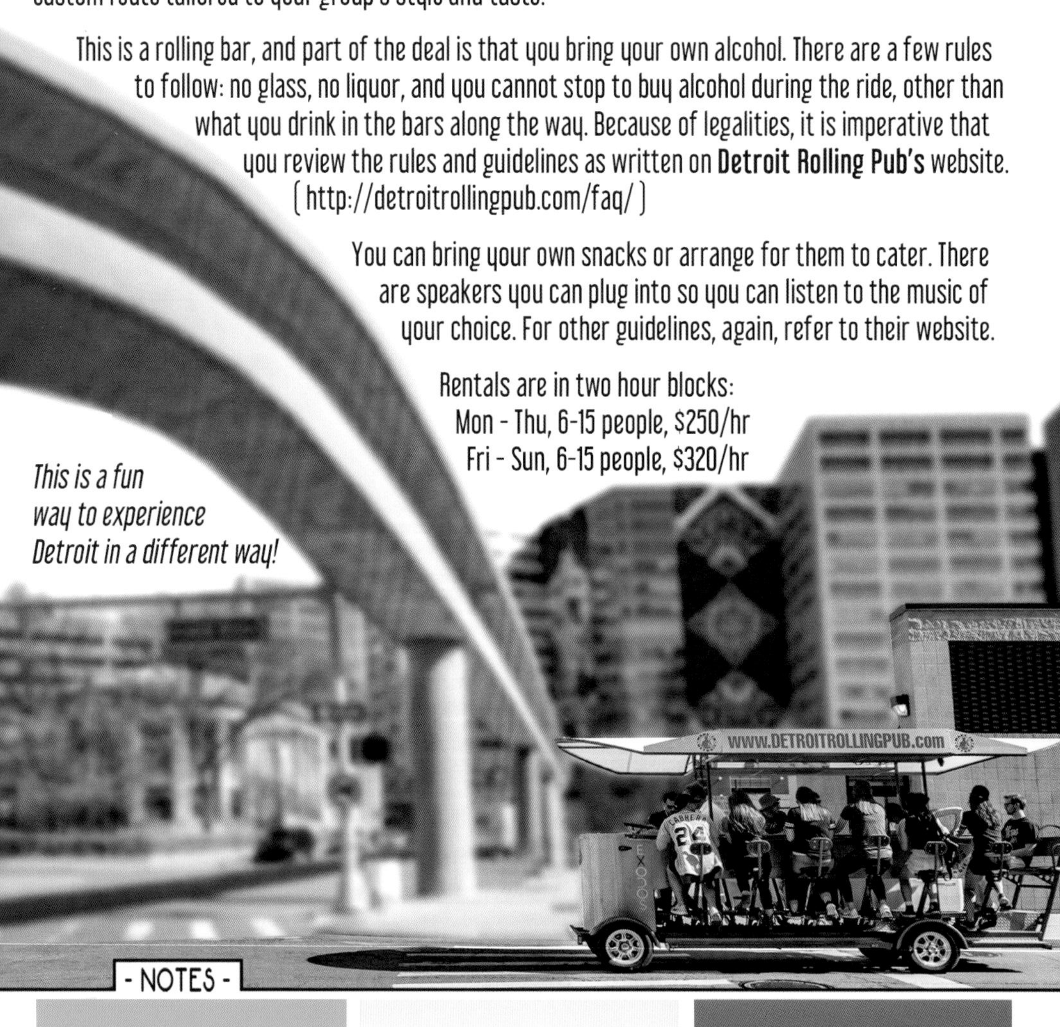


- NOTES -

300 E. Adams Avenue
(313) 962-2337

# Elwood Bar & Grill

Full bar: ☑ Draft beer: ☑ Full kitchen: ☑ Shuttle service: ✗ elwoodgrill.com

**Elwood Bar & Grill** is located between Comerica Park and Ford Field. The bar opened in 1936 at 2100 Woodward Avenue, then the building was moved to its current location in 1997. On game day, whether the Tigers at Comerica Park, or the Lions at Ford Field, the Elwood is a bustling hotspot. They generally do a great job of keeping the drinks flowing and serving good, hot food fast, even when the place is packed. Because of its proximity to the two sports venues, parking is plentiful in parking garages, but can be congested on game days.

HOURS:
Mon - Tue: 11am - 2pm
Wed - Sat: 11am - 8pm
Sun: CLOSED

Author Favorite

This historic little Art Deco bar is one of those places that you have to experience at least once. Their food focus is sandwiches and burgers, and they do them well. There are salads and sides, and in the author's experience, the fries and wings are fresh and hot, all the time.

Draft beers and standard mixed drinks are the norm from the bar at **Elwood**, and the beers are served up nice and cold.

The **Elwood** looks like a diner from the 50s, with the tiled exterior, and the abundance of neon lighted signs. While **Elwood** appears small on the outside, they manage to pack the people in. The atmosphere is electric when there's a game, as the sounds from the fields easily reach the bar.

- NOTES -

Been there! ☐ Foxtown

# Da Edoardo Foxtown Grille

2203 Woodward Avenue
(313) 471-3500

Full bar: ✓ Draft beer: ✗ Full kitchen: ✓ Shuttle service: ✗ daedoardo.net/foxtown-grille

HOURS:
Tue - Thu: 11:30am - 9pm
Fri: 11:30am - 10pm
Sat: 5pm - 10pm
Sun - Mon: during events

*Hours vary seasonally and based on events.*

**Foxtown Grille** is primarily a high-end restaurant, sharing the building with the exquisite Fox Theater. The elegance of the exterior continues inside to the restaurant and bar.

The fully stocked bar offers traditional cocktails, a decent selection of beers, and an extensive wine list, providing many options to pair with your meal.

**Foxtown Grille** offers Northern Italian cuisine, and is considered one of Detroit's premier restaurants. If you are looking to impress, or simply want to enjoy a nice Italian meal in a comfortably eleglant environment, this is the place for you. Because of the variability of their hours, calling ahead is recommended.

Located across the street from Comerica Park and within shouting distance of Ford Field, the Fillmore Theater, and Little Caesars Arena, this is a popular destination.

Parking is plentiful in the immediate area, and the QLine has stops nearby, both up and down Woodward Avenue. There is also a Detroit People Mover stop just across Grand Circus Park.

*Calamari is a crowd favorite at **Foxtown Grille.***

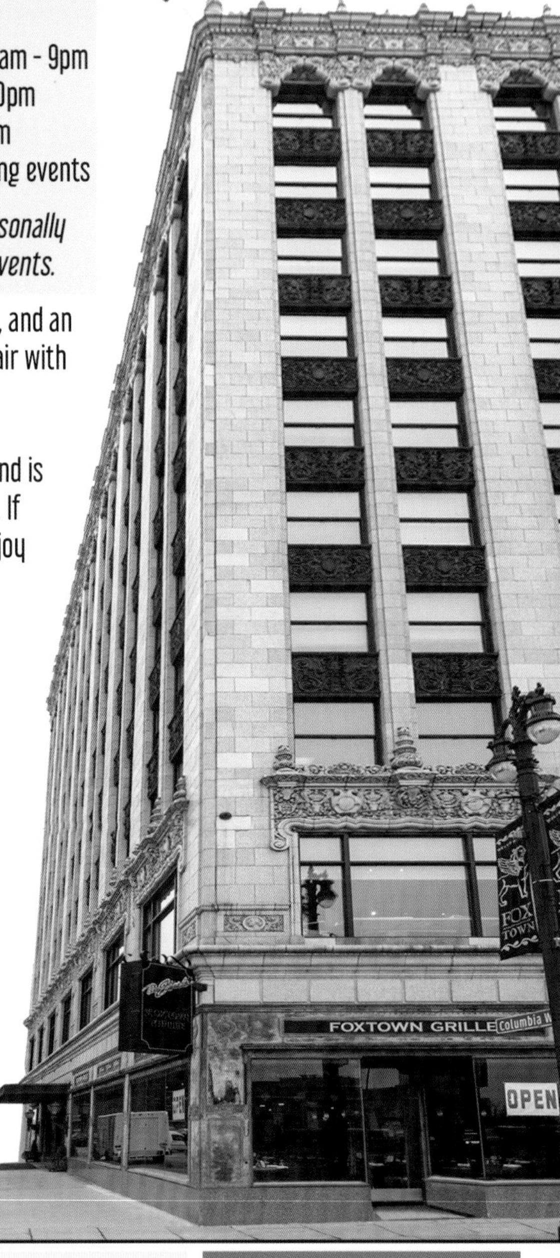


- NOTES -

2482 Clifford Street
(313) 964-1575

# Harry's Detroit Bar

Full bar: ✓ Draft beer: ✓ Full kitchen: ✓ Shuttle service: ✓ harrysdetroit.com

HOURS:
Mon - Sun: 11am - 2am

HAPPY HOUR:
Mon - Sun: 4pm - 7pm

**Harry's** is a big, proud bar standing in the shadow of the new Little Caesars Arena. Inside, the main space has high ceilings, TVs for every angle, and walls adorned with beer mirrors and old pictures and maps of Detroit. Keeping in the bar spirit, there is a pool table, dart board, and a juke box added to the mix.

The long wooden bar stretches most of the length of the back wall, and a large chalk board lists the daily food specials and current draft list. The wear on the bar speaks of the countless fans who have bellied up over the years. **Harry's** has a rooftop open-air patio which doubles the capacity of this time-proven establishment. This is a popular place before, during, and after sporting and entertainment events in Detroit. They also offer an equal opportunity happy hour - everything is $1 off.

The kitchen makes just about everything in-house, including grinding their own burgers, making the sauces, and smoking their own meats. Their smoked chicken wings, burgers, and amazing macaroni and cheese are crowd favorites.

With location being an important factor, you would be hard pressed to get any better than this. **Harry's** is practically an annex to the Red Wings and Piston's new home. Comerica Park, Ford Field, Fox Theater, and the Fillmore Theater are right across I-75, and the Detroit Opera House is only a little further. Besides **Harry's** private parking lot, there are many other parking choices in the immediate area.

***Harry's** rooftop patio can be opened or sealed depending on the weather. It is a fun place to visit with a group.*

- NOTES -

Been there! ☐

Foxtown

# Hockeytown Cafe

2301 Woodward Avenue
(313) 471-3400

**Full bar:** ☑ **Draft beer:** ☑ **Full kitchen:** ☑ **Shuttle service:** ☑ **hockeytowncafe.com**

HOURS:
Mon - Sun: 11am - ?
*They generally open at 11am, but the closing times vary based on the local events.*

**Hockeytown Cafe** has the "cool factor" going. When you walk in, you are faced with a two story lobby, custom motorcycles and sports paraphernalia everywhere you look, a long beautiful bar, and copious seating choices across multiple levels of the restaurant.

In addition to the bar as you enter, there is another full bar upstairs, cutting down wait times to get your drinks. **Hockeytown Cafe** also has a rooftop bar and a street-level fenced in patio, both of which give you the opportunity to enjoy good weather, fresh air, and the sounds from Comerica Park when there is a game going on. Inside, among all of the memorabilia, numerous TVs allow you to catch the games from anywhere on the property.

The beer list is extensive, with twenty or so on tap and dozens more offered in bottles and cans. Of course, the bars offer more than beer, and there is a decent wine list as well. Being one of the biggest sports bars in Detroit, there are generally game day specials.

The menu at **Hockeytown** is impressive, as is the quality of the food. There is sure to be something for everyone, and most everything is made fresh to order. If you are visiting during lunchtime, ask about the daily lunch special.

*This is a great place for large groups, but keep in mind that it is very close to Comerica Park, Little Caesars Arena, and Ford Field, and can fill up quickly when there is a game.*

- NOTES -

# La Casa Cigars & Lounge

**1502 Randolph Street**
**(313) 285-8332**

**Full bar:** ✓ **Draft beer:** ✗ **Full kitchen:** ✗ **Shuttle service:** ✗ **lacasacigars.com/locations/detroit.com**

HOURS:
Mon - Tue: noon - midnight
Wed - Thu: noon - 1am
Fri - Sat: noon - 2am
Sun: noon - 11pm

If you are into cigars, this is the place for you. Retail on one side, and bar with lounge on the other. The rich browns and dark reds used throughout the interior compliment the leather chairs. Hanging lights and a long stone bar complete the decor, creating a warm and comfortable environment. During the day, soft music wafts through the lounge, adding to the soothing mood. On Wednesday through Saturday evenings there is live music. On Wednesday and Thursday, it starts at 8pm, and on Friday and Saturday, at 10pm.

**La Casa** has a full bar with a significant offering of martinis, skillfully mixed cocktails, and a respectable variety of whiskeys. While not their focus, there is also a selection of beer and wine. There is not a happy hour, however Tuesday is ladies' night, with $8 martinis. There is no kitchen here, but food can be ordered in. The bartenders can provide a list of local restaurants who deliver.

**La Casa** is very close to the Detroit Opera House, the Detroit Music Hall, and all of the sports venues. As a direct result, there are many parking garages nearby, surface lots, and metered parking along most of the streets. The Detroit People Mover has a stop a block away, and it's a short walk to Woodward and the QLine. Between the two, just about all of downtown, midtown, and New Center are within reach.

*The second floor of **La Casa** is a VIP Lounge. This is a members only space providing even more elegance, private rooms, a walk-in humidor with private cigar lockers, another full bar, an open air patio, and many comfortable leather chairs and couches. It is really the lap of Luxury. The upstairs can be rented for private events, even by non-members.*

\- NOTES -

Been there! ☐ Foxtown

# MGM Grand Detroit

1777 3rd Avenue
(877) 888-2121

**Full bar:** ✓ **Draft beer:** ✓ **Full kitchen:** ✓ **Shuttle service:** ✗ **mgmgranddetroit.com**

HOURS:
Mon - Sun: 24 hours

**MGM Grand Detroit** is one of Detroit's three casinos. There are table games, both live and digital, as well as around 3,500 slots and digital poker machines.

Besides the roving waitstaff throughout the property, **MGM Grand Detroit** also has several bars around the perimeter of the gaming area, and one, The **Axis Lounge**, right in the middle of everything. It is open from 10am-2am, seven days a week.

**TAP** is the largest of the bars, capable of seating 292 people. **TAP** is open Sun-Thu from 7am - midnight, and Fri-Sat from 7am - 1am. On Friday and Saturday nights, the **V Nightclub** is open at **MGM** from 8pm until 2am. They offer table service, and DJs provide music to fill the dance floor.

**MGM Grand Detroit** offers a variety of live entertainment. Check the website for details and dates.

Finally, food. You don't have to go hungry when you are visiting the **MGM Grand**. You have six different places to choose from: Wolfgang Puck Steak, Wolfgang Puck Pizzeria & Cucina, Palette Dining Studio, TAP, the Breeze Dining Court, and for something light, The Roasted Bean.

***AUTHOR'S NOTE**: Smoking is allowed on the gaming floor throughout the casino. For the non-smokers, they do offer a couple of smoke-free slot rooms.*

There are roughly 400 rooms in the hotel at **MGM Grand Detroit**, a spa, a fitness center, and an indoor pool.

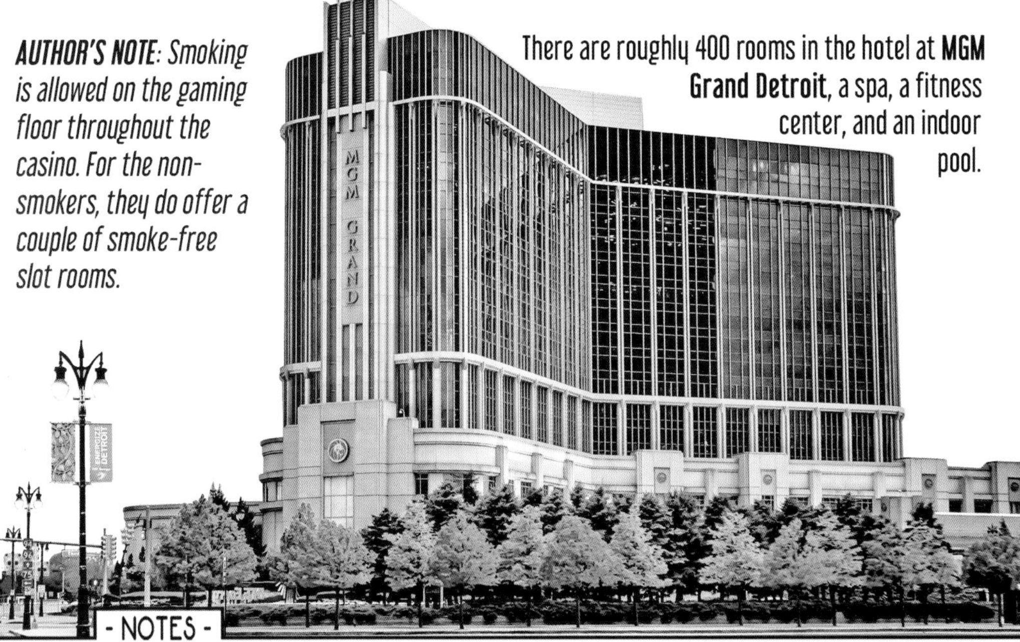


- NOTES -

2208 Cass Avenue
(313) 744-3272

# Michigan Pedaler

Full bar: ✗ Draft beer: ✗ Full kitchen: ✗ Shuttle service: ✗ michiganpedaler.com

HOURS:
Mon - Sun: 9:50 am - 8:10pm

This is one of Detroit's three rolling bars. The home base for **Michigan Pedaler** is Bookies Bar & Grille. Your tour will start and end there.

This is a pedal bar, which means you and your friends - each bar holds 15 - provide the power to make the bar move. But wait! **Michigan Pedaler's** bars have an electric assist which will help you along your way, or if you really get stubborn, can provide all of the power needed to move around town. There are currently 3 bars in this fleet, allowing you to book for a group as large as 45. On each bike you will have 10 pedalers, 4 people sitting on a bench, and one captain.

The deal with the pedal bars is that you supply your own drinks and snacks. No glass bottles and no hard liquor unless it has been pre-mixed. For the specifics, review the rules on their website, or talk to their representatives directly to make sure everything is clear.

There are three tours: Downtown, Midtown and Corktown, and the **Michigan Pedaler** allows groups of all ages on their bikes. The two hour tours are $300 on Sunday through Thursday, and $350 on Friday and Saturday.

Michigan Pedaler has the last word on all of the rules and prices.

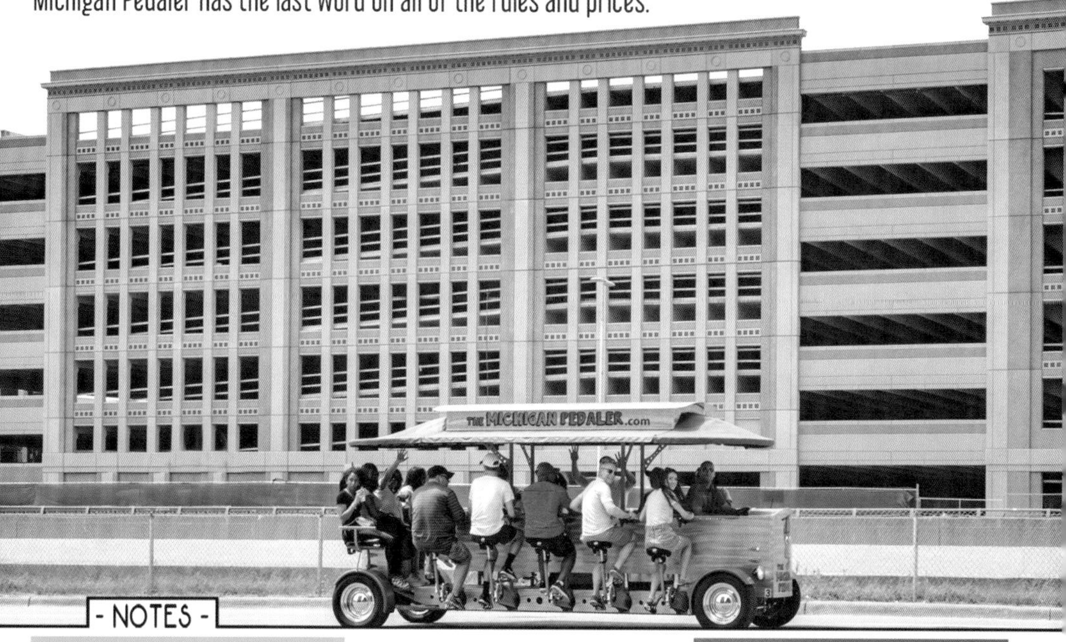


- NOTES -

Been there! ☐

Foxtown

# The Park Bar

2040 Park Avenue
(313) 962-2933

Full bar: ✓ Draft beer: ✓ Full kitchen: ✓ Shuttle service: ✗ parkbardetroit.com

HOURS:
Mon: closed
Tue - Thu: 4pm - 2am
Fri: 11am - 2am
Sat: 1pm - 2am
Sun: 1pm - midnight

**The Park Bar** is a cool space in the corner of a two story building surrounded by taller buildings. Large windows on both exterior sides allow for natural light as well as people watching which can be fun when there is a show at one of the nearby theaters or a game at any of the Detroit sports arenas. The circular wooden bar is in the middle of the room, the main focus from every direction.

**The Park Bar** offers a wonderful selection of craft drafts, and the bartenders are able to mix up everything from standard to trendy drinks. Due to its smaller size, it is better geared for small groups rather than large gatherings.

If you're looking to eat, too, there is a small restaurant, Gogos, in the same space. Gogos serves up Hawaiian style cuisine from a limited menu, and it can be ordered to the bar. On Fridays and Saturdays, they serve up fresh poke (fish salad).

Ford Field, Comerica Park, Little Caesars Arena, the Fillmore and Fox Theater are all within a couple of blocks, making this a popular place to go. With the arenas and theaters come plenty of local parking.

- NOTES -

1331 Broadway Street
(313) 749-9738

# Punch Bowl Social

Full bar: ✓ Draft beer: ✓ Full kitchen: ✓ Shuttle service: ✗ punchbowlsocial.com

**Punch Bowl Social** has been designed to look like a space converted from an old industrial site. It is located under the Z Garage, with entrances on Broadway Street, and it is absolutely HUGE. There are two levels, several full bars, bowling alleys, an 80s style arcade, shuffle board, pool tables, darts, marbles, ping pong, and private karaoke. There is so much energy in this establishment that it feels like a party all the time. It's kind of like an amusement park for adults.

HOURS:
Mon - Fri: 11am - 2am
Sat: 9am - 2am
Sun: 9am - midnight

HAPPY HOUR:
Mon - Sun: 3pm - 6pm
Sun - Thu: 10pm - midnight
Fri - Sat: 11pm - 1am

**Punch Bowl Social** offers a relatively large menu filled with creative culinary items. If you are there for happy hour (3-6pm), make sure you get the happy hour menu. On Saturdays and Sundays, **PBS** offers a brunch. If you are bringing a large group - and this is a perfect place for a large group - call ahead and get a reservation. Multiple bars throughout the facility are capable of handling just about anything you want.

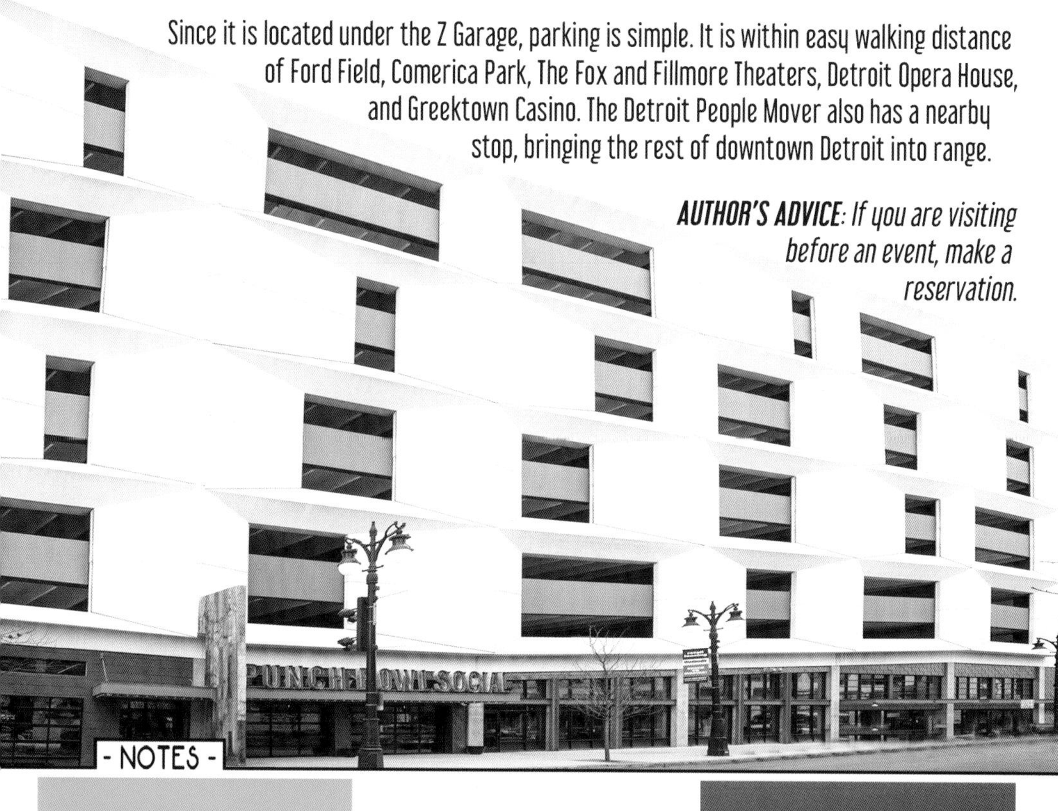


Since it is located under the Z Garage, parking is simple. It is within easy walking distance of Ford Field, Comerica Park, The Fox and Fillmore Theaters, Detroit Opera House, and Greektown Casino. The Detroit People Mover also has a nearby stop, bringing the rest of downtown Detroit into range.

***AUTHOR'S ADVICE***: *If you are visiting before an event, make a reservation.*

- NOTES -

Been there! ☐

Foxtown

# PV Lounge

1435 Randolph Street
(313) 962-4180

**Full bar:** ✓ **Draft beer:** ✗ **Full kitchen:** ✓ **Shuttle service:** ✗

**PV Lounge** is a hot spot for night time entertainment. The upscale, modern environment provides semi-private seating for those looking for a more intimate destination, as well as space to dance and mingle.

**PV Lounge** is connected to the Detroit Seafood Market next door, which provides not only thier food, but also live bands daily. **PV** has DJ entertainment Wednesday through Sunday.

HOURS:
Mon, Wed, Fri: 4pm - midnight
Tue, Thu: 4pm - 1am
Sat - Sun: 4pm - 2am

HAPPY HOUR:
Mon - Sat: 4pm - 7pm

The bar offers classic cocktails, a decent selection of signature drinks, and bottle service. Beer is by the bottle only, wine can be had by the bottle or by the glass, and their wine list is extensive.

To reserve a private booth, there is a commitment to either purchase a bottle of champagne or $100 in drinks, minimum.

**PV Lounge** charges a cover of $10 before 11pm, and it goes up after that. During happy hour, all drinks except champagne are half off, and on Tuesdays bottles of wine are half off.

**PV Lounge** is centrally located in Downtown Detroit, making it accessible from Ford Field, Comerica Park, the theaters (Fox and Fillmore), and Greektown.

Parking is plentiful in the area, with several large parking structures, suface lots, and metered street options.

*For large parties, there is a VIP room which must be reserved in advance.*

- NOTES -

**35 East Grand River Avenue**
**(313) 285-8019**

# Queens Bar

**Full bar:** ✓ **Draft beer:** ✓ **Full kitchen:** ✓ **Shuttle service:** ✗

HOURS:
Mon - Sat: 4pm - 2am
Sun: 4pm - midnight

HAPPY HOUR:
Mon - Sun: all day
($3 PBR, Highlife and Stroh's, and $5 wells)

**Queens Bar** has an appealing yet unassuming look from the outside. The building corner it occupies has a smooth, rounded finish, giving it a unique look in a city filled with hard edges. Inside, the bar follows a similar contour, wrapping around the small kitchen. Modern and clean, this is an inviting location, set up well for casual gatherings, drinks, and some food.

At the bar, the current draft list and the daily specials are recorded on a chalkboard overhead. All in all, there are around a dozen beers on tap, a small wine list, and a well rounded liquor set-up. The bar staff is experienced, and can serve up not only standard fare, but also some creative cocktails if called upon to do so.

The kitchen at **Queens** does not make a lot of offerings, mostly a selection of sandwiches and burgers, a few appetizers, and a soup of the day. Everything is made up fresh in house, and fits with the casual ambiance.

Round tables, nicely spaced throughout, provide a setting well suited to have conversations with your tablemates. A stack of board games is available to take back to your table. When it's warm outside, **Queens'** patio is a popular hang-out spot.

The location is about as central as you can get to most of the hot-spots in Detroit. The sports arenas, theaters, Greektown, and Campus Martius are all nearby, and parking is plentiful in this area.

# Republic Tavern

**1942 Grand River Avenue**
**(313) 446-8360**

**Full bar:** ✓ **Draft beer:** ✓ **Full kitchen:** ✓ **Shuttle service:** ✗ **republictaverndetroit.com**

Author Favorite

HOURS:
Tue - Thu: 4pm - 10pm
Fri: 4pm - 11pm
Sat: 5pm - 11pm
Sun: 5pm - 9pm
Mon: closed

HAPPY HOUR:
Tue - Fri: 4pm - 6pm

Located in the GAR (Grand Army of the Republic) building, one of the coolest looking structures in Detroit with its castle-like appearance, **Republic Tavern** is a large, inviting space. High ceilings and modern finishings give an open feel and the artistic touches throughout add the factor of fun to any visit.

The bar offers a deep selection in every category, from beer through top shelf whiskey. With so much to choose from, every sort of drinker can be appeased. Hand crafted cocktails also grace the menu, and the line-up of house made syrups, infusions, and fresh herbs are visible around the bar, at hand to take the drinks over the top. The cocktail menu changes seasonally, keeping the choices appropriate for the time of year. Come during happy hour, and enjoy select drink and small plates specials.

*The other half of the first floor is occupied by their sister restaurant: Parks & Rec Diner. The entire second floor of the GAR building can be rented for private parties and events.*

The food at **Republic Tavern** is creative, and in their words, "locally sourced, seasonally inspired, and crafted with love". The menu items are varied, including several options for vegans and vegetarians. As with the drinks, some of the dishes are seasonal.

The Fox and Fillmore theaters, Comerica Park, Little Caesars Arena, and Ford Field are walking distance from **Republic**.

Surface lots and metered parking are plentiful in the area.

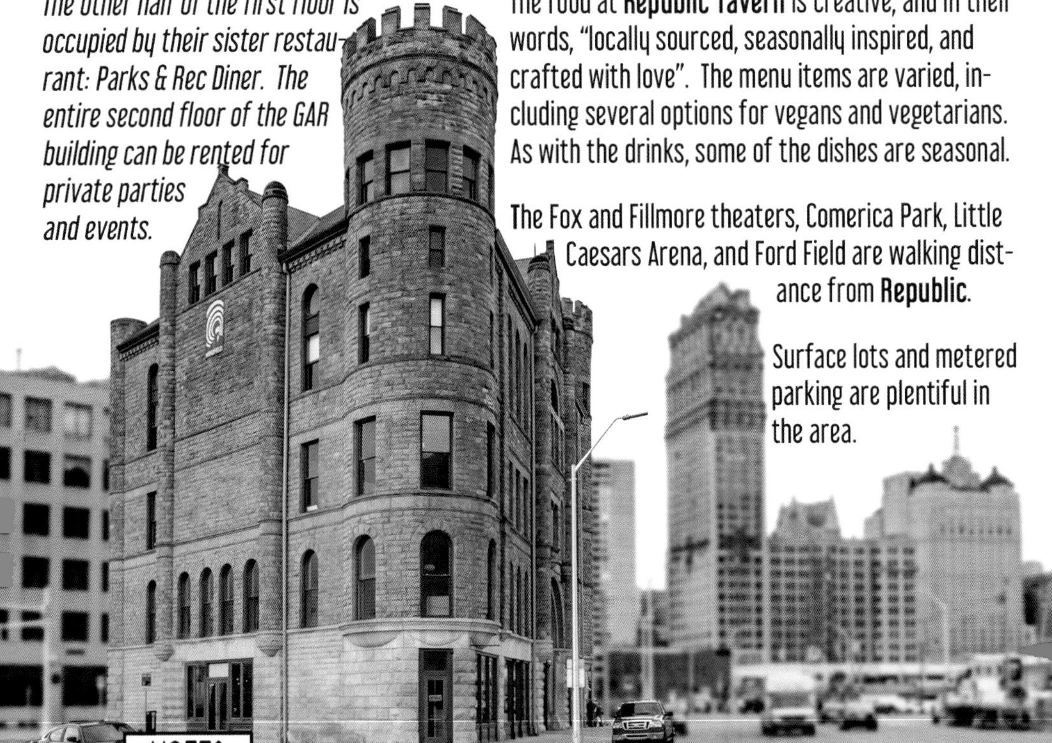

- NOTES -

# Rockefellers Oyster Bar

1315 Broadway Street
(313) 626-5000

**Full bar:** ✓ **Draft beer:** ✓ **Full kitchen:** ✗ **Shuttle service:** ✗

HOURS:

CLOSED

Now the location of Bert's on Broadway.

Tucked into a row of buildings along Broadway, **Rockefellers** is one of the new players in the bar scene of Detroit. They do come with experience, however, as they were previously located in Grosse Pointe prior to a fire in 2016.

**Rockefellers'** space here is large, with soaring ceilings and hardwood floors. There is a long bar down much of the left side of the spacious room. If one of the Detroit sports teams is playing, their game is probably being shown on the TVs over the bar and around the room. As with many places around Detroit, **Rockefellers** has a small seating area out front on the sidewalk.

CLOSED

For your drinking pleasure, the bar carries a fairly standard line-up of liquor, six draft beers, more in bottles and cans, and a few house wines. During happy hour **Rockefellers** offers a handful of drinks at lower prices. Food is limited to six appetizers, although this is rumored to be changing in the future.

Parking is plentiful in this area, with surface lots, metered spots on the street, and several large parking structures nearby. This location is conveniently close to the sports venues, the Fox and Fillmore, the Detroit Opera House, the Music Hall, Greektown, and Campus Martius.

- NOTES -

Been there! ☐

Foxtown

# The Royce - Detroit

76 West Adams Street
(313) 481-2160

**Full bar:** ✓ **Draft beer:** ✗ **Full kitchen:** ✗ **Shuttle service:** ✗ **theroycedetroit.com**

HOURS:
Tue - Thu: noon - 10pm
Fri - Sat: noon - midnight
Sun: 1pm - 9pm
Mon: closed

This warmly decorated business is located in the old Kale's building which was built in 1914. The ceilings at **The Royce** are soaring, allowing for a mezzanine in the middle overlooking not only the tall racks of wine along the perimeter walls, but also the bar area and the guests coming and going.

While this is a wine shop with over 350 wines for sale, there is also a bar where you can order wine and mixed drinks, just not beer. Many of the liquors and mixers are Michigan brands, including fresh juices from Wolf Moon. There is an extensive list of wines which can be ordered by the glass. For a $10 corkage fee, bottles can be purchased and consumed in the store. There is free wine tasting on Wednesdays from 5:30-7pm, and free pinchos (small snacks) on Thursdays from 6pm until 10pm.

There is no kitchen at **The Royce**, but there are small plates of meats, chocolates, seafood, and cheese to accompany your drinks.

*If you buy a bottle of wine and would like it chilled, **The Royce** has a blast chiller which takes about seven minutes to cool a bottle. This is a free service.*

No reservations are needed here. On Sunday evenings there is either live music or a DJ for entertainment, and on the third Thursday of each month, **The Royce** hosts an LGBTQ party (The G Party) with a DJ and drink specials.

**The Royce** is close to Ford Field, Comerica Park, the Fox and Fillmore theaters, and Little Caesars Arena. For more distant destinations, the QLine has a station just around the corner, and the People Mover has a stop across Grand Circus Park.

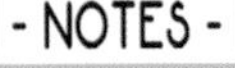

- NOTES -

78 West Adams Avenue
(313) 782-4751

# Rusted Crow

**Full bar:** ✓ **Draft beer:** ✓ **Full kitchen:** ✓ **Shuttle service:** ✗ **rustedcrowdetroit.com**

Cool is the word for the style of this place. The interior decor theme is that of steampunk. Everywhere you look, there are little details that will catch your eye. Along with the repurposed industrial items, they hired a local artist, Josh Keel, to paint some beautiful pictures on a few of the interior walls, and the result is amazing.

HOURS:
Tue - Thu: 11:30 - midnight
Fri - Sat: 11:30am - 1am
Sun: 10am - 10pm
Mon: *closed*

HAPPY HOUR:
Tue - Fri: 3pm - 6pm

**The Rusted Crow** features mixed drinks made with their own distillery's spirits: Detroit Steam Vodka, Davey Jones Rum, Ginstache Gin, and Murder Mitten Moonshine. In addition, they have 20 or so beers on tap, and a bunch more in bottles.

From a food standpoint, their menu is filled with creatively crafted items. Burgers and sandwiches are the main fare, however there are other options as well.

Location is often key to success, and they definitely have that covered, being within sight of Comerica Park and Ford Field, and just around the corner from the Fox and Fillmore theaters. Little Caesars Arena is just a stone's throw across I-75.

Parking on the street is limited, however there are many surface lots and nearby parking garages.

*There is live music every night except Sunday & Tuesday.*

- NOTES -

Been there! ☐ Foxtown

# The Skip

The Belt - 1234 Library Street
- no phone -

Full bar: ☑ Draft beer: ☑ Full kitchen: ☒ Shuttle service: ☒ theskipdetroit.com

Author Favorite

**The Skip** is located in Detroit's coolest alley, The Belt, which is found between Library Street and Broadway, running from Grand River to Gratiot.

HOURS:
Tue - Thu: 4pm - 10pm
Fri - Sat: 3pm - 2am
Sun: 4pm - midnight

HAPPY HOUR:
Tue - Fri: 4pm - 6:30pm

Prior to the formation of **The Skip**, the artist Shepard Fairey had painted a mural on the space that now makes up the back wall of the bar. It sets the tone for the overall decor. The remaining walls, ceiling, and bartop are all done in black, allowing comfort and relaxation to take the lead. To finish it all off, the front wall is a windowed garage door which can be opened.

Drinks from the bar range from beers and delectable frozen drinks to masterfully mixed craft cocktails. Visit during happy hour Tuesday through Friday, and enjoy discounted prices on select drinks.

There is no kitchen at **The Skip**, however don't be surprised to find a food cart from Standby, their neighbor and sister bar. When it's there, so is the opportunity to enjoy culinary excellence.

This location is central to downtown Detroit, allowing Greektown, Campus Martius, Comerica Park, Ford Field, Little Caesars Arena, the Fox & Fillmore theaters, and the Detroit Opera House to be within walking distance. There is a People Mover stop just around the corner, and a QLine station just a block over on Woodward Ave.

There is limited metered parking on the streets, free on Sundays and after 10pm. **The Skip** is actually under a parking garage, with another across Gratiot.

*There is seating in the alley when the walls are open, allowing for more capacity, and more fresh air. It's not your typical alley, it is clean and cool.*

- NOTES -

1521 Broadway Street
(313) 963-0702

# Small Plates Detroit

Full bar: ☑ Draft beer: ☑ Full kitchen: ☑ Shuttle service: ✗ smallplates.com

**Small Plates Detroit** has its space inside a beautiful old building across from the Detroit Opera House. The façade brings forward historic architecture, while the inside has been finished with modern touches. The highlight of the decor is the murals that have been hand-painted by a local Detroit graffiti artist.

HOURS:
Mon - Thu: 11:30am - 10pm
Fri: 11:30am - midnight
Sat: noon - midnight

This is more restaurant than bar, however is still a nice place to stop in for a drink when in the area. **Small Plates** directs some focus to their bar with a large list of craft cocktails, along with a selection of beers, wines, and liquors, many of them Michigan sourced. The sourcing continues right down to their decision to carry Faygo, a Detroit favorite brand of pop.

The food at **Small Plates** is what brings the crowds. The menu is filled with tantalizing dishes created from fresh ingredients, unique enough to be interesting without getting overly trendy. The flavor profiles in the descriptions will have you coming back to try new things. If you are coming in on a weekend or when there is a big event in the city, make a reservation. They fill up quickly.

Centrally located in Detroit, all of the sports arenas, the Fox and Fillmore theaters, and the Detroit Opera House are an easy walk from here. A little more of a walk, or a quick trip on the Detroit People Mover, and you can get to Greektown.

While there are minimal metered spots on the street, and only a few surface lots, parking in the area is abundant thanks to a few large parking structures supporting the sports and cultural venues.

***Small Plates** offers a brunch on some Sundays. Check their website or social media.*

- NOTES -

Been there! ☐

Foxtown

# Standby

225 Gratiot Avenue
(313) 736-5533

Full bar: ☑ Draft beer: ☑ Full kitchen: ☑ Shuttle service: ☒ standbydetroit.com

HOURS:
Mon - Sun: 5pm - 2am

**Standby** is a hidden getaway in Detroit. The entrance is in an alley. Not just any alley, The Belt, an art-filled social alley between Library and Broadway Street, running from Grand River to Gratiot. The entrance is as unique as the menu items you'll find inside. A pair of old wooden folding doors open out into the alley, providing access to the bar. Inside, all of the windows are curtained with thick drapes, providing a somewhat dimly lit oasis, an escape from the outside world. Furnished with comfortable tables and chairs, the small seating area generally fills up quickly, as does the bar space.

While the old standby cocktails and drinks are available, the drink menu leans heavily toward creative blends of top shelf liquors and fresh, house-made juices, syrups, and infusions. There is also a moderate selection of beer and wine, and soft beverages if that is what you are looking for.

Equally as creative as the cocktail menu, the kitchen serves a unique array of skillfully created plates. Prepare to have your palate tickled with each adventure in food at **Standby.**

**Standby** is centrally located in Detroit; walking distance to Greektown, the Opera House, the sports arenas, and the Fox and Fillmore theaters. Parking is plentiful in the area, and the Detroit People Mover and QLine have nearby stations.

*Ask about their "Break Even Bottle", your opportunity to try something from the top shelf without breaking the bank.*

- NOTES -

2101 Woodward Avenue
(313) 961-5441

# State Bar and Grill

**Full bar:** ✓ **Draft beer:** ✓ **Full kitchen:** ✓ **Shuttle service:** ✗ **thefillmoredetroit.com/statebarandgrill**

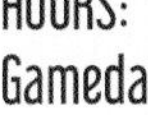

HOURS:
Gamedays: 11am - ?

Show days: 4pm - ?

*Closing times vary.*

**State Bar and Grill** is attached to the historic Fillmore Theater, although it does not share the opulent design of the theater. It is a mid-sized, mostly modern themed bar with a handful of booths, and a long bar which wraps around the interior.

They offer a full bar, including a dozen or so beers on tap, a variety of bottled beers, and a limited selection of wines. While they do not have a traditional happy hour, they do run specials from time to time. About the only thing that comes into question here is closing time. It all depends on the ending time of games and shows, and the volume of customers.

The food menu is consists of sandwiches, wraps, burgers, and nachos.

Parking is plentiful around the area. thanks to the proximity to Comerica Park, Ford Field, the Fox and Fillmore Theaters, and Little Caesars Arena.

*This is a good place for a quick bite and some drinks before a ballgame. It gets crowded, but that is part of the ambiance.*

- NOTES -

# The Town Pump Tavern

100 W,. Montcalm Street
(313) 961-1929

**Full bar:** ✓ **Draft beer:** ✓ **Full kitchen:** ✓ **Shuttle service:** ✗ **thetownpumptavern.com**

BAR HOURS:
Mon - Sun: 11am - 2am

HAPPY HOUR:
Daily: 4pm - 7pm

KITCHEN HOURS:
Mon - Sun: 11am - 11pm

**The Town Pump** is one of those old buildings in Detroit that has been well maintained and well adapted. When you enter the premises, you are greeted with the warm feel of dark wood trim, tin ceilings, and a smooth, inviting ambiance.

Scoot up to the bar or grab a table, and take advantage of 18 beers on tap as well as a full bar. They offer 25% off starters and sharables, and $1 off well drinks, pints, and glasses of wine during their daily happy hour.

**The Town Pump** is best known for burgers and pizza. When it comes to pizza, they offer a whole slew of toppings to personalize your pie according to your taste. In addition, **The Town Pump Tavern** has a full menu of items to chose from. The kitchen is open daily from 11am until 11pm.

On Tiger's opening day and St. Patrick's Day, **The Town Pump** sets up a large outdoor patio, usually complete with a DJ for musical entertainment. If you are looking for a party on one of those occasions, this is a great place to be.

On an ongoing basis, they have live music after Lions and Tigers games, and DJs on the weekend.

Located a block behind the Fox Theater, they are easily within walking distance of Comerica Park, Ford Field, Little Caesars Arena, and the Fox and Fillmore Theaters. Parking in this area is plentiful, with the Fox garage, metered street parking, and a bunch of surface lots.

*This part of town gets really busy during games, so get here early.*

- NOTES -

1314 Broadway
(313) 828-4500

# Truth Music Cafe

Full bar: ✓ Draft beer: ✓ Full kitchen: ✓ Shuttle service: ✗ truthmusiccafe1.com

HOURS:
Thu: 5pm - 10pm
Fri: 5pm - 2am
Sat: 9pm - 2am
Sun - Wed: closed

HAPPY HOUR:
Thu: 5pm - 10pm

**Truth Music Cafe** is located on the edge of Foxtown on Broadway Street, one of the rapidly developing streets in Detroit. Inside, the space has been set up in a way that allows either for a lot of tables and chairs, or a large dance floor with booths around the perimeter. A stage at the front provides a space for DJs and Friday night Karaoke.

The long stone-topped bar stretches back down the left wall, past a sitting area with comfortable couches and a huge projection screen TV. Besides the standard liquors at the bar, **Truth Music Cafe** has a cocktail menu and a list of their own special martinis. There is a decent selection of beers and wines, and for those looking to get a little fancy, **Truth** offers a bottle service.

**Truth** serves food, and the menu contains some of the common bar foods such as wings, french fries and onion rings, while also offering burgers and a few different salads.

It's just a stroll to Comerica Park, Ford Field, the Detroit Opera House and the Music Hall, as well as the Fox and Fillmore theaters. The Detroit People Mover has a station just up the street, and the QLine can be caught over on nearby Woodward Avenue.

There are several large parking structures in the immediate area, and also metered parking along many of the streets, so finding a spot for your car is generally not difficult.

*There is a 2nd floor at* ***Truth****, also with a full bar and a DJ.*

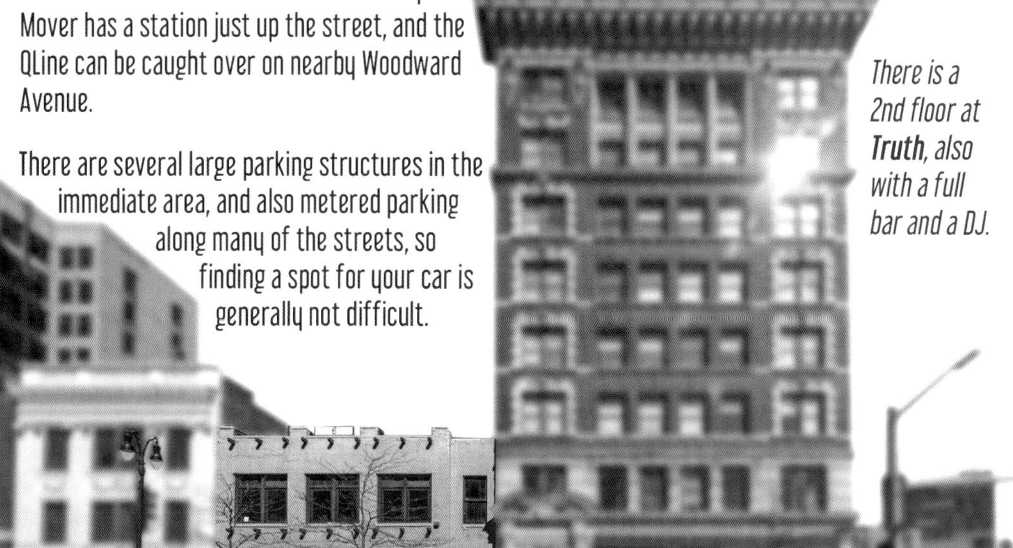


- NOTES -

Been there! ☐ Foxtown

# Vertical Detroit

1538 Centre Street
(313) 732-9436

**Full bar:** ☑ **Draft beer:** ☑ **Full kitchen:** ☑ **Shuttle service:** ☒ **verticaldetroit.com**

HOURS:
Mon - Thu: 4pm - 10pm
Fri - Sat: 4pm - midnight
Sun: 4pm - 9pm

HAPPY HOUR:
Mon - Fri: 4pm - 6pm

Located in the lower level of the beautiful wedge shaped Ashley Hotel, **Vertical Detroit** is a beautiful place. Elegance is the theme, and wine rooms and wine racks dominate the decor. This long and narrow, half underground space has an intimate feel, with low ceilings, dark wood, and dimmed lights.

The focus of the bar is clear: wine. Not only does **Vertical Detroit** have an impressively large wine list, they were recognized by Wine Enthusiast as one of America's top 100 wine restaurants in 2016. In addition, they offer both draft and bottled beer, as well as a craft cocktail list which includes two on draft. The bar is located at the far end of the restaurant in a warm and cozy setting.

The restaurant portion of **Vertical** puts forth a small menu of carefully crafted selections, covering a range of flavors and proteins. As a general rule, reservations are a good idea if you intend to dine.

Proper attire is expected at **Vertical**, as is a certain level of decorum. Don't take that to be snobbery, it's just a nice place. There are plenty of other places where T-shirts and shorts are welcome.

***Vertical** is a great place for a special dinner, a date, or to simply enjoy a fine meal and a great glass of wine.*

- NOTES -

1 Park Avenue
(313) 237-1700

# WXYZ Bar

**Full bar:** ✓ **Draft beer:** ✓ **Full kitchen:** ✗ **Shuttle service:** ✗ **aloftdetroit.com/detroit-bar**

HOURS:
Sun - Thu: 11am - midnight
Fri - Sat: 11am - 2am

Located in the beautifully restored David Whitney Building, **WXYZ Bar** holds a choice spot in the first floor lobby. The bar occupies a relatively small space, however it is cozy and comforatble. The decor is modern and the ambiance is welcoming.

**WXYZ Bar** has a lot going on in the neighborhood. The Fillmore Theater, The Fox Theater, the Detroit Opera House, Comerica Park, Ford Field and Little Caesars Arena are all within view of the front door, easily within walking distance. The Detroit People Mover has a stop at the building as well, bringing much of the rest of downtown Detroit well within reach, including historic Greektown, Cobo Hall, and the Riverfront.

The bar offers seasonal signature drinks, a variety of draft and bottled beers, and wine. They do not have a full menu, however do offer a limited selection of bar-bites. For your entertainment, they often have live musical acts which can be enjoyed from the bar or one of the comfortable couches. In addition, there is a pool table which is free to play.

When the weather cooperates, **WXYZ** has a decent sized sitting area outside.



*The David Whitney building has one of the most beautiful interiors in Detroit.*

- NOTES -

# Greektown

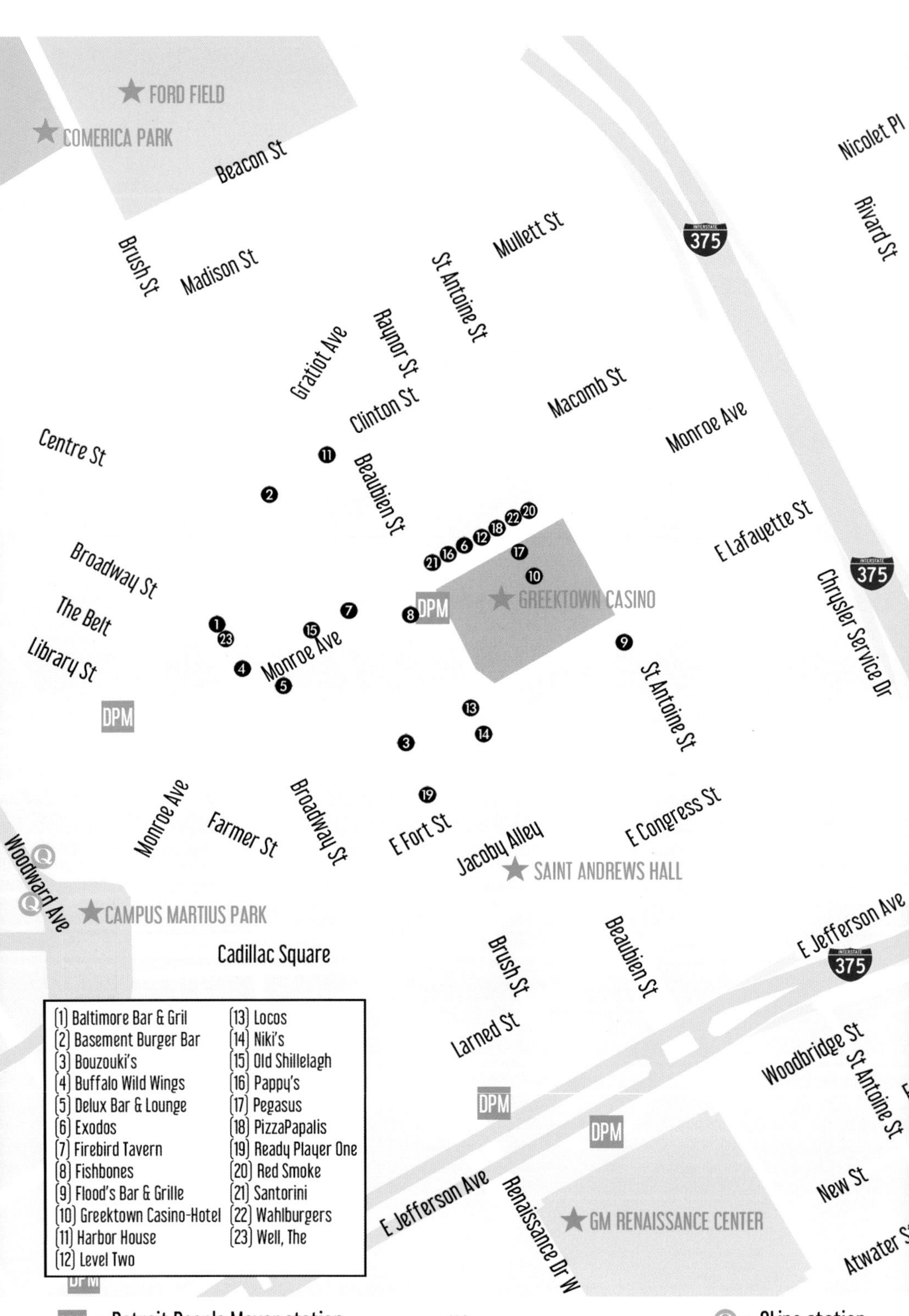


DPM = Detroit People Mover station

Q = QLine station

1234 Randolph Street
(313) 964-2728

# Baltimore Bar & Grill

**Full bar:** ✓ **Draft beer:** ✓ **Full kitchen:** ✗ **Shuttle service:** ✗

HOURS:
Mon - Sun: *vary*

Located on the outer edge of Greektown, **Baltimore Bar & Grill** occupies half of the first floor of an old brick building on Randolph Street. Inside, some of the old details remain, with the majority of the walls being exposed brick. The decorative pressed tin ceiling gives a nod to history.

About half of the space is occupied by the bar. The bar-top is some sort of semi-transparent plastic underlit with moving lights. This allows it to stand out in an otherwise somewhat dimly lit interior. The offerings from the bar are no-frills, with a minimal beer selection and a basic liquor service. It's the kind of bar you can pop into for a few drinks and get out for under twenty bucks.

There is not a full kitchen at the **Baltimore**, however there is food. Sticking with the overall theme of the place, the menu is short, posted on a board in the back, and consists of basic bar fare: burgers, sandwiches, and a couple of sides. These also can be had without breaking the bank.

There is a pool table back by the kitchen, a bar-top video game machine, and an arcade-style punching bag game, all of which can help to make a visit more enjoyable, especially when there with a group of friends.

*There may be more things going for this bar, but when asked, the owner said it was "just a hole in the wall". The bartender was friendly, and they do draw a crowd in the evenings.*

- NOTES -

Been there! ☐

Greektown

# Basement Burger Bar

1326 Brush Street
(313) 818-3708

Full bar: ☑ Draft beer: ☑ Full kitchen: ☑ Shuttle service: ☒ basementburgerbar.com

HOURS:
Sun - Thu: 11am - 10pm
Fri - Sat: 11am - 2am

HAPPY HOUR:
Daily: 3pm - 6pm
and: 10pm - 2am

**Basement Burger Bar** is centrally located between Greektown Casino, Comerica Park, and Ford Field. This is the largest of their three locations, the others being in Farmington and Canton, and they bring their ***build your own burger*** concept that, along with their quality, put them on the map.

If you are not the kind of person who likes to make decisions, there are four pre-designed burgers on the menu, as well as a handful of salads and a whole bunch of starters. The star attraction food-wise is the build your own burger menu. With this you choose everything from the meat, to the bread, to the toppings in between. They give you a dry-erase marker and a wipe off menu, so you can change your mind as much as you want prior to ordering.

It's not just about the burgers here. They also have a bar with daily drink specials, and offer over 20 beers on tap. On game days (any professional Michigan sport), 64oz pitchers are $24 for craft beer, $12 for domestic during the game. During happy hour there are appetizer specials. Make sure to check the menu or ask your server for details.

Seating for well over 100 people makes this a place where you can go with a mid - to large sized group.

- NOTES -

**1218 Randolph Street**
**(313) 961-9453**

# Buffalo Wild Wings

**Full bar:** ✓ **Draft beer:** ✓ **Full kitchen:** ✓ **Shuttle service:** ✗ **buffalowildwings.com**
(Greektown - Monroe Avenue)

HOURS:
Mon - Thu: 11am - 1am
Fri - Sat: 11am - 2am
Sun: noon - midnight

**Buffalo Wild Wings** is a chain with locations across the country. The main reason for their proliferation is their consistency. With over 20 flavors of sauces and dry rubs to choose from, you can match flavors to your mood, your beverage, the season, or just about anything. They have been doing wings for a long time, and they have the process down to a science. Don't want wings? They have other things to choose from on their menu.

The Detroit location is huge, making it a destination where you can go with a large group of people. The restaurant occupies two floors of the old (1874) Temple of Odd Fellows building, maintaining some of the original features, including high ceilings and brick walls. Inside, it has more TVs than can easily be counted. If there is a game being televised, they are sure to have it on. There is also an upper level patio to enjoy when the weather is nice.

**Buffalo Wild Wings** offers a full bar with an abundance of draft beer selections. In addition to popular large brewery national brands, there are also many craft beers to choose from.

Located in the Greektown neighborhood of Detroit, they are close to Greektown Casino, and not too far of a walk from The Fillmore, The Fox, The Detroit Opera House, Comerica Park, Ford Field, and with just a little more effort, Little Caesars Arena. Of course, if you don't want to walk, the Detroit People Mover has a stop at Greektown Casino. On game days, there is a free shuttle you can catch on Monroe Avenue. Don't forget to tip the driver!

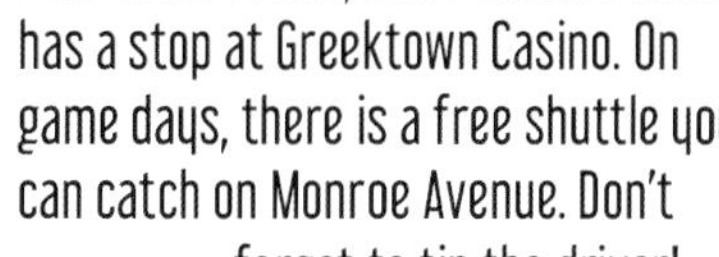

*Parking is plentiful in and around Greektown, with several surface lots and more than a handful of parking structures.*

- NOTES -

Been there! ☐

Greektown

# Delux Lounge

350 Monroe Avenue
(313) 962-4200

Full bar: ☑ Draft beer: ☑ Full kitchen: ☒ Shuttle service: ☒ (Greektown - Monroe Avenue) deluxlounge.com

HOURS:
Tue - Fri: 4pm - 2am
Sat: 6pm - 2am
Sun: 8pm - 2am
Mon: closed

HAPPY HOUR:
Tue - Fri: 4pm - 8pm

**Delux Lounge** has its home on Monroe Avenue in Greektown. Once you pass through the door and down a dimly lit hallway, you enter into an intimate space dominated on one side by a long, well-stocked bar. The rest of the room has long community tables, a small VIP area in the far corner, and a DJ stand.

The bar has plenty of stools for those who prefer to sit. Besides shots and mixed drinks, there are a handful of beers on draft and more in the coolers under the bar. Happy hour is pretty straightforward, offering $1 off all drinks.

There is no kitchen at **Delux**, plan accordingly. There are plenty of places in the area where you can eat.

Entertainment is the name of the game here. On Tuesdays, there are free darts, dice, and shuffleboard, and for $5 you get a PBR and a Jameson. On Wednesday nights, they have Karaoke, no cover, $3 drafts, and $5 all call whiskeys. Thursday nights are free shuffle board, $3 domestic and draft beers, and $4 well drinks. There is a DJ on Friday nights, and while there is a $5 cover, your first drink is free, and there is a $5 martini special. Saturday also has a DJ, and Sunday is service industry night, with 25% off with a work ID.

Their location puts them close the the Greektown Casino and a Detroit People Mover station. St. Andrew's Hall and Campus Martius are within walking distance, as are the sports stadiums, and the Fox and Filmore theaters with a little more effort. Of course, during most home games and major events in the city, there is a free shuttle running from Monroe Street.

Parking is plentiful in this area, with several parking structures, surface lots, and metered spots along some of the streets. As with most places in the city, the parking rates except at meters, go up in proportion to the size, importance, or popularity of the event.

- NOTES -

529 Monroe Avenue
(313) 962-1300

# Exodos Lounge

**Full bar:** ✓ **Draft beer:** ✓ **Full kitchen:** ✓ **Shuttle service:** ✗ (Greektown - Monroe Avenue) **exodosrooftop.com**

HOURS:
Mon: closed
Tue - Sun: 5pm - 2am

HAPPY HOUR:
Tue - Sun: 6pm - 9pm

From down on Monroe Avenue, you would not realize how large a space is occupied by **Exodus Lounge**. They have the second floor above Krema and the party store. The beautiful old brick of the exterior carries over to the interior, defining the look of the indoor part of the lounge. Within the brick walls is a spacious room with ample seating and a large granite-topped bar. Proceed to the back, and transition into the rooftop lounge, complete with its own bar, multiple areas, and different levels separated by a few stairs. It is a great place to party under the stars on a beautiful night.

From the bar comes a standard flow of drinks, including optional bottle service or VIP service. During the daily happy hour, enjoy $2 Bud Light drafts, $4 well cocktails, and $5 Jameson or Jack Fire shots. If you would like to eat, food can be ordered up from the Golden Fleece restaurant, which offers Greek style food.

Entertainment abounds at **Exodos**. Thursday nights are throw-back vinyl nights except in the summer, when they become Techno nights. Friday nights have DJs spinning rap and hip-hop. On Saturday nights, DJs spin all genres. Free entry Thursdays and before 10:30 on Friday and Saturday. Expect a cover after that.

- NOTES -

# Firebird Tavern

419 Monroe Avenue
(313) 782-4189
firebirdtavern.com

Full bar: ☑ Draft beer: ☑ Full kitchen: ☑ Shuttle service: ☑ (Greektown - Monroe Avenue)

HOURS:
Mon - Thu: 11am - midnight
Fri: 11am - midnight
Sat: 2pm - 2am
Sun: *CLOSED*

HAPPY HOUR:
Mon - Fri: 4:30pm - 6:30pm

**Firebird Tavern** is another of Detroit's bars that boasts a warm, old feel, taking residence in a building constructed in the 1880s. The restoration of the building was done in a way that allows both the first and second floor to showcase beautiful wood trim and brick surfaces. Located in historic Greektown, there is plenty of parking, between limited street parking, paid lots, and several nearby parking garages. Firebird Tavern has a bar on each floor, and guests can either mingle or find a table to sit and converse comfortably. There are usually around a dozen beers on tap, with a larger variety available in bottles and cans. Firebird also serves wine, hard cider, and a selection of creative cocktails.

**Firebird Tavern** offers happy hour on weekdays from 4:30pm - 6:30pm. It's a good one, too, featuring 1/2 off all American craft brews and wine by the glass and bottle.

The kitchen is ready to whip up a selection of sandwiches, some entrees, a few soups and salads, and as would be expected, a host of appetizers.

If you are going to a game or major event in downtown Detroit, there is generally a shuttle leaving from Monroe Ave. While the shuttle is free, tipping is encouraged.

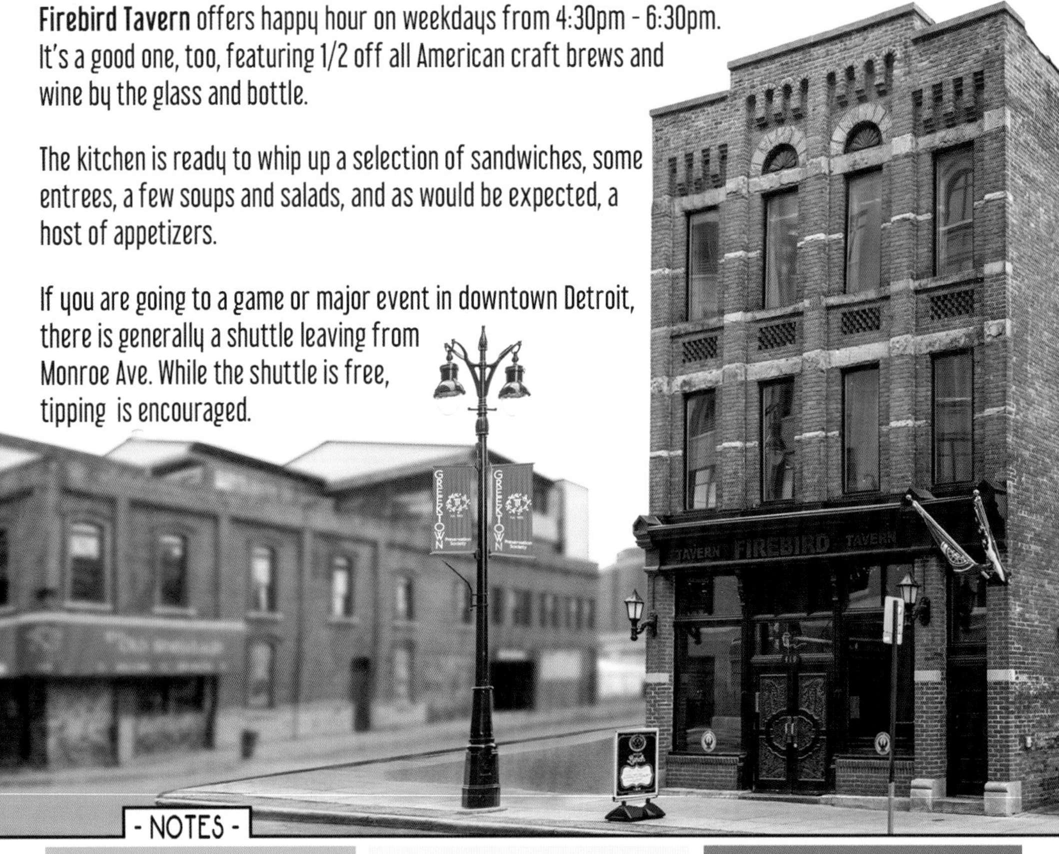


- NOTES -

400 Monroe Avenue
(313) 965-4600

# Fishbone's

**Full bar:** ✓ **Draft beer:** ✓ **Full kitchen:** ✓ **Shuttle service:** ✗ (Greektown - Monroe Avenue) **fishbonesusa.com**

Spacious and elegant, the interior of **Fishbone's** spills out into a multi-story courtyard area with an inter-laced wood beam construction. It's an eye-catching scene, one that preserves the historic nature of the structure.

HOURS:
Sun - Thu: 6:30am - midnight
Fri - Sat: 6:30am - 1am

HAPPY HOUR:
Mon - Fri: 3pm - 6pm

There are two full bars in **Fishbone's**, capable of providing just about any kind of drink patrons might have in mind, with more than 20 beers on tap, more choices in bottles, and an impressive wine list.

Besides the traditional bars, they also have what has to be the largest sushi bar in Detroit. For the sushi lovers out there, this provides the opportunity to watch your sushi being made to order. Aside from the physical size of the sushi bar, the sushi menu is extensive and varied.

**Fishbone's** is primarily a seafood restaurant, and their menus reflect this with a large selection of items. During happy hour, enjoy discounts on select sushi, appetizers, and drinks.

Located in the heart of Detroit's Greektown district, **Fishbone's** is close to all of the action in the city. For games and events in Detroit, you can go on foot, take the Detroit People Mover, utilize the Greektown shuttles, or walk over to Woodward and catch the QLine. Of course, another option is to stay where you are and visit Greektown Casino, which is just across Beaubien Street, a nearby entertainment option.

**Fishbone's** is large enough to handle just about any size group. Reservations are recommended, especially on weekends or when there is a game or large event in the city. Parking in the area is plentiful, with several parking garages, numerous surface lots, and limited metered street parking.

*In addition to sushi, two of their more popular menu items are the Pasta Orleans and the Jambalaya.*

- NOTES -

**Been there!** ☐ **Greektown**

# Flood's Bar & Grille

**731 St. Antoine**
**(313) 963-1090**

**Full bar:** ✓ **Draft beer:** ✗ **Full kitchen:** ✓ **Shuttle service:** ✗ **floodsdetroit.com**

HOURS:
Mon: 4pm - midnight
Tue - Fri: 4pm - 2am
Sat - Sun: 7pm - 2am

HAPPY HOUR:
Mon - Fri: 4pm - 8pm

**Flood's** is located inside a beautiful historic building next to Greektown Casino and is known for good food and live music. The large, marble-topped bar is situated right inside the door, a gathering place for people as they enter. The decor hedges toward elegant, and a sign at the entrance lets everyone know that proper attire is required.

The well stocked bar can provide everything from the basics up through top shelf liquors. Their cocktail list on the back of the menu shows some of the house specialties, and a separate happy hour menu lists the drink and food specials offered from 4pm-8pm Monday through Friday.

The food selection at **Flood's** is broad, and pride is taken in preparation and presentation. While they do offer burgers and other basic dishes, the focus leans toward seafood, with shrimp, lobster, and several different types of fish plates.

Live entertainment is the name of the game here, with a variety of performers Wed-Sat. Check their webpage for specifics.

**555 East Lafayette Street**
**(313) 223-2999**

# Greektown Casino-Hotel

**Full bar:** ✓ **Draft beer:** ✓ **Full kitchen:** ✓ **Shuttle service:** ✗ **greektowncasino.com**
(Greektown - Monroe Avenue)

HOURS:
24 hours a day
7 days a week
365 days a year.

**Greektown** is first and foremost a casino, and you must be at least 21 to enter. They offer two floors of games - slots, tables, a poker room, high limit area, and Synergy, a high energy, ultra-modern gaming area.

Author Favorite

Beyond the games, there are several bars on the property which should allow everyone to find what they want. On the first floor, there is the **Rock Bar**, which, in addition to a wide variety of alcohol, has numerous TVs for watching the current games. On the 2nd floor, there are **Fringe**, **Trapper's**, a bar specializing in craft beer, and a bar in **Prism**, which is the fancy restaurant on property. Finally, back at **Greektown Hotel**, there is a full bar in their restaurant, **Bistro 555**.

Smoking is allowed in most areas within the casino, and there are waitstaff walking the floors, so if you are there to play, you won't even have to get up to get a drink.

Food can be found in several places on site. Just outside the casino on the second floor is Marketplace District. They have five sections: Italian, Chinese, American, a Deli, and a coffee house. The restaurant in the hotel is Bistro 555, and offers a wide variety of dishes. Inside the casino, fine dining is offered at the restaurant, Prism.

**Greektown** has several parking garages as well as valet parking. On game days, shuttle buses run from Monroe Avenue to the events. Comerica Park, Ford Field, Campus Martius, the Fox, and Fillmore are within walking distance. and there is a Detroit People Mover stop at the casino.

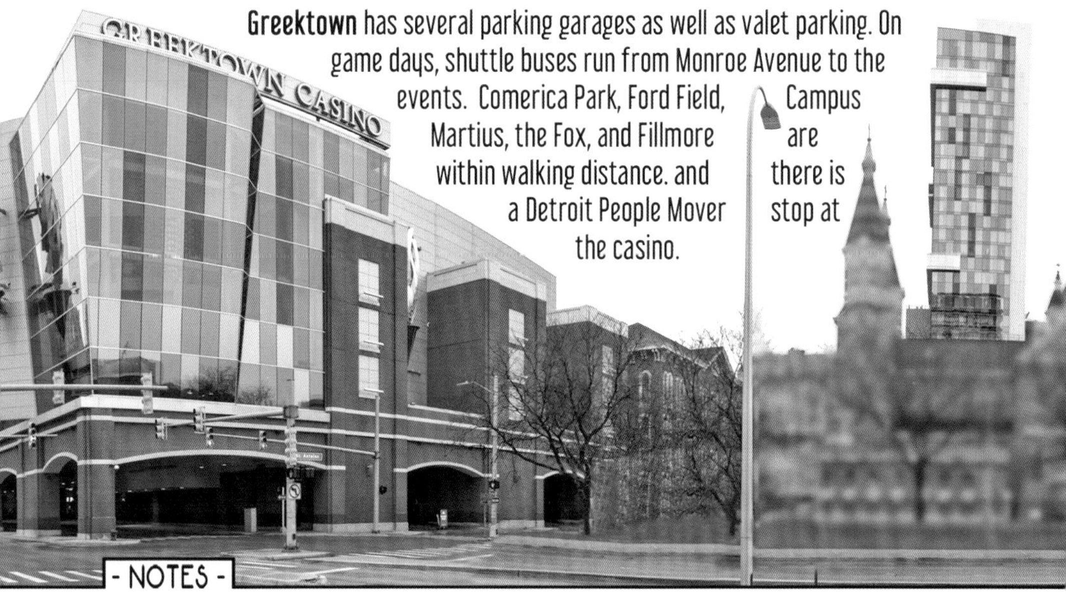


- NOTES -

# Harbor House

440 Clinton Street
(313) 967-9900

**Full bar:** ☑ **Draft beer:** ☑ **Full kitchen:** ☑ **Shuttle service:** ☒ **harborhousemi.com**

**KITCHEN HOURS:**
Mon - Tue: 11am-11pm
Wed: 11am - 1am
Thu: 11am - midnight
Fri: 11am - 1am
Sat: 3pm - 1am
Sun: 1pm - 11pm

**BAR HOURS:**
Mon - Sat: Bar open 'til 2am

**BRUNCH:**
9:30am Lion's Home Games

**Harbor House** is a combination seafood restaurant and bar. Upon entering, you walk into a long room with a 50 foot bar running the length of the left side, and dining tables down the right. If looking for more intimacy, there is another room dedicated to dining.

Throughout the interior the decor is dominated by beautiful, presumably old, stained glass lights and architectural elements. These add some welcome color and beauty.

The long, stocked bar offers enough choices to provide almost any drink ordered. While **Harbor House** does not have a happy hour for drinks, they do have several all-you-can-eat food specials that run all the time. Harbor House is known for this and their seafood, and they also have a wide selection of sandwiches and other menu choices to satisfy your food needs.

**Harbor House** is located close to Greektown Casino, Ford Field, and Comerica Park. Monday, Wednesday, and Saturday nights **Harbor House** has live band performances, some with cover, some without.

*Pay attention to the auto-gratuity rules listed on the menu. There are a few, and it's good to know ahead of time.*

- NOTES -

535 Monroe Avenue
(313) 420-1990

# Level Two Bar & Rooftop

**Full bar:** ☑ **Draft beer:** ✗ **Full kitchen:** ☑ **Shuttle service:** ✗ (Greektown - Monroe Avenue) **leveltwodetroit.com**

HOURS:
Mon - Sat; 4pm - 2am
Sun: 4pm - midnight

HAPPY HOUR:
Mon - Fri: 4pm - 7pm

**Level Two Bar** is located right in the heart of the historic Greektown district on Monroe Avenue across from Greektown Casino. Their rooftop patio is a popular place in the warmer months, offering an open air, semi-private place to party the night away. There is also an inside space, a nice, clean, and comfortable environment with a great view of the street. During the colder months, or when there is inclement weather, the windows in the front portion stay closed, allowing their patrons to still enjoy all that Greektown has to offer. When it is nice out, the windows are open, providing fresh air and connecting to the energy of the city.

There is seating at the bar inside, as well as at tables next to the windows. Happy hour offers $2 domestic beers and $4 glasses of wine. On Thursdays, ladies get half off wine, mules, cosmos, and champagne. **Level Two** also has food available, with appetizers, some small plate offerings, and salads.

DJs pump out the music on Thursday through Saturday nights. There is a $5-$10 cover for guys, and never a cover for the ladies.

There are several surface lots and parking garages in Greektown, and a district shuttle that will take you to games and large events in the city.

*There is a full bar on the outdoor patio at the back of **Level Two.***

- NOTES -

Been there! ☐ Greektown

# Loco's Tex-Mex Grille

**454 East Lafayette Street**
**(313) 965-3737**

**Full bar:** ✓ **Draft beer:** ✓ **Full kitchen:** ✓ **Shuttle service:** ✗ (Greektown - Monroe Avenue) **locosdetroit.com**

HOURS:
Sun - Thu: 11am - 2am
Fri - Sat: 11am - 4am

HAPPY HOUR:
Mon - Fri: 3pm - 6pm

If the name didn't give it away, you'll know you are in a Mexican restaurant when you walk inside. The decor is Mexican from corner to corner.

There is a nice large wrap-around bar where patrons can sit and enjoy a $5 24oz draft or a $10 24oz margarita, two of the bar specials that run all day. The bar at **Loco's** is known for its margaritas, and the recommendation is for on-the-rocks vs. frozen. Happy hour, $1 off all drinks, runs from 3pm-6pm, M-F. You can also get $3 margaritas from 11am-3pm, M-F.

From a food standpoint, the menu is extensive. Mexican and Tex-Mex are the flavors, and the crowd favorites are the Mexican pizzas and deep fried tacos. It is worth noting that the tamales are made in-house.

This downtown location is kitty-corner from Greektown Casino, and just around the corner from St. Andrew's Hall. Campus Martius is a short walk, and there is always the Detroit People Mover, which has a stop at Greektown, to get you around the city.

There are multiple surface parking lots, parking structures, and metered street spots in the area.

On game days (Lions, Tigers, Red Wings, and Pistons) and for big events, there is a shuttle which runs from Greektown. It's free, and can be caught on Monroe Avenue, just a short block away.

*The salsa here is excellent, and it has been my experience that if a Mexican restaurant has good salsa, they will likely have good food, too.*

- NOTES -

735 Beaubien Street
(313) 961-4303

# Niki's Pizza

Full bar: ☑ Draft beer: ☑ Full kitchen: ☑ Shuttle service: ☑ nikisdetroit.com

HOURS:
Sun - Thu: 10am - 2am
Fri - Sat: 10am - 4am

HAPPY HOUR:
Mon - Fri: 2pm - 7pm

Unassuming from the street, when you enter, the size and architecture of the interior space is impressive. The ceilings are high, and most of the seating in the restaurant portion is set up with semi-private booths. The overall feel is welcoming and comfortable.

The bar is at the front, and has everything from a dozen draft beer selections to top shelf liquors. While the general atmosphere is family oriented, the place really picks up when there is a game in town, especially the Lions. Several flat screen TVs give you the option of watching the game right at the bar. During home games for the Lions, Tigers, and Red Wings, the happy hour extends until the game is over. Happy Hour specials are: $5 margaritas and Long Islands, $4.50 sangria and craft pints, and $3 Bud Light and Miller Lite pints.

**Niki's** is best known for its pizza. GQ Magazine agrees with this, voting them as one of the top 25 pizza places in America. Besides their wonderful pizza, the menu is fulled with predominately Greek dishes. Come in on Wednesdays for 1/2 off large pizzas.

***Niki's Lounge****, upstairs, is open from 8pm - 2am on Friday and Saturday nights. They have DJ music and dancing.*

- NOTES -

Been there! ☐

Greektown

# The Old Shillelagh

349 Monroe Avenue
(313) 964-0007

**Full bar:** ☑ **Draft beer:** ☑ **Full kitchen:** ☑ **Shuttle service:** ☑ **oldshillelagh.com**

HOURS:
Mon: 3pm - 2am
Tue - Sun: 11am - 2am

HAPPY HOUR:
Thu: 5pm - 8pm

The **Old Shillelagh** was born to Detroit in 1975, and has been owned by three generations of the same family becoming a Detroit Icon. Two full interior floors plus a third floor rooftop deck gives them one of the larger capacities of all the bars in Detroit. During large events such as opening day for the Tigers and St. Patrick's Day, they also have a large parking lot party tent, increasing their capacity even more. Everything about the decor gives the feeling of being in an Irish pub. On weekends there are DJs and a live Irish band, and during Saturday Tiger home games, the tent will be up in the parking lot, also with a DJ.

When running at capacity, there can be five full bars serving at the same time, keeping drinks in the hands of the patrons, no matter which floor they have chosen. Beers and common pours are generally what get served here, however there is a cocktail list with a few unique concoctions. During happy hour, you can get a pitcher of craft beer and an appetizer for $14.95. Two hours before a Lions or Red Wings game, the offer is a burger and a pint for $15.95.

The kitchen serves up burgers, sandwiches, and appetizers, keeping it tasty and simple. Ask your server about the monthly food specials.

Located in Greektown, parking is plentiful, and the sports arenas and theaters are close. **The Old Shillelagh** offers a free shuttle to all home games and major events in Detroit.

- NOTES -

# Pappy's Bar & Grill

517 Monroe Avenue
(313) 983-4000

**Full bar:** ✓ **Draft beer:** ✓ **Full kitchen:** ✓ **Shuttle service:** ✗
(Greektown - Monroe Avenue)

HOURS:
Mon - Thu: 11am - midnight
Fri - Sun: 11am - 2am

**Pappy's Bar & Grill** is located in the heart of Detroit's lively Greektown district. It is a comfortable place to have a meal, enjoy some drinks and catch a game on one of their TVs. Their location puts them within walking distance of Greektown Casino, which is across the street, and Campus Martius a couple blocks over. Comerica Park, Ford Field, the Fox Theater and the Fillmore are a little bit further, but doable. On game days, there is a Greektown shuttle. It's free just keep in mind the driver works for tips.

**Pappy's** has many drink specials and a huge selection of beer. This is a good place to drop in for some drinks, for a meal, or both. Sandwiches, burgers, wraps and pizza are the main-stays of the menu.

The front of **Pappy's** faces Monroe Avenue, so the ever-present activity is always within view. In summer, the front windows can be rolled up, combining the energy from inside with that on the street, while at the same time bringing in fresh air. For those who are so inclined during warmer weather, a seating area outside is available.

Parking is plentiful, with several nearby pay to park street level lots as well as a couple of parking garages. The Detroit People Mover has a stop at Greektown Casino, bringing more of the city into range without having to worry about moving your car.

***DAILY DRINK SPECIALS:***

*Sunday: $5 Bloody Marys*
*Monday: domestic bottles (beer) $3*
*Tuesday: Bud Light, Coors Light, Miller Lite $2.50 pints*
*Wednesday: $4 well drinks*
*Thursday: $2 PBR and Stroh's (cans)*
*Friday: $5 Cherry Bombs*
*Saturday: $5 Fireball*

- NOTES -

Been there! ☐

Greektown

# Pegasus Taverna

558 Monroe Avenue
(313) 964-6800

**Full bar:** ✓ **Draft beer:** ✓ **Full kitchen:** ✓ **Shuttle service:** ✗ (Greektown - Monroe Avenue) **pegasustavernas.com**

HOURS:
Sun - Thu: 11am - 1am
Fri - Sat: 11am - 2am
Fri - Sat: kitchen open 'til 3am

Cross the threshold and welcome to Greece. The dining area in **Pegasus Taverna** is like a Greek courtyard. Pergolas entwined with grape vines extend above the tables, creating a comfortable, slightly exotic atmosphere.

Equally impressive is the large O-shaped bar, separated from the dining area by a wooden rail and a step. They offer an extensive wine list, a dozen or so beers on draft with many more in bottles, and a full bar. **Pegasus** also has some signature drinks for those wanting something different.

**Pegasus** is a popular restaurant, and has been a fixture in Greektown for over two decades. They offer a large lunch menu with daily specials and a huge dinner menu. With so much to choose from, come with a group so you can share several different dishes ar your table. There is a huge variety of offerings to choose from, and one of the more popular is the Arnisia Paidakia (lamb chops). Of course, you should experience Saganaki (flaming cheese) whenever you get the chance. OPA!

Located in the heart of Greektown, **Pegasus** shares walls with the casino, and is a reasonably easy walk to Ford Field, Comerica Park, the Fox & Fillmore theaters, St. Andrew's Hall, and Campus Martius. If you would prefer not to walk, generally there is a Greektown shuttle running to the games and large events. The free shuttle can be caught on Monroe Avenue; the driver works for tips. There is also a Detroit People Mover stop in Greektown Casino, and that will take you on a 3 mile loop around the city, with 13 separate stops.

Parking is plentiful, with several garages and surface lots in the area.

*Definitely order the saganaki if you haven't had it before. It's a crowd pleaser.*

- NOTES -

553 Monroe Avenue
(313) 961-8020

# PizzaPapalis Taverna

**Full bar:** ✓ **Draft beer:** ✓ **Full kitchen:** ✓ **Shuttle service:** ✗ (Greektown - Monroe Avenue) **pizzapapalis.com**

HOURS:
Sun - Thu: 11am - midnight
Fri - Sat: 11am - 1am

**PizzaPapalis** serves Chicago style pizzas, from a Detroit style restaurant. As with many places in downtown Detroit, **PizzaPapalis** is located in a historic brick building. They have done a good job in carrying forward the beauty of the construction, prividing patrons with a warm and comfortable environment where they can enjoy some of the best pizza around.

Clearly this is a pizza place. That is what put them on the map, and it is what most people come here for. However, their menu does extend beyond pizza to a few pasta dishes, flatbreads, and giant, fresh-made strombolis.

The bar at **PizzaPapalis** is on the smaller side, however the dining area seating is large, with two floors of space. They usually have a featured beer for $2.75, and have a drink list of house specialty concoctions.

Located in the heart of Greektown, parking is plentiful, with a handful of large parking garages and numerous surface lots in the immediate area.

**PizzaPapalis** is across the street from Greektown Casino, and relatively easy walking distance from Ford Field, Campus Martius, Comerica Park, The Fox and Fillmore theaters, and St. Andrew's Hall. There is a shuttle in Greektown for home games and most major events, and a Detroit People Mover stop at the casino.

***AUTHOR'S FAVORITE:** The Michigan Bourbon Chicken Wings are probably the best wings I've had. I also love the Bacon Cheeseburger pizza.*

- NOTES -

# Red Smoke

573 Monroe Avenue
(313) 962-2100
redsmoke.net

**Full bar:** ☑ **Draft beer:** ☑ **Full kitchen:** ☑ **Shuttle service:** ☒
(Greektown - Monroe Avenue)

HOURS:
Sun - Thu: 11am - 11pm
Fri - Sat: 11am - midnight

Sure, **Red Smoke** is more restaurant than bar, however they do have a bar, and that qualifies. As soon as you walk in, you'll know this is a barbecue joint. The rich smell of the smoke greets you like a warm handshake.

**Red Smoke** has a fair to average selection of beer, both on tap, and in bottles. For the most part, the craft beers are drafts, served by the pint, and the standard national fare come in the bottles. Not here for a beer? There is a list of signature cocktails; Red Smoke Mixers, that can be ordered in either normal or **colossal** sizes.

Located in the heart of Greektown, this is a good place to grab a meal or a drink, or both, whether you are in the city for the Casino, a game, concert, or other event. Parking is plentiful, with several nearby parking structures, as well as surface lots. The Detroit People Mover has a stop at Greektown Casino, and on game days, there is a shuttle running from Monroe Avenue to the venues in a constant loop. Don't forget, the shuttle drivers work for tips. Comerica Park, Ford Field, The Opera House, The Fillmore, St. Andrew's Hall, and the Fox are all within walking distance. Some a little closer than others.

***AUTHOR'S FAVORITE:*** *Ribs and brisket. Seriously good stuff. Seriously.*

- NOTES -

501 Monroe Avenue
(313) 962-9366

# Santorini Estiatorio

**Full bar:** ☑ **Draft beer:** ☑ **Full kitchen:** ☑ **Shuttle service:** ☒ **santorinidetroit.com**
(Greektown - Monroe Avenue)

HOURS:
Mon - Thu: 11am - midnight
Fri - Sat: 11am - 2am
Sun: 11am - 11pm

HAPPY HOUR:
Mon - Fri: 3pm - 7pm
Sat - Sun: noon - 4pm

**Santorini** is a large nautical themed Greek restaurant in Greektown on the corner of Monroe Avenue and Beaubien Street. The front wall in the dining room is made up of windows which are often open on nice days. Their use of linens, both tablecloths and napkins, are a nice touch in an increasingly casual world. The restaurant is bright and family friendly with a welcoming staff and good food.

The large oval shaped bar takes up about a quarter of the floor space, and is situated in a way that allows a view of the activity outside and a little people watching. During happy hour, the drink specials, which vary by day, are only available at the bar. Check their website, or ask your server for the specials of the day. There are also some food specials during happy hour, and these can be had either at the bar or at your table. For anyone with a taste for wine, **Santorini** has an extensive list.

**Santorini's** menu is filled with a wide variety of Greek dishes, appropriate, considering its location. Monday though Saturday, there is a separate lunch menu from 11am - 3pm, mainy consisting of Greek specialties and burgers. While there are a lot of delicious menu offerings, the Lamb Chops and Lemon Chicken are among the most popular items.

Being in Greektown, the arenas are within walking distance, and there is a free shuttle for games and major events. There is also a Detroit People Mover station at the casino. Parking is plentiful, with surface lots and more than a couple parking garages in the area.

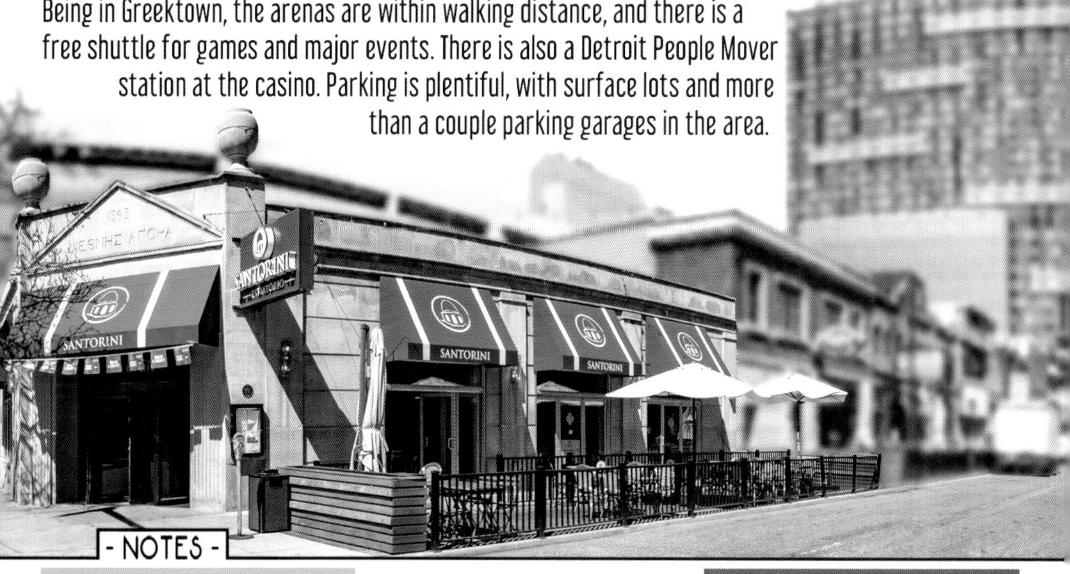


- NOTES -

Been there! ☐ Greektown

# Wahlburgers

569 Monroe Avenue
(313) 209-4499

Full bar: ☑ Draft beer: ☑ Full kitchen: ☑ Shuttle service: ☒ wahldetroit.com
(Greektown - Monroe Avenue)

HOURS:
Sun - Thu: 10:30am - midnight
Fri - Sat: 10:30am - 1am

**Wahlburgers** is located in Greektown, under the overhead crosswalk in the shadow of Greektown Casino-Hotel. Unassuming from the street, inside is modern, clean, bright, and spacious. There are two floors, with downstairs being the smaller of the two spaces. Framed movie posters featuring the Wahlbergs (they are musicians and actors) adorn the walls.

There is a full bar upstairs as well as downstairs, both with a large selection of draft beer, and knowledgable bartenders. There are a few large flat-screen TVs throughout **Wahlburgers**, and they are oriented more toward the bar crowd, although they are also visible to patrons at the tables.

Located in the middle of Greektown, walking to Comerica Park, Ford Field, the Fox Theater, St. Andrew's Hall, the Fillmore, and Campus Martius is reasonable. Shuttles are available during home games and major events. The shuttles can be caught on Monroe Avenue, and are free.

*Everything is made from scratch here, and the onion rings are amazing!*

- NOTES -

Been there! ☐ Greektown

1228 Randolf Street
(313) 964-0776

# The Well

Full bar: ☑ Draft beer: ☑ Full kitchen: ✗ Shuttle service: ✗ thewellbars.com

HOURS:
Mon - Fri: 4pm - 2am
Sat: 5pm - 2am
Sun: 7pm - 2am

HAPPY HOUR:
Mon - Fri: 4pm - 8pm

**The Well** is a small dive bar on the edge of the Greektown district, built into a space that was once a clothing store. Former display windows now house tables allowing them to have a small open-air offering to their bar. It may not be fancy, but neither is it grungy. It does the trick, serves well as a bar, and is a decent place to hangout and grab some drinks at lower prices than you will find at most of the other downtown bars.

Inside, half of the space is the bar itself, long and wood-topped running down the right side of the room all the way to the back. The rest of the space has small tables and room to mingle. Daily drink specials bring some of the prices even further down. These change, so check at the bar to find out what they are. During happy hour, they offer $2 well drinks and $2 domestic beers.

There is no kitchen at **The Well**, however they allow you to bring food in from other places.

Besides mingling with friends or meeting new people, there are a couple of dart boards, a few TVs, and on Friday and Saturday nights a DJ provides musical entertainment.

*As far as dives go, this one is all right. "Dive" is just a category, and does not mean that there is anything wrong with the bar.*

- NOTES -

# Midtown / Cass Corridor

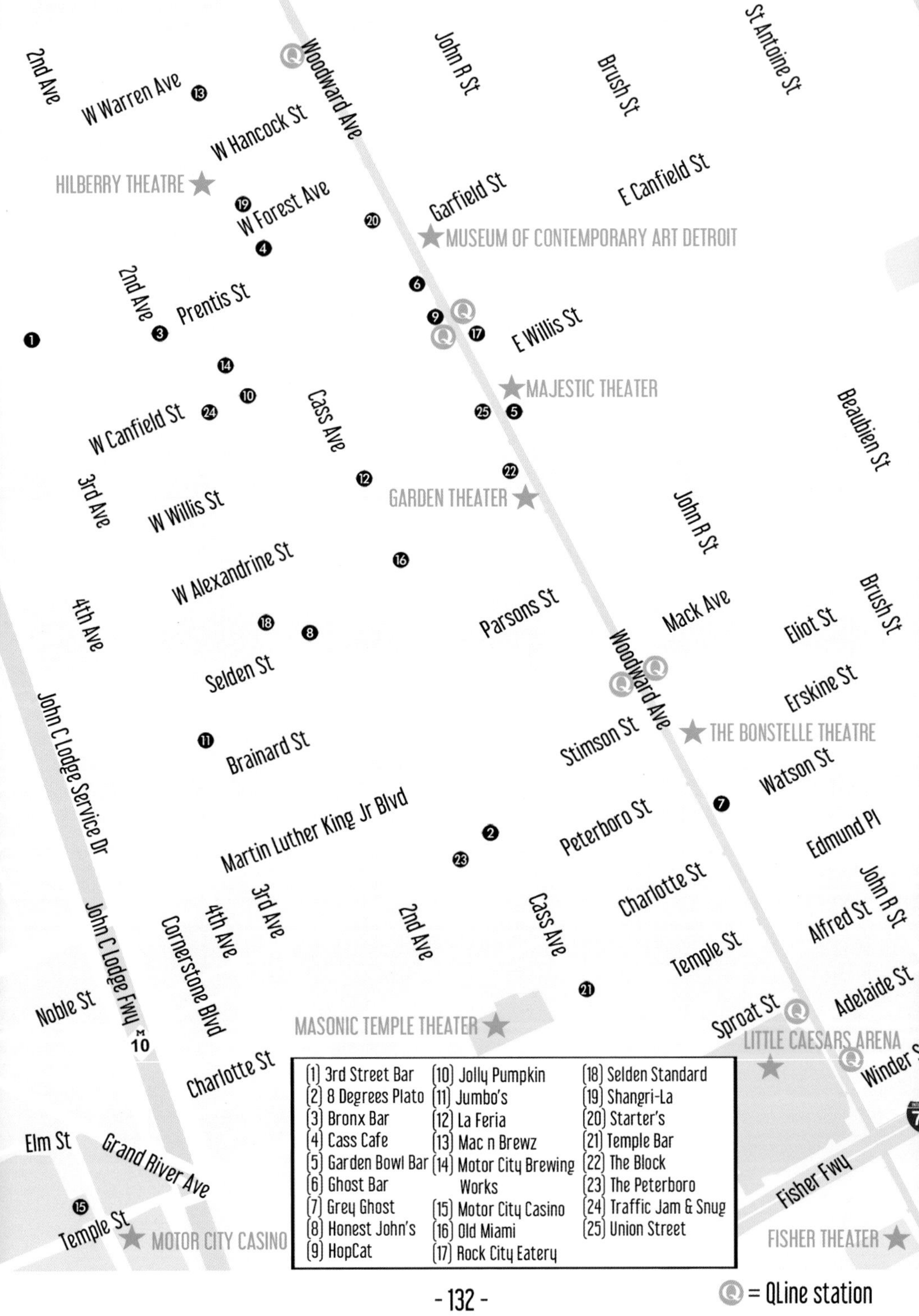

**Been there!** ☐ **Midtown / Cass Corridor**

# 3rd Street Bar

**4626 3rd Avenue**
**(313) 833-0603**

**Full bar:** ✓ **Draft beer:** ✓ **Full kitchen:** ✓ **Shuttle service:** ✗

HOURS:
Mon - Fri: 3pm - 2am
Sat: noon - 2am
Sun: noon - midnight

HAPPY HOUR:
Mon - Sun: 4pm - 6pm

The inside of **3rd Street Bar** is a large space broken up only by rows of tables and chairs. On the back wall, there is a somewhat different feature - a wood burning fireplace. Overall, it's a rather basic place, a dive to many, a welcome hangout to all. There is also a large, covered outside patio at the back of the building.

The bar covers little more than the basics. There are a half dozen beers on tap, more in cans and bottles. Happy hour offers discounts on everything, and college night is on Wednesdays. It's $3 wells from 7pm - close, $2 10oz. Coors, and bomb shots for $4.

The food from the kitchen consists of a fistfull of sides and a few sandwiches. Having been without food offerings for nine months or so, it is nice to see the kitchen in operation again. **3rd Street** is a good place to enjoy some cheap drinks, play some shuffleboard, darts or skeeball, or watch the current game on one of the TVs. The fine sounds of karaoke enhance the air here on Tuesday nights after 10pm. Take that as an invitation or a warning.

There is a small parking lot behind the building, as well as parking on the street. It is a short walk to Woodward Avenue, where the QLine runs. It can take you down to the sports venues and theaters, as well as up to the Detroit Institute of Arts and the Science Center.

This is an ideal place for large groups, especially before games. **3rd Street** offers free shuttles to the games and major events in the city.

*The rumor on the street is there is some sort of allegiance to the New England Patriots at **3rd Street**. If that's your thing, go for it. Otherwise, Go Lions!*

- NOTES -

**Been there!** ☐

**Midtown / Cass Corridor**

# 8 Degrees Plato

**3409 Cass Avenue**
**(313) 888-9972**

**Full bar:** ✗ **Draft beer:** ✓ **Full kitchen:** ✗ **Shuttle service:** ✗ **8degreesplato.com**

Author Favorite

HOURS:
Sun - Wed: 11am - 8pm
Thu - Sat: 11am - 9pm

HAPPY HOUR:
Mon - Fri: 4pm - 6pm

If you were to cross a beer store with a bar and throw in a bunch of coolness, you would end up with **8 Degrees Plato**. Tucked away in a little, somewhat non-descript building, is the 3rd best beer bar in the United States, according to USA Today.

Upon entering, the initial impression is that this is a beer store with a HUGE selection of beers. Racks and coolers fill much of the interior space, and they are loaded with more varieties than you'll find just about anywhere else. Three quarters of the way to the back of the store, the racks give way to tables and then a bar on the back wall.

The bar has 15 beers on draft, the description of what they are is on a chalkboard on the left rear wall. There are also a couple of house wines, but no booze. The focus is on the beer at **8 Degrees Plato**. If you want, any of the beer sold in the store can be consumed in the taproom for a corkage fee. For the dedicated consumer, there is a mug club, which gets you a buck off each draft, and a buck off growler fills. You also get invites to special events, and 10% off merchandise (not beer).

There's no food here, however you can bring your own, and eat it in the taproom.

On the 1st Tuesday of each month, there is a euchre tournament at **8 Degrees Plato**. Besides that, there is no set event schedule. In the past they have had movie night, anniversary parties, and music. To learn about any future events, follow them on Instagram (@8dplatodetroit) or on Facebook.

There is free parking curbside and in the lot across the street.

*This is a dog-friendly establishment. Feel free to bring your pup with you!*

- NOTES -

Been there! ☐

3919 Woodward Avenue

(313) 832-0892

Full bar: ✓ Draft beer: ✓ Full kitchen: ✓ Shuttle service: ✗

Midtown / Cass Corridor

# The Block

theblockdet.com

**The Block** is more of an upscale restaurant with a bar in it. The modern decor is balanced out with a large brick wall covered in a Detroit themed mural which faces the bar. Everything is clean, spacious, and carefully positioned and constructed to be consistent with the type of food and drinks that are offered.

The wood-topped bar is toward the back of the restaurant, next to the busy kitchen area. Despite the proximity, the hustle and noise does not diminish the ambiance. **The Block** has an ever-changing menu of seasonal drinks, a strong selection of top-shelf liquors, a well-rounded selection of beers both on draft and in bottles, and a good-sized wine list. Happy hour offers $1 select drafts, $3 select wines, calamari, and Alfredo mac 'n' cheese, and $5 you call-its, wings, and chicken quesadillas.

HOURS:
Tue - Thu: 11am - 9pm
Fri: 11am - midnight
Sat: 4pm - midnight
Sun: 11am - 9pm
Mon: *closed*

HAPPY HOUR:
Tue- Fri: 4pm - 7pm

BRUNCH:
Sun: 11am - 3pm

Food at **The Block** is not your standard fare. Care and creativity have been applied when creating the recipes, and many items on the menu bring intriguing sets of flavor profiles together. Some of the more popular dishes are the Block Mac 'n' Cheese, calamari, Cilantro Lime Chicken Salad, Shotgun Shrimp, and the Loaded Chicken. Everything is made fresh here, down to grinding the meat for the burgers.

Located near the Detroit Medical Center, parking is plentiful in the area, and the QLine connects you to downtown with just a short ride.

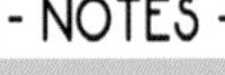

- NOTES -

Been there! ☐

# Bronx Bar

**Midtown / Cass Corridor**
**4476 2nd Avenue**
**(313) 832-8464**

**Full bar:** ✓ **Draft beer:** ✓ **Full kitchen:** ✗ **Shuttle service:** ✗

HOURS:
Mon - Fri: 11am - 2am
Sat - Sun: noon - 2am

BLOODY MARY BAR:
Sat - Sun: noon - 5pm

The **Bronx Bar** is a bit of a dive, but a comfortable one. Established in 1938, it is safe to say it has survived the test of time. Because of its small size, it is a perfect place for gathering a small group of friends.

The decor is mostly a throw-back to the 50s without being too kitschy. There are a dozen or so tables inside, and seating outside for the warmer months. If you are looking for entertainment outside of conversation, they have a pool table and a juke box.

They are best known for their burgers, and have a loyal following for that reason. This proves you don't have to be fancy to be good. Not a fan of beef? They also offer a bean burger and a turkey burger, both of which are quite popular. **Bronx Bar** does not have a big kitchen or a big menu, but they do seem to care about the quality of their food, and that goes a long way.

There's no trivia night, no live bands, there's not even a happy hour. It is a dive bar, but it's not the kind that creeps you out or makes you feel dirty when you walk in the door. It's a pleasant little place where you can pass some time with cold drinks, simple good food, and a few of your friends.

It's relatively close to Wayne State, The DIA, Detroit Science Center, and Detroit's medical center. Parking is limited to metered street spaces and a few nearby surface lots.

*Make sure you look at both sides of the menu.*
*You will understand once you do it.*

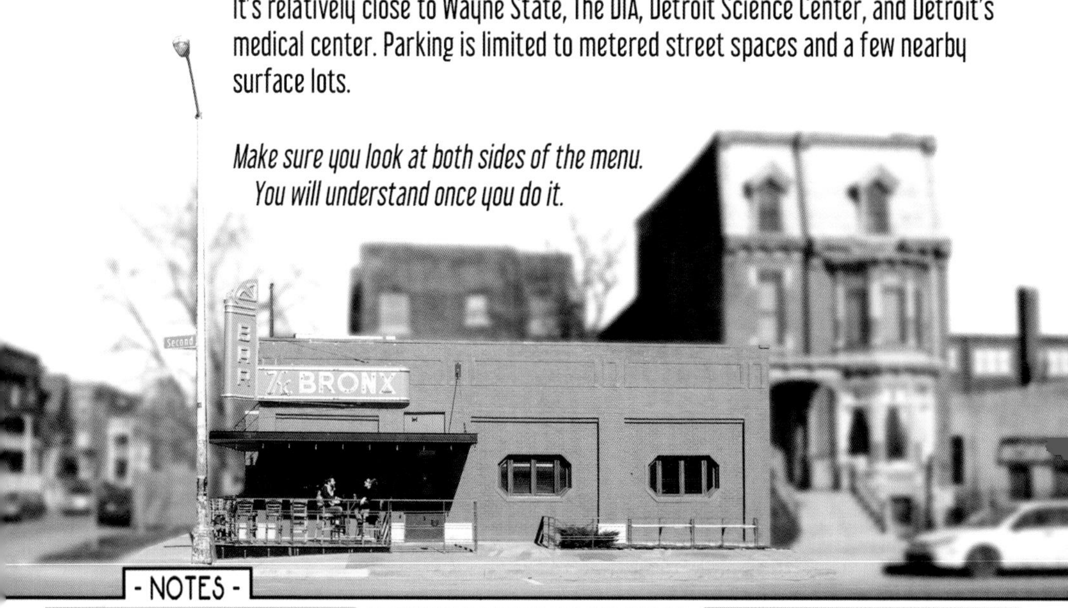


- NOTES -

Been there! ☐

4620 Cass Avenue
(313) 831-1400

Full bar: ☑ Draft beer: ☑ Full kitchen: ☑ Shuttle service: ✘

Midtown / Cass Corridor

# Cass Cafe

casscafe.com

HOURS:
Mon - Thu: 11am - midnight
Fri - Sat: 11am - 1am
Sun: 5pm - 10pm

**Cass Cafe** is an open, warm and inviting location that feels more like a coffee house than a bar or restaurant. There are two levels to the space. The lower level has a bar in the middle and seating both front and back. The upper level is a mezzanine over the bar, set up with tables, and overlooks the lower area from both ends. Several large skylights and a full bank of windows in the front provide wonderful natural light inside during the day.

From a bar perspective, **Cass Cafe** is capable of meeting your cocktail and cordial needs, with trained bartenders and a large selection of liquors. They also have a dozen beers on draft, with more in bottles and cans. You can get locally brewed craft beers and imports from around the world. There is also a moderate selection of wines to choose from.

The menu is filled with wonderfully creative food, including many vegan and vegetarian options. There are daily food specials, bringing seasonal ingredients to your plate.

In the back of the restaurant, the walls are decorated with local art. The gallery rotates every three months, and 100% of the proceeds go to the artists.

**Cass Cafe** is located on the edge of Wayne State University campus, just a block away from Hilberry Theatre. For parking, they have a private lot behind the building. There are also metered spots along the street and surface pay lots in the area.

*Try the lentil burger, one of their most popular menu items.*

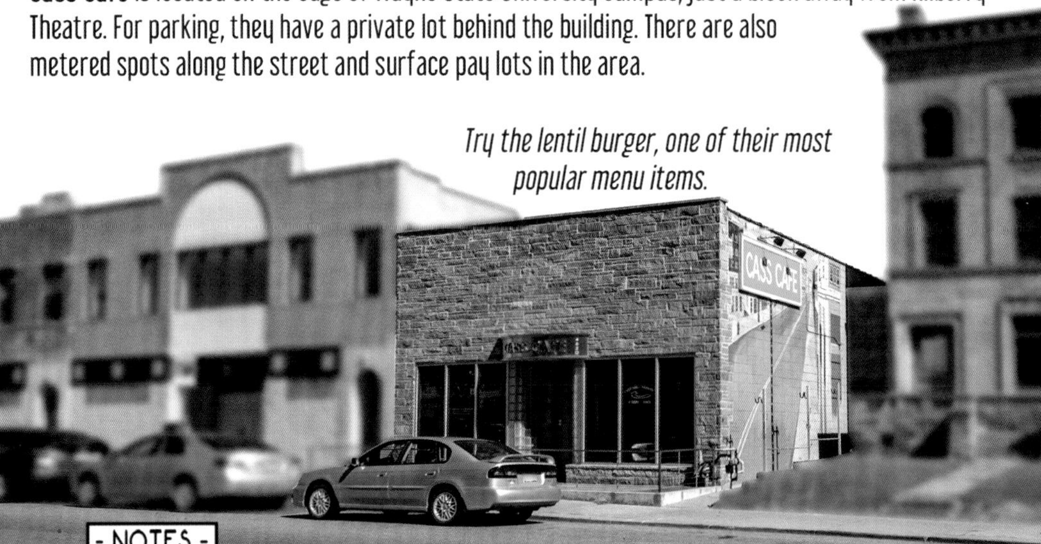


- NOTES -

Been there! ☐

Midtown / Cass Corridor
4120 Woodward Avenue
(313) 833-9700 x205

# Garden Bowl Bar

**Full bar: ✓ Draft beer: ✓ Full kitchen: ✓ Shuttle service: ✗** majesticdetroit.com/garden-bowl-detroit

Author Favorite

HOURS:
Mon - Sun: 11am - 2am

HAPPY HOUR:
Mon - Fri: 3pm - 6pm

Located in the front of Garden Bowl, the oldest continuously operating bowling alley in the country (1913), **Garden Bowl Bar** is a divey place with a lot of character. The bar, refrigerator, and much of the wall space is covered with stickers of all sorts, and the bar top was built using the wood from an old bowling lane. The remaining wall space is mostly filled with show flyers for events at the adjoining Majestic Theater and the Magic Stick. The decor is eclectic, maintaining a cool, open and welcome feel. A large section of windows accordion out of the way to allow the front to be open to the fresh air and constant activity of Woodward when the weather is nice.

The bar has a large selection of reasonably priced beers, including 16 mostly Michigan drafts, with a bunch more in bottles and cans, and a full line-up of booze. During happy hour (M-F 3-6pm), they offer $2 well drinks, $2 Bud and Bud Light, and $3.50 Jäger shots.

Technically, the bar does not have food, however inside the establishment is Sgt. Pepperoni's, a pizza and stromboli place with good, fresh made food that can be ordered and brought into the bar.

**Garden Bowl** is in the heart of Midtown, a natural place to drink when attending a show at the Majestic. Of course, it is cool enough to be a destination itself, a place to go and hang out. It is also close to the Detroit Medical Center, and a ride on the QLine will get you easily anywhere up and down Woodward Avenue.

Since it is located at a bowling alley, you can also build bowling into your evening.

*The Woodward Stromboli from Sgt. Pepperoni's is awesome!*

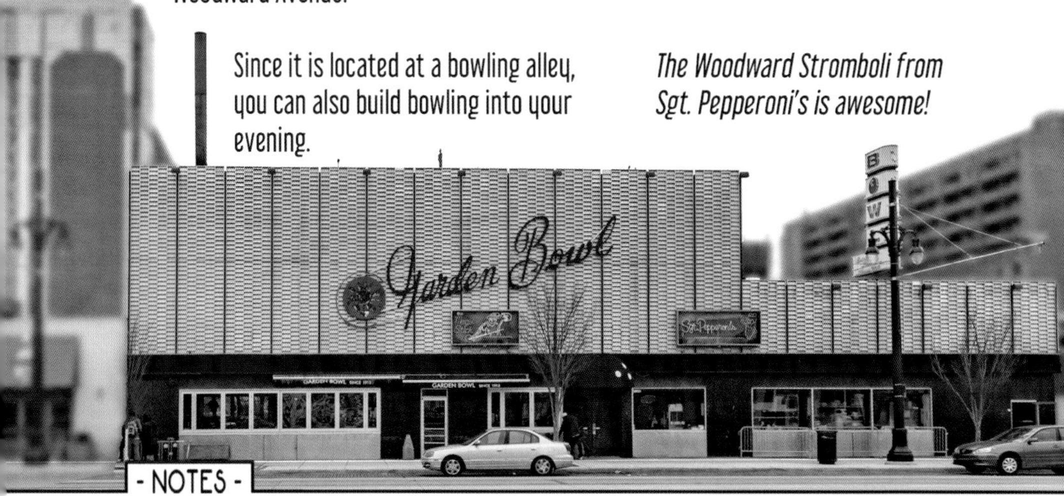


- NOTES -

**Been there!** ☐

**4421 Woodward Avenue**

**(313) 832-5700**

**Midtown**

# The Ghost Bar

**Full bar:** ☑ **Draft beer:** ☑ **Full kitchen:** ✗ **Shuttle service:** ✗ **whitneyghostbar.com**

While many streets in Detroit were once lined with opulent mansions, there are relatively few left, and even fewer that have been either maintained or restored. The Whitney Mansion is one such survivor, restored in 1986. The 21,000 square foot, 52 room beauty was built from 1890-1894 in the style of Romanesque Revival. Now a fully functioning restaurant and bar, the interior has kept most of the wonderful details from the past.

HOURS:
Mon - Sat: 4:30pm - 1:30am
Sun: 11am - 4pm

HAPPY HOUR:
Mon - Fri: 4:30pm - 6:30pm

**The Ghost Bar** is located on the third floor, allowing all who enter to experience the elegance of the mansion as they ascend the central stairway. A domed ceiling over the ornate wooden bar is the scene awaiting, and while there are seats at the bar, there are also a couple of nearby rooms with tables, and a sitting room with comfortable chairs and sofas where patrons may enjoy their drinks. The bar stock is on the limited side, with a small selection of wine, three draft beers, and although many top-shelf brands, few choices within each type of liquor. One standout category is Absinthe, of which there are seven to choose from.

There is a limited bar menu, with just eight food items offered.

For those who are interested in eating, The Whitney Detroit is a restaurant on the first floor, preparing a variety of different dishes. On the third level, The Woodward Room serves only prime rib.

- NOTES -

Been there! ☐

Midtown / Cass Corridor

# Grey Ghost Detroit

47 Watson Street
(313) 262-6534

**Full bar:** ✓ **Draft beer:** ✗ **Full kitchen:** ✓ **Shuttle service:** ✗ **greyghostdetroit.com**

HOURS:
Mon - Thu: 4pm - midnight
Fri - Sat: 4pm - 1am
Sun: 4pm - midnight

BRUNCH:
Sun: 10am - 2pm

One of Detroit's elegant new hotspots, **Grey Ghost** is a breath of calm sophistication in a busy city. The decor is modern without being kitschy, and elegant without being pretentious. Between the large windows and the ample lighting within, the setting is quite comfortable.

The bar at the **Grey Ghost** is impressive in its size as well as its content. A large shelving system displays the wide variety of alcohol available, while at bar level, there are rows of bottles containing house made infusions and syrups which are used to make the creative cocktails offered, or to construct a custom drink based on a desired flavor profile. Wines and beers, the latter only in bottles, are available, however the focus is on cocktails.

The kitchen at **Grey Ghost** presents a variety of creative dishes, designed and prepared under the watchful eyes of chefs John Vermiglio and Josef Giacomino. The food has been met with rave reviews, and the popularity of the restaurant has soared, making it mandatory to have a reservation to sit at a table. If you plan on dining here in the future, make a reservation now, as they are generally booked solid over a month out. Walk-ins may eat at the bar or on the patio, depending on availability.

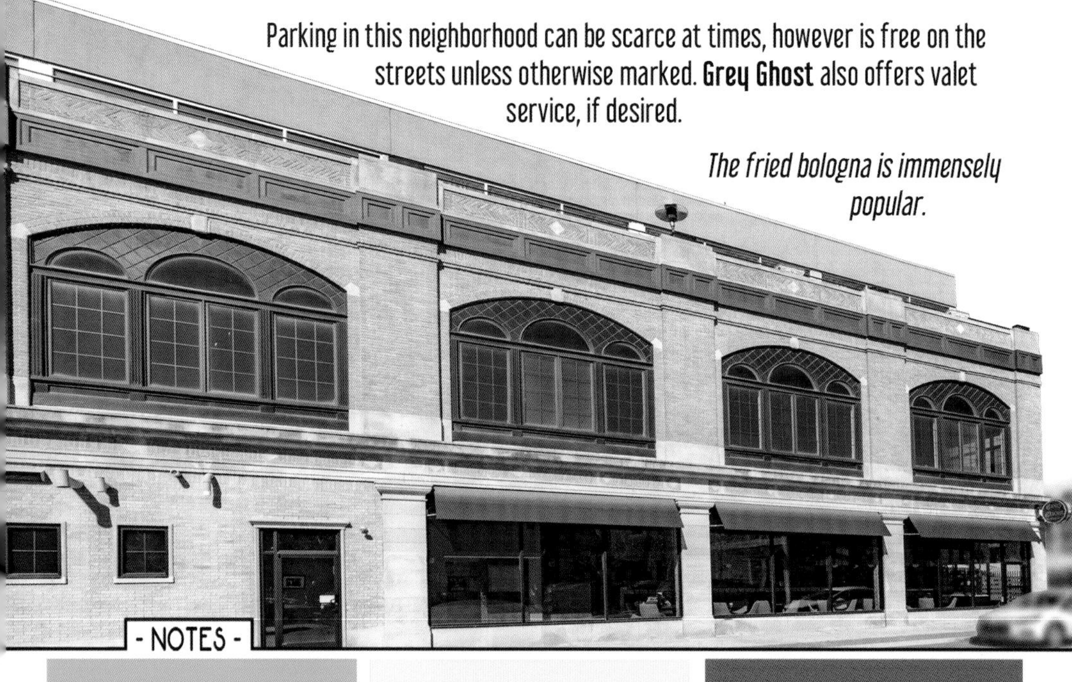

Parking in this neighborhood can be scarce at times, however is free on the streets unless otherwise marked. **Grey Ghost** also offers valet service, if desired.

*The fried bologna is immensely popular.*

- NOTES -

**Been there!** ☐

**488 Selden Street**
**(313) 832-JOHN**



# Honest ? John's

**Full bar:** ✓ **Draft beer:** ✓ **Full kitchen:** ✓ **Shuttle service:** ✗ **honestjohnsdetroit.com**

HOURS:
Mon - Sat: 7am - 2am
Sun: 9am - 2am

HAPPY HOUR:
Mon - Fri: 4pm - 6pm

Walking into **Honest John's** brings you into a warm, inviting space. Comical neon signs and holiday lights set a comfortably light mood immediately after passing through a set of swinging doors. It's the kind of place that has a familiar feel, even if it's your first time. If the weather is cooperating, there is also the option of sitting out on their patio. If you need to be entertained, there is a pool table, a few TVs, and a juke box.

They have a full bar, a dozen or so beers on tap with more varieties in bottles, and a selection of wines. If you need something to take with you, they also offer the option of buying some for the road (beer and wine only).

From a food standpoint, **Honest John's** is probably most known for offering a full breakfast menu, seven days a week. For the lunch and dinner crowd, the menu consists mostly of burgers, sandwiches, and wraps, as well as a selection of appetizers, soups, salads, and sides.

There are a few specials at **Honest John's**. Happy Hour on weekdays is between 4-6pm, during which draft beers are $4. College Nights are Friday and Saturday from 7-9pm. With a valid college ID, select 40oz beers are $5, and appetizers are half off.

Parking is pretty easy - there is a private fenced-in lot behind the bar. When that's full there are ample spots, both metered and not, along the surrounding streets.

*Want something yummy? Try the Chicken and waffles.*

- NOTES -

**Been there!** ☐

**Midtown / Cass Corridor**
**4265 Woodward Avenue**
**(313) 769-8828**

# HopCat

**Full bar:** ☑ **Draft beer:** ☑ **Full kitchen:** ☑ **Shuttle service:** ☒ **hopcat.com/detroit**

Author Favorite

**HopCat** is two floors of excitement. The upstairs has ample seating, and is where the music comes from. Called the Huma Room, there is a stage, 30 beer taps, and a full bar.

The downstairs is dominated by the huge and impressive bar which has more taps than you can easily count; over 130 according to the menu. That should be enough to allow everyone to find something they like. It will probably take longer to choose your beer than your food. Of course, the bar offers liquor, too.

HOURS:
Mon - Wed: 11am - midnight
Thu - Fri: 11am - 2am
Sat: 10am - 2am
Sun: 10am - midnight

HAPPY HOUR:
Mon - Thu: 3pm - 6pm

LATE NIGHT HAPPY HOUR
Sun - Wed: 10pm - close

Speaking of food, **HopCat** has a well constructed menu that will take you on an adventure from appetizers through entrees. All of their food is made from scratch. They tend to do very well with their burgers and sandwiches, especially when accompanied by their quite possibly world famous CRACK FRIES. If you end up at **HopCat**, you *must* give the fries a try. Trust me.

**HopCat** is located on Woodward, near the Majestic Theater and the Museum of Contemporary Art Detroit. The M1 Rail (QLine) allows people to easily move up and down Woodward, bringing a lot of downtown Detroit into reach.

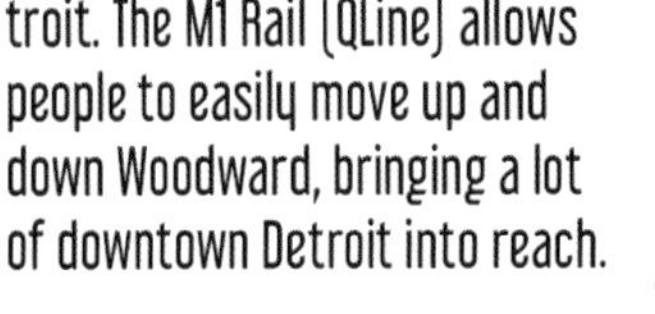

There are a few options for parking. **HopCat** has a valet lot, and there is metered parking on the street.

- NOTES -

**Been there!** ☐

**441 West Canfield Street**

**(313) 262-6115**

**Midtown / Cass Corridor**

# Jolly Pumpkin

**Full bar:** ✓ **Draft beer:** ✓ **Full kitchen:** ✓ **Shuttle service:** ✗ **jollypumpkin.com**

HOURS:
Mon - Thu: 11:30am - 11pm
Fri - Sat: 11:30am - 1am
Sun: 11:30am - 10pm

HAPPY HOUR:
Mon - Fri: 4pm - 6pm

When you walk through the front door, you enter a modern-industrial style bar/restaurant. The space is roomy, with high ceilings and a front wall of windows which help create a comfortable atmosphere.

The bar itself is rather impressive, with over 30 drafts made up of beers from **Jolly Pumpkin** and their sister brewery, North Peak. **Jolly Pumpkin** is known for authentic sour beers. They were the first brewery to specialize in making them. The brewing itself happens at their Dexter, Michigan location.

In addition to the ample selection of beers, Jolly Pumpkin has a line of signature mixed drinks utilizing Civilized liquors, a brand made in Traverse City, Michigan, exclusively for them. Staying with the theme, **Jolly Pumpkin** serves wine made for them by Peninsular Cellars, also in Traverse City.

The menu consists mostly of gourmet sandwiches, along with a dozen or so creatively topped pizzas, providing some tasty food selections to accompany the bar fare. If you are there on a Tuesday, they offer pizza specials and trivia.

Parking is generally pretty easy, with surface lots and metered street options all around. Located in Midtown, The **Jolly Pumpkin** is not far from the DIA, Wayne State, The Science Center, Detroit's Medical Center, and the Detroit Historical Museum.

*Want something a little different? Try the Korean shortrib pizza. It's a good one!*

- NOTES -

Been there! ☐

# Jumbo's Bar

Midtown / Cass Corridor
3736 3rd Street
(313) 831-8949

**Full bar:** ✓ **Draft beer:** ✗ **Full kitchen:** ✗ **Shuttle service:** ✗

HOURS:
Mon - Fri: 11am - 2am
Sat: noon - 2am
Sun: 1pm - 8pm (ish)

King of the dive bars in Detroit. Is that a bad thing? Not if you ask the regulars. **Jumbo's** has maintained its style for years, and is not looking to change. It first opened in 1940, and has been owned and run by the same family ever since.

There are no windows in **Jumbo's**. When you enter, you find yourself in a clubhouse style bar. There is a long straight bar down one side of the room, and the other side is taken up by a few tables and chairs, a pool table, a jukebox, video games, darts and pinball. There is a small outdoor patio, which is mainly used as a smoking area.

The bar is no frills, and the drinks are inexpensive. Well drinks start at $3.50, and beers start at $2.50. Because of the low prices, it's basically happy hour all the time.

There is no kitchen at **Jumbo's**, and therefore no food, at least not on a regular basis. On game days for the Detroit Lions, there is often food brought in for the drinking guests, although it is not guaranteed for every game.

**Jumbo's** has a small stage and schedules local bands from time to time. Parking is avaiable in the lot next to the building, and on the street out front. Both are free.

*It's a simple and friendly place. Not all places need to be trendy.*

- NOTES -

**Been there!** ☐

**Midtown / Cass Corridor**

**4130 Cass Avenue**
**(313) 285-9081**

# La Feria

**Full bar:** ☑ **Draft beer:** ☑ **Full kitchen:** ☑ **Shuttle service:** ✗ **laferiadetroit.com**

HOURS:
Mon - Thu: 11am - 11pm
Fri - Sat: 11am - midnight

HAPPY HOUR:
Mon - Thu: 3pm - 6pm

Much like the exterior, the interior of the building for **La Feria** is modern and angular. The space is small, with a few tables set for diners and a short bar across the front of the kitchen. Large windows on the front and side of the building allow natural light to bring warmth to the overall ambiance.

The primary funtion of **La Feria** is not to be a bar, however the way it has been designed allows for it to be a welcoming destination for some drinks and tapas (small plates). They have a couple of beers on draft, one of which rotates frequently with local brews. The cocktail list brings forward a variety of Spanish inspired drinks, true to form with the type of food served here. For those who desire wine, **La Feria** has a batch to choose from. During happy hour, for $3 you can get a glass of house white or red wine, a draft beer, or Patatas Bravas, one of the most popular food items.

The menu is filled with food of Spanish persuasion served in small portions, aka tapas. Tapas are snacks or appetizers, served hot or cold. The variety from the kitchen is wide, and the taste combinations range from expected to unusual. There are options for vegetarians and vegans, and some menu items are gluten free.

**La Feria** is close to Wayne State campus and the Detroit Medical Center. Parking options include a paid lot next door and metered curbside spots on surrounding streets.

*Of the many delicious dishes on the menu, two items stand out for their popularity: The Gambas al Ajillo, seared shrimp with garlic and dried chilis, and the Patatas Bravas, fried potatoes with a spicy tomato sauce and alioli.*

- NOTES -

Been there! ☐

# Mac n' Brewz

Midtown / Cass Corridor
4870 Cass Avenue
(313) 782-4180

**Full bar:** ☑ **Draft beer:** ☑ **Full kitchen:** ☑ **Shuttle service:** ☒ **macncheez.com/midtown**

HOURS:
Mon - Thu: 10am - 10pm
Fri - Sat: 10am - 11pm
Sun: 10am - 9pm

HAPPY HOUR:
Mon - Sun: 11am - 4pm

**Mac n' Brewz** takes some of its design cues from the traditional diners of the 1950s, yet with a modern twist. It's quite open inside, with high exposed beam ceilings, and windows which wrap all the way across the front of the building and down one side. This brings beautiful natural light inside.

At first appearance, it does not look like there is much of a bar, however, once you get to the counter, it comes into view. There are a dozen beers on tap, with more in bottles and cans, a small selection of wines, and the ability to "design your own cocktails." For the young at heart, **Mac n' Brewz** offers you *Boozie Smoothies*. Although the prices are already quite reasonable, they have a happy hour every day from 11am - 4pm when draft beers are $2.75.

Your food and drinks are ordered up at the counter, and the menu is posted overhead. Food-wise, their claim to fame is variations of macaroni and cheese, of which they have many. There is also a selection of wraps and salads to choose from, and everything offered is prepared fresh.

There are several TVs in this establishment, bringing local games to you when the seasons are active. Located near Wayne State, parking is plentiful in the area. Campus is just across the street, and the Hilberry Theatre and Detroit Institute of Art are within walking distance. The QLine has nearby stops on Woodward, bringing much of the city into reach.

- NOTES -

Been there! ☐

470 West Canfield Street
(313) 832-2700



# Motor City Brewing Works

Full bar: ✓ Draft beer: ✓ Full kitchen: ✓ Shuttle service: ✗ motorcitybeer.com

HOURS:
Mon - Thu: 11am - midnight
Fri - Sat: 11am - 1am
Sun: noon - midnight

**Motor City Brewing Works** has been crafting excellent beer since 1994. With several varieties on tap, there is something for everyone who likes beer. In addition to the site-made beer, they also have a pizza oven in which they make hot, fresh pizzas, appetizers, and other delicious items. This is a place locals bring visitors to for a consistently good experience. On Mondays and Tuesdays, you can get a growler filled for only $6, and most Wednesdays a local artist is featured, their work decorating the walls and up for sale.

The ambiance at **MCBW** is comfortable and inviting. Everything revolves around the u-shaped bar in the middle of the main room. There is an upper deck and a beer garden, both of which are only open during the warmer months. It is a relatively small place, so getting a large group in can be challenging. If you are a small group, this is a great place to go.

Author Favorite

They are known for their amazing pizzas as well as their house-made beers. Ghettoblaster, "the beer you can hear" has been their mainstay since 1995, and their least known, best beer is quite possibly a Nut-Blaster, which is half Nut Brown, and half Ghettoblaster.

Parking requires some education. In the lot that faces Canfield, the ONLY free spots are the five designated for **Motor City Brewing Works**. If you park in one of the other spots in the lot, you will have to pay the attendant $5. Besides the spots there, metered street parking is available, and there are reserved parking spots (free) behind the restaurant off Prentis Street.

Their location makes them conveniently close to Wayne State Universty, the Detroit Institute of Arts, Detroit Science Center, Detroit Historical Museum, Center for Creative Studies, Detroit's Main Library, Hilberry Theatre, Opera House, Max Fisher Theater and Detroit's Medical Center.

*Get creative and build your own pizza!*

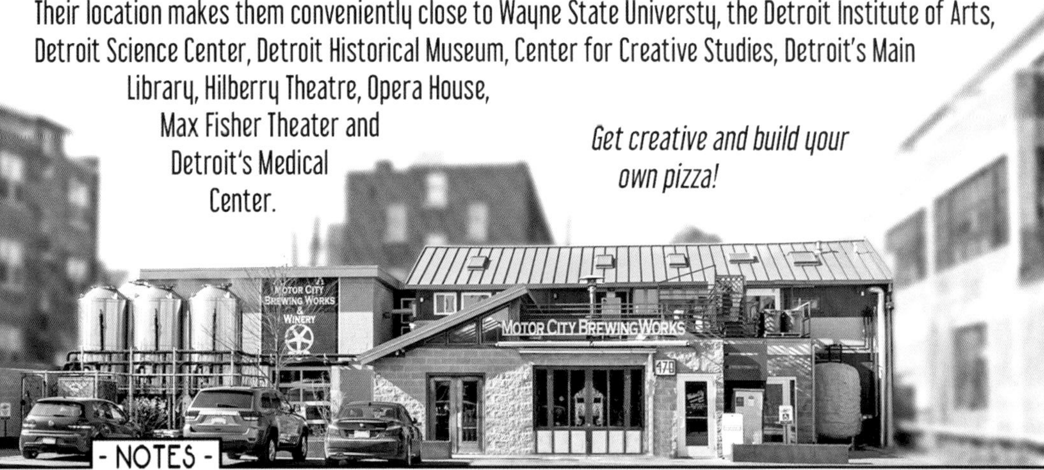


- NOTES -

Been there! ☐

# Motor City Casino

Midtown / Cass Corridor
2901 Grand River Avenue
(866) 782-9622

Full bar: ☑ Draft beer: ☑ Full kitchen: ☑ Shuttle service: ☒ motorcitycasino.com

HOURS:
Mon - Sun: 24 hours

**Motor City Casino** is one of the three casinos in Detroit, and you must be 21 to enter. It's big and opulent, as you would expect from a casino. You will find over 2,800 slot machines, a smoke free, twelve table poker room, and 59 table games spread across two floors for your gambling entertainment.

**Motor City Casino** has seven bars between the hotel and the casino. **Strut** is centrally located on the 2nd floor, has a large curved bar with gaming consoles built in, multiple TVs, and comfortable padded seating around the perimeter. **Spectators** is more sports oriented, located on the 1st floor of the casino, and has many TVs to bring in all of the games. **Headlights Lounge** is also on the 1st floor of the casino, near the poker room, and has gaming units built into the bartop. **Radio Bar** is located on the 2nd floor, and features DJs and live broadcasts.

The other three bars are outside of the gaming area. **The Lounge** is a small bar on the hotel side. **Overdrive** is a larger bar over by Sound Board on the 2nd floor. Finally, **Pit Stop** is another small bar on the 2nd level, hotel side, near the Assembly Line food court. Safe to say, there are lots of choices here. Bar hours vary, please check the website for specifics.

The food offerings are wide and deep thanks to six different restaurants throughout the property. The high-end food experience comes from Iridescence with modern American cuisine and an award winning wine list. The Assembly Line is **Motor City's** food court and buffet, offering a wide variety of choices. The Lodge Diner is open 24 hours, and serves everything from breakfast through dinners and late night snacks. Grand River Deli & Burgers has sandwiches and burgers. Little Caesar's is there for pizza cravings, and Sweet Ride is ready to tackle your sweet tooth. with pastries, cupcakes and cakes.

- NOTES -

Been there! ☐

Midtown / Cass Corridor

# The Old Miami

3930 Cass Avenue
(313) 831-3830

Full bar: ☑ Draft beer: ☑ Full kitchen: ☒ Shuttle service: ☒

HOURS:
Mon - Sat: 11am - 2am
Sun: noon - midnight

Author Favorite

On the awning out front are the words, "Thank you veterans". Go through the front door, and you enter a wall to wall tribute to veterans. **The Old Miami** was opened in 1973 by a Vietnam vet, and militaria covers the walls, columns, and just about every niche and corner throughout the interior. Above the bar are hundreds of pins and patches, many donated by past and current patrons. As a final touch, there are several guns, reduced to ornamental accents only, hanging from the ceiling and walls. While this is definitely a dive bar, it scores high on the coolness scale.

This is not the place to come for a fancy or trendy drink. Keep it simple, keep it real. **The Old Miami** offers a few beers on draft, many in bottles and cans, and all of your basic liquors. Do you want food? There are 3-4 different flavors of single serving chips available, that's it. No kitchen. The exception to this is on Thanksgiving and Christmas, when they offer free meals to anyone and everyone - *very cool!*

There is room for a dozen or so people to sit at the bar, then there are sofas and comfortable seats in the main room. These are set up around the fireplace, jukebox, pool table, dartboard, and three old-school pinball machines. At the far back part of the interior is a stage where rock and roll bands play Thursday - Sunday. Check the Metro Times and Facebook for details. There is also a chalkboard in the bar showing the current week's list of events.

To the side and behind **The Old Miami** is one of the largest outdoor patios in the city. There's a section that is a traditional style patio, then a large area right behind the bar that is like a back yard, complete with grass, flowers, and room to roam. All of this space is surrounded by a privacy fence.

- NOTES -

Been there! ☐

# The Peterboro

Midtown / Cass Corridor
420 Peterboro Street
(313) 833-1111
thepeterboro.com

Full bar: ☑ Draft beer: ☒ Full kitchen: ☑ Shuttle service: ☒

HOURS:
Mon: *closed*
Tue - Thu: 5pm - 11pm
Fri: 5pm - midnight
Sat: 4pm - midnight
Sun: 4pm - 11pm

HAPPY HOUR:
Tue - Fri: 5pm - 7pm

The name of the business tells you nothing about what to expect here. **The Peterboro** is a Chinese restaurant complete with a trendy bar. The location is somewhat appropriate, as it is in what has been Detroit's official Chinatown since the 1960's.

Enter the nondescript building into a neo-industiral setting with high ceilings and tubular ductwork, all painted black. High tables and wooden stools take up the central portion of the restaurant, with low tables on the perimeter.

The bar is at the far right of the restaurant, most noticable by the tall shelves in the center which hold the liquor. **The Peterboro's** bar is a craft cocktail kind of place, with homemade syrups and infusions, and an assortment of fresh garnishes. Some of the more creative cocktails are listed on the bar menu, as is a list of available sakés and whiskeys. If the latter is enticing to you, each day of the week except Monday has a $4 whiskey pour. While there is no draft beer, a small assortment of beer in cans and bottles is available. Happy hour specials change, so ask your server about the current deals.

The food coming out of the kitchen is not your typical Chinese fare. Many of the items are familiar, then have some sort of twist. For example, they have a Cheeseburger Spring Roll. Unlike many other Chinese restaurants, the menu is not large. It covers all the bases without overwhelming you with choices.

There is parking on the street out front, and in the dirt lot next to the building.

***The Peterboro's*** *location is a fair distance from almost all of Detroit's entertainment venues, and is not near the QLine or the Detroit People Mover.*

- NOTES -

**Been there!** ☐

**4216 Woodward Avenue**
**(313) 265-3729**



# Rock City Eatery

**Full bar:** ✓ **Draft beer:** ✓ **Full kitchen:** ✓ **Shuttle service:** ✗ **rockcityeatery.com**

HOURS:
Mon - Sat: 11am - midnight

BRUNCH:
Sun: 10am - 4pm

Author Favorite

**Rock City Eatery** has never been about having a fancy, trendy space. They focus on providing unique and excellent food. The building is on the plain side, a long, rectangular construction. Inside is clean and tidy, however still relatively non-descript. Concrete floors, simple yet functional furniture, and sparsely decorated walls are what you will find here. Once you order something, you will appreciate the subjects of their focus.

The bar space is small. The shelves with the liquor are welded steel with lights to highlight the bottles. **Rock City** has a dozen taps, more beer offerings in bottles and cans, a moderate wine list, and a list of quite creative cocktails. Every week there is a new specialty cocktail, just about guaranteed to be something you have not tried before.

The seating area is large at this location, at least three times the size of their first place. This is good. as it improves the liklihood of being able to get a table. The kitchen offers a unique menu for each service. The brunch menu is available from 10am-4pm on Sunday, and has everything from hot breakfast meals to a large selection of cold cereals with optional toppings. Lunch runs from 11am-4pm Monday through Saturday, getting into housemade sandwiches and pizzas. Finally, after a soft transition from 4pm-5pm we move from the lunch to the dinner menu, filled with imaginative hot entrees and continuing with fresh pizzas. The menus change with some frequency, so come back to find new favorites.

Located on Woodward Avenue, downtown is within reach using the QLine. This will also get you up Woodward to the Detroit Institute of Arts, the Michigan Science Center, the Charles H. Wright Museum of African American History, and the Detroit Medical Center, among other things.

*Pies put them on the map originally, so make sure to save room!*

- NOTES -

Been there! ☐

# Selden Standard

Midtown / Cass Corridor
3921 2nd Avenue
(313) 438-5055
seldenstandard.com

Full bar: ✓ Draft beer: ✓ Full kitchen: ✓ Shuttle service: ✗

HOURS:
Mon - Fri: 11am - 2:30pm
4:30pm - 11pm

Sat - Sun: 10am - 2pm
4:30 - 11pm

Fitting with the appearance of the outside of the building, the interior of **Selden Standard** is contemporary, warm, and inviting. Casually elegant in its design, the appearance foreshadows for the experience you are sure to have.

As for libations, there is more than just beer and booze. Aside from the fully stocked bar, **Selden Standard** offers a robust beer list, both on draft and in bottles, a handful of special craft cocktails, and a moderate wine list. If this is not enough, they suggest you ask your server about "fine wines, crazy beers, cognac, champagne, and rare whiskey".

On the food side, you are in good hands here. **Selden Standard** won *Restaurant of the Year* two years in a row, had a chef who was a 2017 James Beard nominee, and now has Rebecca LaMalfa from Bravo's Top Chef, running the kitchen. Everything is made fresh, and they do their best to source locally, practicing a "farm to table" concept. The menu changes along with the seasons as different inredients become available. The result of all of this is a menu filled with creative dishes, not the same old stuff that is available anywhere else.

**Selden Standard** has a small, private parking lot, and there is a fair amount of both metered and free parking on the surrounding streets.

***Selden Standard*** *is a popular place. If you plan to eat, it is highly recommended you make a reservation. It is not uncommon to find a two or three hour wait for a table on weekends.*

- NOTES -

Been there! ☐

Midtown / Cass Corridor

4710 Cass Avenue
(313) 974-7669

# Shangri-la

Full bar: ✓ Draft beer: ✓ Full kitchen: ✓ Shuttle service: ✗ midtownshangri-la.com

HOURS:
Mon - Thu: 11am - 10pm
Fri - Sat: 11am - 11pm
Sun: closed

**Shangri-La** is a relatively small place, however they make the most of what they have. The dining room is split by the entrance, and there is a mezzanine level to handle any extra diners. The decor is modern minimalism, unique when compared to some of the more historic locations around the city.

The bar itself is cozy, with only a handful of seats. They do offer a cocktail list, with a selection of draft and bottled beers, draft sake (yes, draft sake), hot sake, unique craft cocktails, and a selection of wines. They also have a full range of liquor to handle more traditional drink orders. While they do not have a happy hour, there is a daily drink special, a daily beer special, and a daily wine special from 4:30pm until closing time.

Food-wise, **Shangri-La** is most known for its wide selection of dim sum. Additionally, they have a large sushi menu, all freshly rolled to order. If neither one are your thing, they also have a menu full of Chinese dishes and a few Thai dishes.

Located in Midtown on Cass Avenue, **Shangri-La** is close to Wayne State's campus, and not far from The Hilberry Theatre and Children's Hospital. Woodward and the QLine are just a couple of blocks away, making an easy connection into the city.

Parking is metered on the streets, for the most part, and there is a $5 lot next to **Shangri-La**. There are also a couple of parking garages in the area.

***Dim sum** is a style of Chinese cuisine prepared as small bite-sized portions of food served in small steamer baskets or on small plates.* (Wikipedia)

- NOTES -

Been there! ☐

# Starter's Bar

Midtown / Cass Corridor
4501 Woodward Avenue
(313) 831-3100

Full bar: ✓ Draft beer: ✓ Full kitchen: ✓ Shuttle service: ✗ startersdetroit.com

HOURS:
Mon - Wed: 11am - 1am
Thu - Sat: 11am - 1:30am
Sun: noon - 1am

HAPPY HOUR:
Mon - Fri: 2pm - 7pm
Sun - Thu: 11pm - close

**Starter's Bar** is a large (6,500sf) bar located less than a half mile from the Detroit Institue of Arts, down Woodward Avenue. The decor is modern and clean, with an abundance of tables and a very large, circular, granite-topped bar. This family-friendly establishment is capable of handling large groups.

The bar appears to have everything one would need, and then some. Their drink menu is larger than most dinner menus at other restaurants. In addition to the booze, they carry 20-some beers on draft, plus many more varieties in bottles and cans. Beer drinkers, rejoice! **Starter's** offers a 22oz pour, and during happy hour, you can get Bud Light, Budweiser, Miller Lite and MGD in that size for only $3.25. There are a lot of other options during happy hour, too.

The menus are filled with relatively inexpensive, American style food items. They have a special lunch menu (11am-2pm), and daily dinner specials. Fresh baked buttered rolls complete the food picture.

**Starter's** is close to the DIA, Wayne State, the Detroit Medical campus, and the Detroit Science Center. Parking in the area is mostly parking structures, although there is some street parking. With the QLine running up and down Woodward, a jaunt into the city is easy from here.

- NOTES -

**Been there!** ☐

**2906 Cass Avenue**

**(313) 832-2822**

**Midtown / Cass Corridor**

# Temple Bar

**Full bar:** ☑ **Draft beer:** ☑ **Full kitchen:** ✗ **Shuttle service:** ✗

HOURS:
Mon - Sun: 1pm - 2am

**Temple Bar** is one of Detroit's classic dive bars. Part of its charm comes from the neighborhood, which isn't exactly posh, although that might be changing due to the new Little Caesars Arena nearby, and all of the change that will bring. Outside, the appearance is rough. Inside, it's worn. The space inside the bar is on the dark side, certainly not fancy, but not dirty, either. It's friendly, simple, and the prices of drinks are low.

Sticking with the theme, the bar is no-frills, with two beers on tap, and twenty or so in bottles and cans. Safe to say that drinks at the bar tend toward the old standards, not so much toward trendy cocktails. On the weekends, there are often Jello shots available for a buck each.

Other than a rack of potato chips, there is no food here. Food can be brought or ordered in.

For entertainment, there is a pool table, a dart board and a juke box. On Friday and Saturday nights, and some Thursdays in the Summer, there is a DJ, and consequently, dancing. These DJ nights are what they are known for. Every other Saturday is "THOTs and Prayers", and the 3rd Saturday of the month is "Haute to Death", a vinyl driven DJ dance party.

**Temple** has a private lot, and there is parking on Cass Avenue.

*While* ***Temple Bar*** *is a gay bar, all are welcome equally here.*

- NOTES -

Been there! ☐

# Traffic Jam & Snug

**Midtown / Cass Corridor**
**511 West Canfield Street**
**(313) 931-9470**

**Full bar:** ✓ **Draft beer:** ✓ **Full kitchen:** ✓ **Shuttle service:** ✗ **trafficjamdetroit.com**

HOURS:
Mon - Thu: 11am - 10:30pm
Fri - Sat: 11am - midnight
Sun: 11am - 8pm

HAPPY HOUR:
Mon - Thu: 7pm - 10pm

Restaurant, bar, bakery, micro brewery, and dairy; they've got all of that and more at **Traffic Jam & Snug**. In business since 1965, **Traffic Jam & Snug** is well established in the Midtown community of Detroit, and professes to be Michigan's first brew-pub. They also make just about everything from scratch, using local ingredients whenever possible. They even have a rooftop garden where they grow many of their herbs, spices and tea. Guy Fieri from Food Network featured them on his show *Diners, Drive-Ins & Dives*, which certainly helped bring awareness to this already popular establishment.

The taps at the bar are generally occupied by five flavors of **TJ&S** house-brewed craft beer, although they will occasionally rotate another Michigan beer through. The bar at **Traffic Jam** is small compared to the restaurant. If you have any more than a handful of people, you're better off to get a table and enjoy some food with your drinks.

The menu at **Traffic Jam & Snug** is large and creative, providing ample selections at every level from appetizers through dessert. A couple of their more popular dishes are the lasagna and the meatloaf, both of which have stood the test of time without much if any change to the recipes in years. When **TJ&S** was featured on *Diners Drive-Ins and Dives*, the star of the show was the BBQ Beef Brisket Panini.

Located in Midtown, **TJ&S** is not too far from the DIA, the Detroit Science Center, Wayne State campus, Detroit's Medical Center, the Hilberry Theatre, Max Fisher Theater, and the Detroit Historical Museum.

Conveniently, there is metered parking on the streets, as well as a guarded lot across Canfield Street.

***Traffic Jam & Snug** has their own dairy, and makes their own cheese and ice cream!*

- NOTES -

Been there! ☐

4145 Woodward Avenue

(313) 831-3965

Midtown / Cass Corridor

# Union Street

Full bar: ✓ Draft beer: ✓ Full kitchen: ✓ Shuttle service: ✗ unionstreetdetroit.com

Author Favorite

**Union Street** is a comfortable, old-feel, neighborhood-style bar and restaurant. The dark tones of the wood throughout and open seating area provide a welcome environment for all who enter.

This is a place where you can scoot up to the bar and chat with the people around you while you enjoy any variety of drinks, from the wide selection of beers on draft to a mixed cocktail.

HOURS:
Mon - Thu: 11:30am - 10pm
Fri: 11:30am - midnight
Sat: noon - midnight
Sun: 11:30am - 8pm

HAPPY HOUR:
Mon - Fri: 11:30am - 6:30pm

**Union Street** also offers an extensive menu filled with creatively constructed selections. On Sundays, they have a special brunch menu in addition to the normal menu, and claim to have Detroit's largest Bloody Mary bar. It's huge, and it is delicious.

Parking is available in the lot next door, or in designated, metered street spaces. With the QLine in operation, there is now an option to park Downtown and ride up and back easily.

*From the menu: Dragon Eggs. Let me tell you... One of my absolute favorite dishes anywhere. Order the rasta sauce on the side, so you get to control the amount of heat.*

- NOTES -

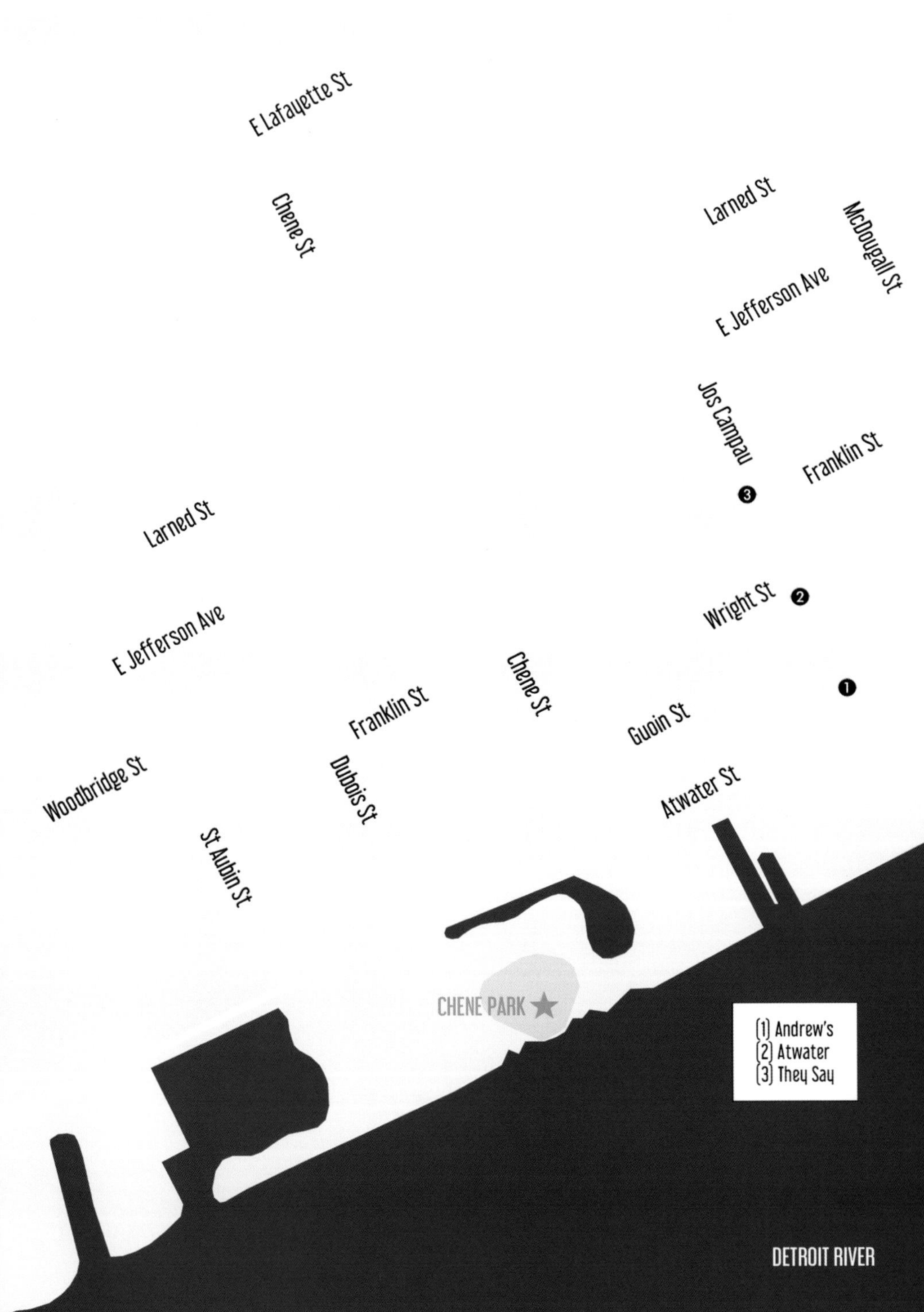
E Lafayette St
Chene St
Larned St
McDougall St
E Jefferson Ave
Jos Campau
Franklin St
3
Larned St
Wright St
2
E Jefferson Ave
Chene St
1
Franklin St
Guoin St
Woodbridge St
Dubois St
Atwater St
St Aubin St
CHENE PARK
(1) Andrew's
(2) Atwater
(3) They Say
DETROIT RIVER

201 Joseph Campau Street
(313) 259-8325

# Andrews on the Corner

**Full bar:** ✓ **Draft beer:** ✓ **Full kitchen:** ✓ **Shuttle service:** ✓ **andrewsonthecorner.com**

HOURS:
Mon - Thu: 11am - midnight
Fri: 11am - 2am
Sat: noon - 2am
Sun: 11am - 10pm

On the divey end of the bar spectrum, **Andrews on the Corner** has been around longer than the Detroit Red Wings. This bar has been family owned and operated since 1918. The old brick building is a beautiful glimpse into the past when the neighborhoods along the Detroit River were flourishing.

100 years of being in business indicates, at least on some level, that people like your business. For **Andrews on the Corner**, they have kept their prices down, and they serve good food. The main fare is burgers and sandwiches, and they offer a list of bar-style sides/appetizers. They do run daily specials; they change, so check in to see what they are. Some of the more popular menu items are the fish dishes, including their fish and chips.

As for the bar itself, **Andrews** has a full line-up of liquor, and offers up Atwater craft beers on draft. Seeing that they are next door to the Atwater brewery, this makes a lot of sense, and should assure fresh kegs are always on hand. Not to worry, if you are not an Atwater or craft beer fan, the cooler is stocked with cans and bottles of the more common varieties of suds.

**Andrews** offers shuttle service to Tigers, Red Wings, and Lions games in Detroit as well as to most major events, which is always a plus. With their secured parking lot, you can go to Andrew's before the game, eat, have a few drinks, and not worry about having to drive to the game or pay expensive parking fees. As with any service like this, don't forget to tip the shuttle driver.

*No tour of Detroit's Dive bars is complete without a visit to* ***Andrews on the Corner****.*

- NOTES -

**Been there!** ☐ **Riverfront**

# Atwater Detroit Tap House

**237 Joseph Campau**
**(313) 877-9205**

**Full bar:** ☑ **Draft beer:** ☑ **Full kitchen:** ☑ **Shuttle service:** ☒ **atwaterbeer.com**

HOURS:
Mon - Thu: 1130am - 10pm
Fri: 11:30am - midnight
Sat: 11am - midnight
Sun: 11am - 10pm

HAPPY HOUR:
Mon - Fri: 3pm - 6pm

The beer is going to be fresh here, the brewery is in the back of the building. In fact, you can see the vats through the wall of windows behind the bar when you walk through the door. The design of the taproom is modern, open, and inviting. With high ceilings, light colors, and lots of windows, it is a very comfortable environment.

There are as many as 20 **Atwater** brews on tap at any given time, but if beer is not your thing, they also have a full bar and a wine list to satisfy your cravings.

They do offer food, however at the time of publication, their menu was in the process of being changed. Check their website to see what the current offerings are.

This is a good place to come with a group. Aside from the variety of drinks and food, there are several large TVs for sports, they do trivia on Mondays, and Bar Bingo on Tuesdays. There is also a selection of games you can take to your table, such as Jenga, Connect 4, Boggle, Cranium, etc.

If you are going to be a regular, they offer a mug club membership, which gets you cheaper beer, 10% off on Mondays, and exclusive events and tours.

Happy hour (M-F 3p-6p) gives you $2 off beers, craft cocktails for $6, wine, cheese and crackers for $7, and 2 sandwiches and a beer for $9.

*I have been a fan of the beer for years. They are constantly coming up with new flavors, so visit often and get familiar with their style.*

- NOTES -

## They Say

267 Jos Campau Street
(313) 446-4682

theysayribs.com

**Full bar:** ✓ **Draft beer:** ✓ **Full kitchen:** ✓ **Shuttle service:** ✗

**They Say** occupies a beautiful old building just up from the Detroit River. Like so many of the old buildings, the brickwork on the exterior is a joy to see, and it carries over to the interior. On the first floor, the look is a mix of old exposed brick, and a modern flare. The second floor, where there is dancing and parties, is mostly exposed brick surfaces, and has a full bar.

HOURS:
Mon - Wed: 11am - 11pm
Thu: 11am - midnight
Fri: 11am - 2am
Sat: noon - 2am
Sun: noon - 11pm

HAPPY HOUR:
Mon - Fri: 4pm - 7pm
and 9pm - 11pm

The bar at **They Say** has a pretty standard offering of drinks, from drafts through top shelf liquor and a selection of wines. Though not a focus of the bar, a stand-out item is the "ski-shots". This is a ski with four shot holders on it, allowing four people to do a shot at the same time.

From the standpoint of food, the kitchen is full, offering a good variety of American comfort food. They have separate menus for kids, lunch, and dinner, with daily specials. A self-described gastropub, **They Say's** kitchen is known for its chicken wings, considered the best in Detroit by many, as well as plenty of other delicious items to choose from.

On Mondays and Tuesdays, there is ballroom dancing upstairs. Thursdays are open mic nights with old school music on the 1st floor. On Friday and Saturday nights, there is a DJ upstairs, and room to dance.

Parking is available for free along the street and there is a private lot behind the building, with the entrance on Franklin Street.

*TVs at the bar bring the games to the patrons.*

- NOTES -

# Southwest

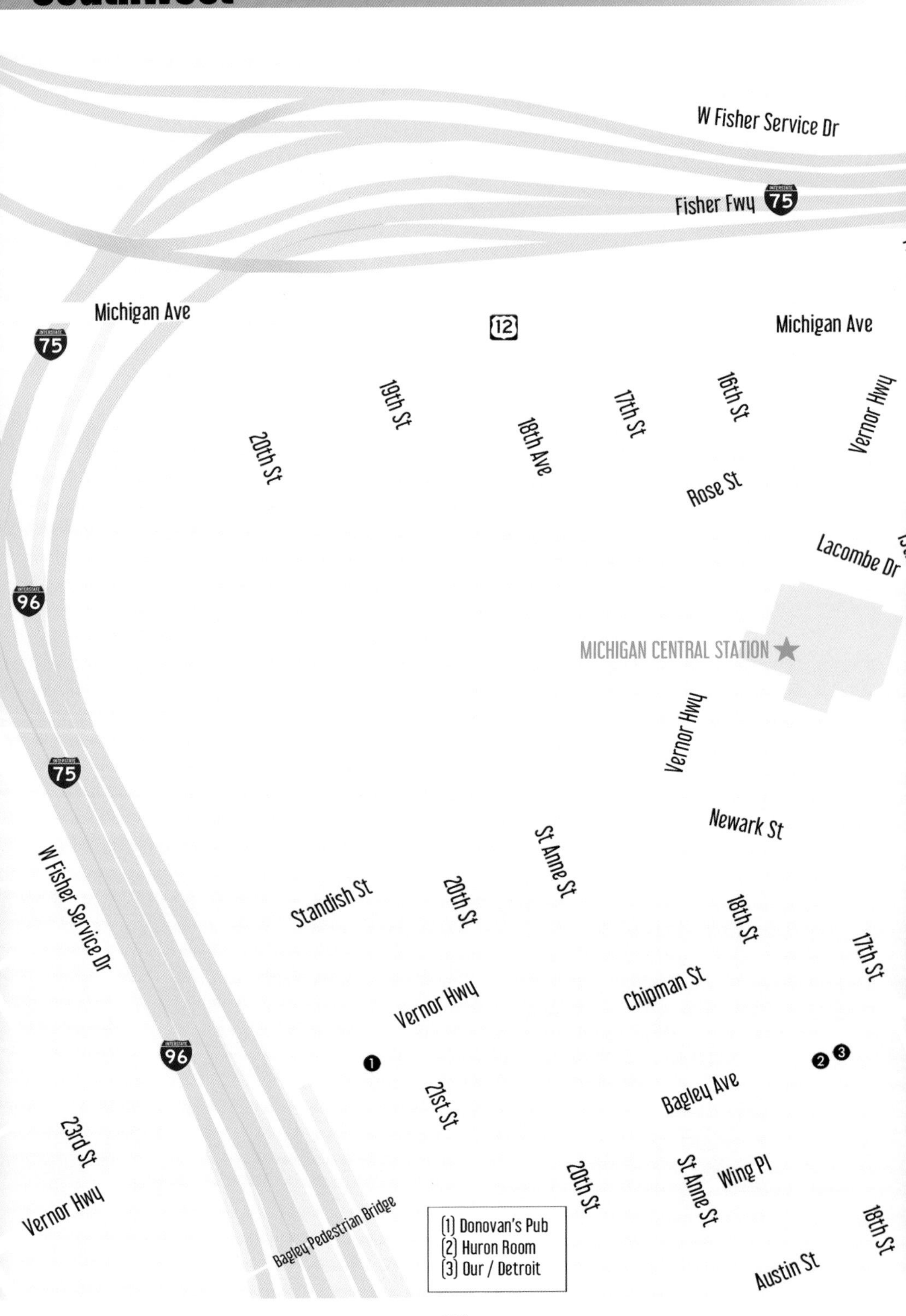

W Fisher Service Dr
Fisher Fwy
75
Michigan Ave
75
12
Michigan Ave
19th St
18th Ave
17th St
16th St
Vernor Hwy
20th St
Rose St
Lacombe Dr
96
MICHIGAN CENTRAL STATION
Vernor Hwy
75
Newark St
St Anne St
Standish St
20th St
18th St
17th St
W Fisher Service Dr
Vernor Hwy
Chipman St
96
Bagley Ave
21st St
23rd St
20th St
St Anne St
Wing Pl
Vernor Hwy
Bagley Pedestrian Bridge
18th St
Austin St
(1) Donovan's Pub
(2) Huron Room
(3) Our / Detroit

3003 Vernor Highway
(313) 964-7418

# Donovan's Pub

**Full bar:** ✓ **Draft beer:** ✗ **Full kitchen:** ✗ **Shuttle service:** ✗

HOURS:
Mon - Sun: 4pm - 2am

This small pub is located not too far from the Ambassador Bridge. If not for the prominent signage on the exterior, it would be easy to miss and drive right on by. If you do stop and go inside, once your eyes adjust to the dim interior, you will find a well maintained, clean establishment. The bar is along the far wall, and there are a handful of tables, a large flatscreen TV in the far back corner, and a pool table.

The beer list at **Donovan's** is written on a dry-erase board near the door. There are around thirty to choose from; all in bottles or cans. If you're lucky, there are also $1 jello shots. You're not likely to get a trendy cocktail here, but you can get a solid mixed drink or a shot if that's your thing.

There are a few food items available, and they are listed on another board, this one by the kitchen. There are some bar sides, wing dings, burgers, and shrimp. They also have pierogis, one of the more popular choices. Of course if you just want something to snack on while you have some drinks, there is a popcorn machine by the TV, and the popcorn is free.

**Donovan's** has its own parking lot next to the building. Although the parking lot is small, there are also places to park along the side streets.

From the standpoint of location, this bar gets the award for being the furthest away from downtown Detroit of any of the places in this guide. It's a quaint, clean, friendly place to throw back a couple of cold ones.

*While there are people who were born and raised here, this is Southwest Detroit, not South Detroit.*

- NOTES -

Been there! ☐

Southwest

# Huron Room

2547 Bagley Avenue
(313) 265-3325
huronroom.com

Full bar: ☑ Draft beer: ☑ Full kitchen: ☑ Shuttle service: ☒

HOURS:
Mon - Thu: 3pm - 10pm
Fri - Sat: 11am - 11pm
Sun: 11am - 10pm

HAPPY HOUR:
Mon - Fri: 3pm - 6pm

BRUNCH:
Fri - Sun: 11am - 3pm

Located in Southwest Detroit inside a small, modern building is this pleasant gem of a place. Above the entrance is a large salmon, appearing to swim through the facade. Inside is a quaint restaurant and bar, finished in a contemporary fashion. On most Spring and Summer days they set up tables and chairs out front, allowing people to enjoy the day while they eat and drink.

The cozy little bar positioned in the front of the building takes full advantage of the large windows. What they serve is heavy on Michigan brands, with many local spirits and a good selection of Michigan craft beers. The beers are available on draft, in cans, and in bottles. **Huron Room** also has a decent selection of hard ciders, both in can and on draft. If you are looking for cocktails, there is a specialized list on the menu, and the bartender is capable of making others that are not listed. Finally, if you are interested in beer to go, they offer growlers. Buy the 64oz bottle for $5, then pay four times the glass cost to have it filled. Since their glasses are 12oz, you are getting a deal. Happy hour, M-F, 3-6pm has an abbreviated menu, however the prices of the items are among the lowest in Detroit.

Author Favorite

As one might guess based on the fish on the front of the building, the main dishes from the kitchen are seafood-based. They do offer non-seafood choices, both in appetizers and in their entrees. Fish and chips are one of the biggest draws here.

The location is close to the Ambassador Bridge and not far from Corktown, a popular and busy part of Detroit for bars and restaurants.

Parking is easy here. **Huron Room** has its own parking lot behind the building, and there is some parking available on the street.

*The homemade Bloody Mary mix is awesome!*

- NOTES -

2545 Bagley Avenue
(313) 656-4610

# Our / Detroit

Full bar: ☑ Draft beer: ☒ Full kitchen: ☒ Shuttle service: ☒ ourvodka.com/ourdetroit

HOURS:
Thu: 5pm - 11pm
Fri: 5pm - 1am
Sat: 1pm - 1am
Sun: 1pm - 6pm
Mon - Wed: *closed*

HAPPY HOUR:
Thu - Sat: 5pm - 7pm

**Our/Detroit** is a nano-distillery that only makes vodka. It is located in Southwest Detroit in a small building it shares with the Huron Room. In fact, the two are connected by a hallway. For the curious, the distillery operations can be viewed through a window in the tasting room.

The tasting room is at the front of the building, and has a couple of community style tables, some bar stools along the windows, and a small bar. While they only make drinks with their vodka, which is also for sale, they prepare a few different infused flavors for use at the bar. The cocktail list is of a size sufficient to provide a range of options. Besides the vodka, these drinks use house-made syrups, fresh herbs and juices, and a few sweet candy accessories.

There is no kitchen at **Our/Detroit**, however food can easily be brought over from the adjoining Huron Room, or ordered or brought in from other places. The one food item they do offer is popcorn, and it's free. Occasionally there is a pop-up food event from a local restaurant, food truck, or chef. Keep up with **Our/Detroit** on social media to learn about these.

In addition to the delicious drinks, there are events. Thursday nights are movie nights, starting at 8pm. Friday nights are for Karaoke, running from 9pm until 1am. The 1st Saturday of the month is generally an art opening featuring art from a new artist. Finally, the 3rd Saturday of the month is DJ night.

Free parking is available on the streets, and in the lot behind the building.

***Our/Detroit's** version of the Moscow mule is excellent!*

- NOTES -

# Honorable Mentions

There were some decisions that had to be made regarding inclusion in this guide. This page lists many of the bars that were not included. It is not a reflection on quality, just part of the vetting that was needed to keep the guide at a manageable size and consistent in terms of content.

**AFTER HOURS / LATE NIGHT**
211 Ultra Lounge: 211 West Congress Street. 4pm-9pm, Thu. 8pm-4am, Fri-Sat. (313) 965-7822
3Fifty Terrace: 350 Madison Street. 9pm-2am, Wed. 10pm-2am, Thu & Sat. 4pm-2am, Fri. (313) 687-4350
Bleu Detroit: 1540 Woodward Avenue. 10pm-2am, Thu-Sun. (313) 974-7799
Leland City Club: 400 Bagley Street. 10pm - 4:30am, Fri-Sat. (313) 962-2300
TV Lounge: 2548 Grand River Avenue. 9pm-2am, Wed-Sat. (313) 965-4789
Whitehouse Nightclub, The: 625 Shelby Street. 9:30pm-2am, Thu-Sat. (313) 347-9820
Works, The: 1846 Michigan Avenue. 10pm-5am, Thu-Sat. (313) 961-1742

**GENTLEMEN'S CLUBS**
Bouzouki's: 432 East Lafayette Street. (313) 964-5744
Legends: 415 East Congress Street. (313) 961-5005

**HOTEL BARS** (*Those that are there basically to serve the hotel guests*)
Chrome Bar & Grille, Hilton Garden Inn - Detroit: 351 Gratiot Avenue. (313) 967-0900
Downtown Courtyard Marriott: 333 East Jefferson Avenue. (313) 222-7700
Motor Bar, Westin Book Cadillac Hotel: 1114 Washington Boulevard. (313) 442-1600
Red Dunn Kitchen, Trumbull and Porter: 1331 Trumbull Street. (313) 496-1400
Round Bar, DoubleTree Suites by Hilton Hotel: 525 West Lafayette Boulevard. (313) 963-5600
Urban Cellars, Crowne Plaza Detroit - Downtown Riverfront: 2 Washington Boulevard. (313) 965-2000
Volt, Detroit Marriott at the Renaissance Center: 400 Renaissance Drive. (313) 568-8000

**VENUE BARS** (Open during performances and/or special events only)
Alley Deck: Garden Bowl/Magic Stick, 4140 Woodward Avenue (313) 833-9700
Café 78: MOCAD, 4454 Woodward Avenue. (313) 784-9636
Jazz Cafe: Music Hall. 350 Madison Street. (313) 887-8501
Majestic Cafe, The: Magic Stick, Majestic Theatre. 4140 Woodward Ave. (313) 833-9700
Paradise Lounge: The Max M. & Marjorie S. Fisher Music Center. 3711 Woodward Ave. (313) 576-5111
Shelter, The: St. Andrew's Hall. 431 East Congress Street. (313) 961-8961
Skydeck: Detroit Opera House. 1526 Broadway. (313) 965-4146

211 Ultra Lounge, 166
24 Grille, Downtown, 35
3Fifty Terrace, 166
3rd Street Bar, Midtown / Cass Corridor, 133
8 Degrees Plato, Midtown / Cass Corridor, 134
*About the Author*, 170
*Acknowledgements*, 169
*After Hours Bars*, 166
Alley Deck, 166
Anchor Bar, Downtown, 36
Andrews on the Corner, Riverfront, 159
Apparatus Room (The), Downtown, 37
Athens Souvlaki, Downtown, 38
Atwater Detroit Tap House, Riverfront, 160
Axis Lounge (The), MGM Grand Detroit, 92
Bad Luck Bar, Downtown, 39
Baltimore Bar & Grill, Greektown, 111
Basement Burger Bar, Greektown, 112
Batch Brewing Company, Corktown, 15
Bath Tub Pub (St. Brigid's), Downtown, 40
BBs Butchers Inn, Eastern Market, 69
Bert's Entertainment Complex, Eastern Market, 70
*Bicycle Pubs*: Detroit Rolling Pub, 86. Handlebar, 53. Michigan Pedaler, 93.
Big City Bar & Grille, Downtown, 41
Bistro 555, Greektown Casino, 119
Bleu Detroit, 166
Block (The), Midtown / Cass Corridor, 135
Bobcat Bonnie's, Corktown, 16
Bookies Bar & Grille, Foxtown, 76
Bouzouki's, 166
Brass Rail Pizza Bar, Foxtown, 77
*Breweries*: Batch Brewing Company. 15. Detroit Beer Company, 85. Motor City Brewing Works, 147.
**Bricktown Neighborhood Map**, 2
Briggs Detroit, Bricktown, 3
Broderick Grille, Foxtown, 78
Bronx Bar, Midtown / Cass Corridor, 136
Buffalo Wild Wings, Greektown, 113
Buhl Bar, Downtown, 42
Café 78, 166
Café D'Mongo Speakeasy, Downtown, 43
Calexico, Downtown, 44
*Casinos*: Greektown, 119. MGM Grand, 92. Motor City, 148
Cass Cafe, Midtown / Cass Corridor, 137
Caucus Club, Downtown, 45
Centaur Bar, Foxtown, 79
Central Kitchen & Bar, Downtown, 46
Centre Park Bar, Foxtown, 80
Checker Bar Detroit, Bricktown, 4
Cheli's Chili Bar, Foxtown, 81
Chrome Bar & Grille, 166
Cliff Bell's, Foxtown, 82
Coaches Corner Bar & Grill, Foxtown, 83
Cobo Joe's Bar & BBQ, Downtown, 47
Colors, Foxtown, 84
**Corktown Neighborhood Map**, 14
Corktown Tavern, Corktown, 17
Cornerstone Barrel House, Downtown, 48
Cutters Bar & Grill, Eastern Market, 71
Delux Lounge, Greektown, 114
Detroit Beer Company, Foxtown, 85
Detroit City Distillery, Eastern Market, 72
Detroit Rolling Pub, Foxtown, 86
Detroiter Bar, Bricktown, 5
Dime Store, Downtown, 49
Distilleries: Detroit City Distillery, 72. Two James Spirits, 32. Our/Detroit, 165.
Donovan's Pub, Southwest, 163
Downtown Courtyard Marriott, 166
Downtown Louie's Lounge, Downtown, 50
**Downtown Neighborhood Map**, 34
Drive - Table Tennis Social Club, Downtown, 51
**Eastern Market Neighborhood Map**, 68
Elwood Bar & Grill, Foxtown, 87
Exodus Lounge, Greektown, 115
Firebird Tavern, Greektown, 116
Fishbone's, Greektown, 117
Flood's Bar & Grille, Greektown, 118
Foxtown Grille (Da Edoardo), Foxtown, 88
**Foxtown Neighborhood Map**, 75
Fringe, Greektown Casino, 119
Garden Bowl Bar, Midtown / Cass Corridor, 138
*Gentlemen's Clubs*, 166
Ghost Bar (The), Midtown / Cass Corridor, 139
Gold Cash Gold, Corktown, 18
Grand Trunk Pub, Downtown, 52
Granite City Food & Brewery, Bricktown, 6
Greektown Casino-Hotel, Greektown, 119
**Greektown Neighborhood Map**, 110

# Index


Green Dot Stables, Corktown, 19
Greenwich Time Pub, Bricktown, 7
Grey Ghost Detroit, Midtown / Cass Corridor, 140
Handlebar Detroit (The), Downtown, 53
Harbor House, Greektown, 120
Hard Rock Cafe, Downtown, 54
Harry's Detroit Bar, Foxtown, 89
Headlights Lounge, Motor City Casino, 148
Hockeytown Cafe, Foxtown, 90
Honest ? John's, Midtown / Cass Corridor, 141
*Honorable Mentions*, 166
HopCat, Midtown / Cass Corridor, 142
*Hotel Bars*, 24 Grille, 35. Apparatus Room (The), 37.
Big City Bar & Grille, 4. Bistro 555, 119.
Lounge (The), 148. WXYZ Bar, 109. *166*
Huron Room, Southwest, 164
Jacoby's German Biergarten, Bricktown, 8
Jazz Cafe, 166
Jolly Pumpkin, Midtown / Cass Corridor, 143
Jumbo's Bar, Midtown / Cass Corridor, 144
Keep (The), Bricktown, 9
La Casa Cigars & Lounge, Foxtown, 91
La Feria, Midtown / Cass Corridor, 145
La Lanterna, Downtown, 55
*Late Night Bars*, 166
Legend's, 166
Leland City Club, 166
Level Two Bar & Rooftop, Greektown, 121
LJs Sweetheart Bar, Corktown, 20
Locos Tex-Mex Grille, Greektown, 122
London Chop House, Downtown, 56
Lounge (The), Motor City Casino, 148
*Maps*: Bricktown, 2. Corktown, 14. Downtown, 34.
Eastern Market, 68. Foxtown, 75. Greektown, 110.
Midtown/Cass Corridor, 132. Riverfront, 158.
Southwest, 162.
M!X Bricktown, Bricktown, 10
Mac n' Brewz, Midtown / Cass Corridor, 146
Majestic Cafe (The), 166
Maru Sushi, Downtown, 57
McShane's Irish Pub, Corktown, 21
Mercury Burger & Bar, Corktown, 22
MGM Grand Detroit, Foxtown, 92
Michigan Pedaler, Foxtown, 93
**Midtown / Cass Corridor Neighborhood Map**, 132
Mo' Better Blues, Bricktown, 11 - CLOSED
Motor Bar, 166
Motor City Brewing Works, Midtown / Cass Corridor, 147
Motor City Casino, Midtown / Cass Corridor, 148
Motor City Wine, Corktown, 23
Mudgie's, Corktown, 24
Nancy Whiskey, Corktown, 25
Nemo's Bar, Corktown, 26
Nick's Gaslight Restaurant, Downtown, 58
Niki's Pizza, Greektown, 123
Old Miami (The), Midtown / Cass Corridor, 149
Old Shillelagh (The), Greektown, 124
Ottava Via, Corktown, 27
Our / Detroit, Southwest, 165
Overdrive, Motor City Casino, 148
Pappy's Bar & Grill, Greektown, 125
Paradise Lounge, 166
Parc, Downtown, 59
Park Bar (The), Foxtown, 94
Pegasus Taverna, Greektown, 126
Peterboro (The), Midtown / Cass Corridor, 150
Pit Stop, Motor City Casino, 148
PizzaPapalis Taverna, Greektown, 127
PJs Lager House, Corktown, 28
Prism, Greektown Casino, 119
Punch Bowl Social, Foxtown, 95
PV Lounge, Foxtown, 96
Queens Bar, Foxtown, 97
Radio Bar, Motor City Casino, 148
Ready Player One, Bricktown, 12
Red Corridor, Corktown, 29 - CLOSED
Red Dunn Kitchen, 166
Red Smoke, Greektown, 128
Republic Tavern, Foxtown, 98
**Riverfront Neighborhood Map**, 158
Roast, Downtown, 60
Rock Bar, Greektown Casino, 119
Rock City Eatery, Midtown / Cass Corridor, 151
Rockefellers Oyster Bar, Foxtown, 99 - CLOSED
Round Bar, 166
Royce-Detroit (The), Foxtown, 100
Rusted Crow, Foxtown, 101
Santorini Estiatorio, Greektown, 129
Savannahblue, Downtown, 61
Selden Standard, Midtown / Cass Corridor, 152

# Index

Shangri-La, Midtown / Cass Corridor, 153
Shelter [The], 166
Skip [The], Foxtown, 102
Skydeck, 166
Slows Bar B Q, Corktown, 30
Small Plates Detroit, Foxtown, 103
**Southwest Neighborhood Map**, 162
Spectators, Motor City Casino, 148
Standby, Foxtown, 104
Starters Bar, Midtown / Cass Corridor, 154
State Bar and Grill, Foxtown, 105
*Strip Clubs*, 166.
Strut, Motor City Casino, 148
Sugar House, Corktown, 31
*Sushi*: Fishbone's, 117. Maru Sushi, 57. Shangri-La, 153.
Sweetwater Tavern, Bricktown, 13
TAP, MGM Grand Detroit, 92
Temple Bar, Midtown / Cass Corridor, 155
Texas de Brazil, Downtown, 62
They Say, Riverfront, 161
Thomas Magee's Sporting House Whiskey Bar, Eastern Market, 73
Tommy's Bar & Grill, Downtown, 63
Town Pump Tavern [The], Foxtown, 106
Townhouse, Downtown, 64
Traffic Jam & Snug, Midtown / Cass Corridor, 156
Trapper's, Greektown Casino, 119
Truth Music Cafe, Foxtown, 107
TV Lounge, 166
Two James Spirits, Corktown, 32
UFO Factory, Corktown, 33 - REOPENING in 2018
Union Street, Midtown / Cass Corridor, 157
Urban Cellars, 166
V Nightclub, MGM Grand Detroit, 92
*Venue Bars*, 166
Vertical Detroit, Foxtown, 108
Vivio's Food & Spirits, Eastern Market, 74
Volt, 166
Wahlburgers, Greektown, 130
Well [The], Greektown, 131
Whiskey Disco, Downtown, 65
Whisky Parlor, Downtown, 66
Whitehouse [The], 166
Works [The], 166
Wright & Company, Downtown, 67
WXYZ Bar, Foxtown, 109

# Acknowledgements

I would like to thank the following people for their help and contribution to the creation of this guide: First and foremost, my wife for putting up with me making dozens and dozens of trips to Detroit to find the bars, take all of the pictures needed, and the countless scores of hours that were spent in the bars gathering the information that was required to complete the text portion of *Watering Holes: Your Guide to Detroit's Bars, Pubs, and Taverns.* I would like to thank Mamie Sepulveda for her willingness to pour through all of the details, editing, proofreading, fact-checking, and offering her input. Her contributions were invaluable. My gratitude also extends to many of my friends who so graciously offered to be research assistants. Who knew that so many people would want to go bar-hopping with me? While none accompanied me on all of the trips, quite a few were able to join me for a few bars here and there. Thank you to the achievers: Marty West, Yerko Sepulveda and Bjorn Olson for your guidance and encouragement, and for holding me to task. Finally, and certainly a key to everything, I would like to express my appreciation to the people in the bars - the bartenders, managers, owners, and other staff who were very gracious in their willingness to share the information I needed to put this thing together. I found the people of the bar industry in Detroit to be friendly, helpful, knowledgeable, and just plain fun to be around.

Thank you!

Mike

# About the Author

I am Mike Kline. a freelance photographer living in Canton, Michigan. I found my passion for photography in Detroit, and through this developed a love for the city. After several years and hundreds of visits, I had identified a handful of bars/restaurants that I liked and would visit with some frequency. Because of my experience in Detroit, it was common to have friends ask me where they should go when they were in the city for a ball game, concert, show, event, or just adventure. Realizing that different people have different tastes, and that Detroit was quickly becoming a hot spot for new and trendy bars while at the same time being home to scores of well established places, I decided there was a need for a guide.

As I conducted my research, visiting each of the bars, I had a lot of volunteers for the role of research assistant. With only a couple of exceptions, the responsibility of assistant fell on my wife's shoulders. She soldiered through with barely any complaints, and after over a hundred trips to the city, I can say with confidence that I visited all of the bars I could find that were between Warren Avenue and the Detroit River north to south, and between Jos Campeau and I-96 east to west. It has been a labor of love.

While I am new to book writing, I have been fortunate to have my photography published all over the world, and rarely go anywhere without at least one of my cameras.

You can see and follow my work at the following:

Flickr: www.flickr.com/photos/notkalvin/
Instagram: @notkalvin
Facebook: www.facebook.com/NotkalvinPhotography/

or at my website;
www.notkalvinphotography.com

Thank you for your support,
Mike Kline
mike@notkalvinphotography.com

# Notes

See you at the bar.